ID 114646 BC 119641

362.
76
WOO

AF837873

Contesting Stories of Childhood Sexual Abuse

Contesting Stories of Childhood Sexual Abuse

Jo Woodiwiss
University of Huddersfield, UK

U.W.E.
2 7 JAN 2010
Library Services

palgrave
macmillan

© Jo Woodiwiss 2009

All rights reserved. No reproduction, copy or transmission of this publication may be made without written permission.

No portion of this publication may be reproduced, copied or transmitted save with written permission or in accordance with the provisions of the Copyright, Designs and Patents Act 1988, or under the terms of any licence permitting limited copying issued by the Copyright Licensing Agency, Saffron House, 6-10 Kirby Street, London EC1N 8TS.

Any person who does any unauthorized act in relation to this publication may be liable to criminal prosecution and civil claims for damages.

The author has asserted her right to be identified as the author of this work in accordance with the Copyright, Designs and Patents Act 1988.

First published 2009 by
PALGRAVE MACMILLAN

Palgrave Macmillan in the UK is an imprint of Macmillan Publishers Limited, registered in England, company number 785998, of Houndmills, Basingstoke, Hampshire RG21 6XS.

Palgrave Macmillan in the US is a division of St Martin's Press LLC, 175 Fifth Avenue, New York, NY 10010.

Palgrave Macmillan is the global academic imprint of the above companies and has companies and representatives throughout the world.

Palgrave® and Macmillan® are registered trademarks in the United States, the United Kingdom, Europe and other countries.

ISBN-13: 978–0–230–57404–5 hardback

This book is printed on paper suitable for recycling and made from fully managed and sustained forest sources. Logging, pulping and manufacturing processes are expected to conform to the environmental regulations of the country of origin.

A catalogue record for this book is available from the British Library.

A catalog record for this book is available from the Library of Congress.

10 9 8 7 6 5 4 3 2 1
18 17 16 15 14 13 12 11 10 09

Printed and bound in Great Britain by
CPI Antony Rowe, Chippenham and Eastbourne

To my dear friends Dave, Chris and Liz

Contents

Acknowledgements

There are many people I would like to thank for their help and support, but I would like to start by thanking the women who took part in the research on which this book is based. They gave generously of their time and energy, and shared their stories, their thoughts and their feelings with me. They did so with strength, courage and humour, and I hope I have done justice to their words.

Thank you also to the women at Support and Survival (Wakefield) and York Women's Aid not only for their support and encouragement but also for acting as a constant reminder of why, as feminists, we should conduct research into women's lives.

The research for this book was funded by the Economic and Social Research Council, award No. R42200034452, for which I thank them. I would also like to thank those who, through their comments and suggestions on earlier drafts and other papers, have contributed to this work – particularly Eleanor Formby, Stevi Jackson, Lynne James, Ken Plummer, Anthony Woodiwiss and all those at the Centre for Women's Studies at the University of York. I would also like to thank Matthew Waites for his support and encouragement in the early stages of writing this book.

I also want to thank my family and friends who have supported and encouraged me throughout, including Min Cooper, Audrey Lawrence, Liz Lewis, Wendy Morgan, Chris Windell, Dave Windell, Mary Woodiwiss, Michael Woodiwiss and Simon Woodiwiss.

Finally a special thank you to Eleanor Formby whose love, support and sense of fun have helped me through the writing of this book.

The author and Palgrave Macmillan gratefully acknowledge permission from Routledge to reprint edited extracts from Jo Woodiwiss (2008) 'Compulsory sexuality': a guide to healing?, *Culture, Health & Sexuality* 10(4 May): 345–359.

List of Acronyms

bfms	British False Memory Society
CSA	Childhood Sexual Abuse
DID	Dissociative Identity Disorder
FMS	False Memory Syndrome
FMSF	False Memory Syndrome Foundation
MPD	Multiple Personality Disorder
MPS	Multiple Personality Syndrome
PICT	Parks Inner Child Therapy
RCC	Rape Crisis Centre

1
Introduction

> *The marriage of feminism and the phenomenally popular recovery movement is arguably the most disturbing (and influential) development in the feminist movement today*
>
> (Kaminer 1993)

Set against the background of the recovered memory wars, this book explores women's engagement with narratives of childhood sexual abuse (CSA), recovery and therapeutic discourses and the role they themselves play in the construction and use of abuse narratives whether they have, by their own definition, continuous, recovered or false memories. These are the women whose voices have been largely absent from the debates around recovery and the recovered memory wars and who are mostly constructed as weak, vulnerable and at the mercy of misguided therapists or the ongoing effects of abuse. This is not a book about childhood sexual abuse. Nor is it a book on the recovered memory wars, or on memory. It is also not a general book about therapeutic or self-help culture. Yet these themes do form part of the background against which the research for this book was carried out. They also form part of the background against which women engage in the ongoing process of (re)constructing their own narratives of childhood sexual abuse.

The main debate in the recovered memory wars is largely based on the view that the recovered memories in question are recall memories and the debate itself is primarily centred on whether therapists help their clients uncover buried memories of sexual abuse in childhood or plant false memories of such abuse in the minds of weak and vulnerable women. However, recall memories are rarely recovered (Bass and Davis 1988) and the memories in question are usually 'symptoms' redefined as 'alternative memories'. The memory wars are located within a therapeutic culture (Furedi 2004), in which the 'reflexive self' is seen as a project to be worked on (Giddens 1991). Within this culture we are encouraged to engage with therapeutic and self-help literature and to reconstruct ourselves as damaged and in need of healing (Furedi 2004, Showalter 1997). It is against this background that women, and it is primarily women, engage with the body of knowledge surrounding CSA, recovery and healing that constitutes the 'harm story' (O'Dell 2003) and its therapeutic corollary, the 'healing discourse' (Davies 1995).

The aim of the research on which this book is based was not to question the memories of those women who come to recover and, in some cases later reject, memories of childhood sexual abuse, or the validity of their stories, but to place the tellers of sexual abuse narratives at the centre of their telling. My intention is to go beyond their narratives to look at how individuals draw on culturally circulating stories and narrative frameworks to construct their own stories. I do however take issue with some of the principles which underpin the arguments on both sides of this great divide, without which women would not be able to tell the particular stories of childhood sexual abuse that they have come to tell in the twenty-first century. Central to the recovered memory movement is the belief that there is no positive or neutral experience of CSA. It is said to be a psychologically devastating experience, the effects of which can be identified in the lives of adult victims. The symptoms, which include a 'failure to thrive' and repeat victimisation, help to construct victims as psychologically damaged and in need of healing without which the cycle of abuse is likely to continue into the next generation. Within this understanding the answer to sexual abuse and the way to prevent it in the future is through healing, and victims owe it to others as well as themselves to heal from what they believe to be a sexually abusive childhood.

This is not the only story that can be, or has been, told of sexual abuse in childhood but it is the story that has come to dominate, not only within the psy professions but also within feminism and wider contemporary understandings. Until the 1970s the consensus within psychology was that the experience of child sexual abuse had few, if any, long-term negative effects. In the feminist moment of the 1970s and 1980s a different story could be told in which sexual abuse was not constructed as an individual problem needing an individual solution but a social problem in need of a political solution (Armstrong 1978, Driver 1989, Kelly 1988, Kitzinger 1993, Rush 1980, Ward 1984). It was also a story which showed 'the other side of being a victim' (Kelly

1988), and recognised that male violence was not just about male power but also women's and children's resistance (Kelly 1988, Kirkwood 1993, Maguire 1992). It was a story that challenged the construction of victims as passive and powerless and allowed for the possibility that 'the process of coping with negative effects may, in the long term, have positive outcomes' (Kelly 1988:159).

Faced with feminist discourses psychology was forced to reassess its understanding and in doing so it consolidated its position to define the problem and solution to sexual violence (Kitzinger 1993). The story to emerge in the late 1980s and 1990s portrayed sexual abuse in childhood as a 'profoundly deforming experience' (Contratto and Gutfreund 1996) which left victims 'not well adapted to adult life' (Herman 1992:110), and allowed for 'evidence' to be identified in the lives of adult women. This story not only dominates the sexual abuse recovery literature but permeates other strands of self-help literature, where sexual abuse is often seen as an underlying cause. This is also a story which enables women to identify 'symptoms' of sexual abuse in their adult lives, reinterpreted as 'alternative memories', and therefore construct a history of childhood sexual abuse, whether or not they recall memories of such abuse (Woodiwiss 2009).

The 'harm story' may dominate the recovery literature but it is not the only narrative framework available to those looking to make sense of and improve their lives. Women are not forced to construct a narrative based on childhood and/or sexual abuse but they are constrained by the limited number (Lawler 2002) of stories currently in circulation (Bauman 2001, Jackson 1998, Lawler 2002, Plummer 1995, 2001). We may not be free to tell any story, or have our stories heard, but we can draw on material from beyond the sexual abuse recovery literature. However, when narrating ourselves, the therapeutic scripts in circulation do exert a considerable influence on our lives (Furedi 2004). These scripts tell us of a self to be worked on as we are subjected to a barrage of advice on self-improvement and self-development and increasingly on healing, recovery and survival.

This book, like the majority of stories based on continuous, alternative or false memories of childhood sexual abuse is based on the accounts given by women. Women do not represent the totality of adults who were formerly abused as children or the totality of those who engage with the CSA recovery and recovered memory literature. However, they do represent the majority, both in terms of victims of sexual abuse in childhood and as the readers and writers of personal stories of sexual abuse. Women are encouraged to recognise symptoms that identify them as passive, weak, vulnerable and most importantly as victims, in which the telling of a sexual abuse narrative can be used to construct them as responsible for perceived failures in their lives including victimisation in adulthood. Men are provided with similar lists of symptoms but alongside symptoms that encourage them to identify anger, aggression and perpetrating abuse as evidence, in which the telling of a sexual abuse narrative can be used to excuse or justify abusive behaviour. Therefore, whilst we can see that aspects of the stories available to, or told by, women are also relevant to men it is important to recognise that the overall frameworks, as well as many of the individual plot lines, available to men and women are, in important ways, very different and therefore so too are their stories.

The women whose stories feature in this book

The research on which this book is based sought to look at how and why women engaged with CSA recovery and therapeutic discourses, and why they entered therapy or read self-help manuals aimed at victims of sexual abuse in childhood, often with no knowledge of having been abused. There is now a large body of literature aimed at adults who believe they are (based on continuous or recovered memories) victims, and a large body of literature written about them. This book, based on research which explored women's engagement with discourses of childhood sexual abuse, multiple personalities or false memory syndrome, aims to give some of those women a voice. It is their stories that are at the centre of this text. I am not concerned with whether their stories are 'true' or 'false', except in the degree to which women believe the stories they tell, but in the way women come to (re)construct these narratives. Of course, constructing a narrative is much more than simply telling a story of a life. Constructing a sexual abuse narrative, whether based on continuous, recovered or false memories, is about making sense of a life and of the person who has and continues to live it. It is also about trying to devise a strategy for the future with a self one is happy, or at least content. In the following pages I look at how women do not simply adopt ready-made narratives or step into the shoes of ready-made selves, but engage with these discourses with creativity and imagination to construct a story that gives meaning to their lives and the selves that live (in) them.

I use data from interviews and written accounts conducted with women who had, by their own definition, 'continuous', 'recovered' or 'false' memories of sexual abuse in childhood. I contacted women through an article in a national newsletter produced by a survivor's organisation named Cisters, through the British False Memory Society (bfms) newsletter, and through a letter sent to female members of the bfms. The research was based primarily on 11 in-depth, semi-structured interviews, and five written accounts which followed a similar structure, in which women were asked about their lives and what led them to engage with the sexual abuse recovery literature, their experiences of therapy/counselling, their experiences of self-help literature, and the role they themselves played in the re/construction of their own life stories or narratives. A total of 16 women took part in the research, 11 of whom replied to the article in Cisters and five to material they received from the bfms. Of these 16 women only five entered adulthood with continuous memories of having been sexually abused in childhood. I wanted a method that would allow women to talk freely about their experiences but which precluded a focus on their experiences of abuse whilst allowing those experiences to be taken as given. I decided on a two-stage approach using a questionnaire followed by either an interview or written account. The questionnaire was designed to provide some autobiographical details together with a brief outline of participants' abuse, including, if known, their age, the time and place the abuse occurred and the perpetrator(s), as well as information on the therapeutic material and childhood sexual abuse recovery literature they engaged with. I then used in-depth, semi-structured interviews based on a small number of open-ended questions that would allow follow up questions and prompts. This also had the flexibility to be used as guidelines for those who wished to provide a written account. The interview schedule was designed to encourage a conversational style in which women were able to talk more freely than if responding to rigid questions (Burgess 1982, 1984, Whyte 1982), and allowed them to determine the nature and depth of their responses. I also drafted two different versions of the interview structure/written account guidelines: one for self-identified victims of childhood sexual abuse and one for self-identified victims of FMS. The interviews themselves lasted between two and six hours, were conducted by the author, tape-recorded, later transcribed and analysed thematically.

Before going on to look at their accounts I believe it is important to say something about these women – not as a way of judging their stories or the validity of their accounts but as a way of knowing something about them and how they came to tell the stories they did. In the following short biographies their names have been changed and identifying details removed. I have also included whether they participated by way of an interview or a written account.

Angela (36) entered adulthood with continuous memories of being sexually abused by her brother together with memories of emotionally abusive parents. She accessed counselling and therapy on a number of occasions as well as alternative therapies/healing. She also read general self-help books and those aimed at survivors of CSA and survivor biographies of which she found the self-help books aimed at survivors especially helpful. (Interview)

Anne (56) entered adulthood with continuous memories of a traumatic childhood, in which she witnessed the death of a younger brother and the mental health problems of her mother and another brother. It wasn't until later that Anne recovered memories of incest and ritual abuse. From the age of 34 Anne accessed various counsellors, therapists and religious teachers, and read self-help books aimed at survivors although she has found these difficult to use without support. (Interview)

Beccy (30) recovered memories of sexual abuse, possibly perpetrated by her father and his friend, during therapy she had in her 20s, after she came to work in England. She identified 'the main problem' as a sexual problem in her relationship. Beccy read general self-help books and those aimed at survivors, as well as survivor biographies, of which she found the self-help books aimed at survivors helpful, although not necessarily without the help of a therapist. (Interview)

Daisy (49) had an unhappy childhood during which she developed anorexia/bulimia, overseen by an alcoholic father and a resentful mother. In her 30s she recovered what she later believed to be 'false memories' of sexual and satanic abuse, whilst under hypnosis. Although she did read much of the survivor literature before and after rejecting her memories Daisy says she found none of it helpful. (Written Account)

Emma (32) had continuous memories of being sexually abused between the ages of 10 and 15. She ran away from home at the age of 15 and this led to the involvement of social services and the arrest of her abuser. Emma, when still a teenager, found support and group therapy for the whole family very useful, but found a second period of counselling unhelpful. She also read self-help books of which she found the general ones especially helpful but the ones aimed at survivors less so. (Written Account)

Fiona (37) recovered memories of sexual abuse perpetrated by her father when she was 21. Fiona was sexually assaulted by her long-term boyfriend and suffered from depression, and it was following this that she recovered memories of sexual abuse. She then began counselling, and left her parental home and university. She has accessed counsellors and therapists on a number of occasions over the last 20 years. She has read general self-help books as well as those aimed at survivors of CSA and survivor biographies, and visited Internet sites but found these very disturbing. Fiona also briefly attended a survivor group but found it to be of limited help. (Interview)

Frances (36) recovered memories of minor sexual abuse when she was 17 and recovered memories of more serious sexual abuse between the ages of 25 and 31. Frances says she has had an unsettled life since leaving home and going to college and has a history of drinking, drugs, self-harm and an eating disorder. She was also physically and sexually attacked which she believed helped her recover repressed memories. Frances accessed a variety of counsellors, therapists, psychiatrists, psychologists and spiritualists over a 20-year period, and has read general self-help books and those aimed at CSA/recovered memories all of which she found helpful, but was not aware of therapy groups or survivor biographies and does not use the Internet. (Written Account)

Hazel (48) recovered 'false memories' of sexual abuse by her father during hypnosis which she went to in her late 20s to lose weight. She has since rejected the idea that her father abused her but remains unsure if she was sexually abused by someone else. She read self-help material for survivors and survivor biographies during the time she believed her memories, which she found very helpful, but did not read self-help material after she rejected her memories. (Interview)

Jay (45) entered adulthood with continuous memories of a traumatic childhood which included being sexually abused by a number of different men over a number of years, together with physical and emotional abuse by different people. Jay has spent the last 3 years in recovery and has received counselling through a rape crisis centre (RCC), attended an anger management course, a writing self-help group and regularly reads the Cisters newsletter, along with survivor biographies which she found very helpful. Jay was also able to access self-help books through RCC but found these very difficult to use. (Interview)

Jenny (45) recovered memories of sexual abuse whilst in her 30s during a meditation/visualisation. Jenny started therapy at 32 and has continued with therapy and healing and is now involved with a group running healing workshops. She has been involved in group and individual therapy and counselling and self-help groups, and has also read a lot of general self-help books, and those aimed at survivors, and survivor biographies all of which she has found very helpful. (Written Account)

Julie (41) entered adulthood with continuous memories of having been sexually abused by her brother, together with memories of an aggressive and verbally abusive father. Julie has had two periods of counselling in her late 30s both involving Parks Inner Child Therapy (PICT) and has read both general advice books and those aimed at survivors of childhood sexual abuse, all of which she has found helpful. (Interview)

Nicole (61) believed she was illegally hypnotised by a psychiatrist who implanted false memories of sexual abuse in her mind. She also believes this doctor emotionally, verbally, physically and sexually abused and tortured her. It was not clear why she first saw a psychiatrist. (Written Account)

Pat (45) recovered what she came to reject as 'false' memories of sexual abuse perpetrated by her father in her late 20s and early 30s during a series of scientology sessions which she went to to deal with 'ME-type symptoms'. Her ME symptoms improved immediately and she also recovered memories of sexual abuse which she believed in for about 5 years. Although Pat came to reject her memories of having being sexually abused by her father after watching a television programme, she did not necessarily reject the idea that she had been abused by someone else. She has read general self-help books as well as those aimed at survivors of both CSA and FMS along with survivor biographies, all of which she found helpful. (Interview)

Rae (61) entered adulthood with memories of a difficult childhood which included one incident of abuse when she was 9 which she did not feel was particularly significant, but it was not until her 40s, when she went to a hypnotist to lose weight, that she recovered what she later believed to be false memories of sexual abuse committed by her father. However, like Pat and Hazel, she did not reject her memories completely but believed she may have been sexually abused by someone other than her father. On rejecting her memories Rae went to see a therapist, read self-help books aimed at survivors of FMS and became involved in a support group, all of which she found helpful. (Interview)

Sarah (37) recovered memories of being sexually abused as a child by her uncle when, at the age of 20, she was in hospital following an accident. Sarah had been diagnosed with schizophrenia and hospitalised on a number of occasions but since recovering her memory of abuse she had accessed counselling and alternative healing, read a number of self-help books and was no longer on medication for schizophrenia. She was the only participant who entered adulthood without memories who recovered a 'recall' memory of their abuse (later validated by her mother). (Interview)

Tracey (30) entered adulthood with continuous memories of having been sexually abused by her uncle and physically and emotionally abused by her mother. She moved to England in her 20s with her boyfriend and like Julie entered Parks Inner Child Therapy (PICT). She also read self-help books and survivor biographies, often with her boyfriend, and in some respects found these to be more useful than therapy. (Interview)

Organisation of the book

In Chapter 2, 'A story for our time', I introduce the idea of narratives or storytelling as a way of making sense of our lives before going on to look at the currently circulating stories and available narrative frameworks that have led to the widespread telling of what has become a story for our time. I also introduce some of the key characters and plotlines that have contributed to our contemporary storying of childhood sexual abuse. In Chapter 3, 'Beyond the recovered memory wars', I analyse the key debates in the recovered memory wars and show the limitations of focusing on that aspect of the debate which seeks to establish the truth or falsity of women's stories of abuse whilst failing to explore the experiences of those who, in the process of making sense of their lives, come to engage with narrative frameworks of childhood sexual abuse.

In the remaining chapters I present an analysis of the empirical data from the research. In Chapter 4, 'Choosing a story: Making sense, finding evidence', I look at the processes by which the women came to tell their own sexual abuse narratives and the extent to which they were able to use a sexual abuse narrative to make sense of their lives. Chapters 5 and 6 focus on the inner child. In Chapter 5 I look at the role of the inner child in holding and accessing knowledge and in Chapter 6 I explore what it was like for women to live with an inner child, and how such a child enabled them to engage in activities that they might otherwise find difficult. In Chapter 7, 'Problems with the children', I look at some of the potential problems with inner child work and living with the inner child including the experiences of Anne the only participant who lives with multiple personalities. In this chapter I also offer an alternative understanding for the emergence of Multiple Personality Syndrome (MPS), or Dissociative Identity Disorder (DID) as it is now called, to that which claims that hypnosis is nearly always used in the diagnosis and treatment of MPS and constructs those with multiple personalities as victims of either extreme childhood trauma or of misguided therapists.

Chapters 8 and 9 look at the self and healing. In Chapter 8, 'The contradictory self', I look at the self as a project to be worked on and the contradictory formulations of this self found in the self-help and

CSA recovery literature before going on to explore the variety of ways women engaged with these different formulations of the self in the process of rewriting their life stories. In Chapter 9 I look at how the CSA recovery literature encourages women to write their narratives with a view to healing and recovery and examine what this means for those who attempt to construct such stories, particularly for those whose lives do not neatly fit. One of the key measures of healing within the CSA recovery literature is to be able to live a happy, fulfilled and healthy sexuality, and in Chapter 10, 'Compulsory sexuality', I explore the implications of using sexuality as a measure of well being. In the final chapter I reflect on some of the key findings from this research and argue for the creation of a space in which women, whether they were sexually abused in childhood or not, are no longer directed to look inward for the cause of and solution to their unhappiness or dissatisfaction, but encouraged to look outwards and in doing so acknowledge and address the external conditions of their lives.

2
A Story for Our Time

> *Everywhere we go, we are charged with telling stories and making meaning – giving sense to ourselves and the world around us.*
>
> (Plummer 1995:20)

Introduction

In making sense of our lives, each of us is engaged in the continuous process of telling and retelling their own life story or stories. In doing so we draw on the stories that are currently circulating but these are themselves both culturally and historically specific (Bauman 2001, Jackson 1998, Lawler 2002, Plummer 1995, 2001). In his 1995 book *Telling Sexual Stories* Plummer suggested that 'different moments have highlighted different stories: puberty stories, marriage-bed stories, perversion stories coming out stories, abuse survivor stories women's fantasy stories, men's tribal fairy stories, stories of living – and dying – with AIDS' (Plummer 1995:4). The late twentieth and early twenty-first century can be identified as a moment when it became possible to tell of ones life as a story of childhood sexual abuse (CSA) based on recovered or alternative memories. It is a world in which the stories we tell about ourselves are increasingly informed by a therapeutic culture (Furedi 2004), which has seen an explosion of self-help and self-development literature and where greater and greater emphasis is placed on looking inward for possible causes of and solutions to our troubles (Simonds 1996, Showalter 1997, Woodiwiss 2007a). These stories are constructed in a 'cultural moment' in which we place great 'causal and explanatory, that is, psychological, significance on victimization in people's lives' (Davis 2005:4). One such story, or narrative framework, to emerge in this cultural moment, which not only dominates much of the self-help literature but also permeates many aspects of our everyday lives, is the 'harm story' (O'Dell 2003) of CSA. This is a story that increasingly draws on psychological and therapeutic language (O'Dell and Reavey 2001) and encourages those who are in some way unhappy or dissatisfied with their lives to reinterpret those lives within a narrative framework of CSA at the expense of the circumstances within which they live. It is a story that is retold not only in the self-help and CSA recovery literature and survivor auto/biographies, but also in other contemporary cultural texts from the 'problem pages' of women's magazines to episodes of popular soaps, films, novels and (increasingly celebrity) auto/biographies (Baker 2002, Haaken 1998b, 1999, Showalter 1997).

In its telling this is a story that claims to be based on childhood memories but it owes more to contemporary culture than it does to memories of childhood sexual abuse. It is also a story that is not only more readily available to women but also more likely to be told by them. However, women do not simply slot themselves into ready-made narratives, but they are constrained by the stories that can be told (Bauman 2001, Gergen 1994, Plummer 1995, 2001) or, to borrow from Marx, women construct stories but not in the conditions of their choosing. At the beginning of the twenty-first century the genre of story telling that has taken centre stage derives from a therapeutic culture which, in competition with rival cultural claims, 'provides a script through which individuals develop a distinct understanding of their selves and of their relationship with others' (Furedi 2004:23). This culture has, according to Lasch, 'replaced religion as the organizing framework of American culture' and 'threatens to displace politics as well' (Lasch 1979:13). Whilst it may not be an organising framework of British culture in quite the same way, therapy or counselling has become increasingly visible and influential within British society. Within this therapeutically informed culture individuals increasingly retreat from the public to the private sphere (Sennett 1976, 1993), and this is reflected in the personal stories they tell in public. It is a culture with an authoritarian and coercive dimension (Furedi 2004, Lasch 1979, Sennett 1993) but also where we are 'educated in a therapeutic discourse of the emotions' which we can use 'to turn our own "cases" into stories, and become the authors of our own plot' (Rose 1989:257) albeit a plot that is constrained by those narrative frameworks currently in circulation.

Women can find examples of the 'therapeutic ethos' (Furedi 2004) beyond the consulting rooms of counsellors and the pages of self-help and self-improvement literature, as it increasingly permeates their everyday lives. It is not only individuals but also communities and societies that, damaged and in pain, are identified as in need of healing (Furedi 2004) as we are bombarded with a therapeutic language diagnosing harm and promoting healing for all aspects of everyday and not so everyday life. Within this culture of therapeutically informed story telling, the genre of the confessional biography has not only come of age but is being superseded by stories of survival (Furedi 2004, Rose 1989). Here, authors tell us of their addictions, illnesses, issues of self-esteem and troubled relationships and mental health problems which are often the result of what, in retrospect, are perceived as traumatic childhood experiences. These 'acts of sharing' (Furedi 2004) take place on chat shows, reality T.V. programmes and docudramas, on the radio and in newspapers and magazines, and in the numerous published auto/biographies, many of which are co written with a therapist or counsellor. They not only enter our private worlds but, with live interactive T.V. and television and radio phone-ins, we are encouraged to join in and air our own confessional narratives live to the nation. In doing so we are engaged in an act of telling the self, of constructing a story that gives meaning and sense to our lives and ourselves but we do so within the constraints of currently circulating narrative frameworks and these may not be as empowering as they at first appear.

Life stories, suggests Bauman, 'must confine themselves to toing and froing among the options on offer' (Bauman 2001:7) but these stories 'rarely, if ever, reach beyond the narrow and painstakingly fenced-off enclosure of the private and the "subjective self"' (Bauman 2001:12). The childhood sexual abuse narrative is one such story. It is a story which claims to portray the experiences of (mainly) women who were sexually abused in childhood but which speaks more to women's general unhappiness and dissatisfaction, or simply their desire, often fuelled by the self-help and self-improvement literature, for a 'better' life. This was a story of psychological damage, the 'harm story' (O'Dell 1997, 2003), supported by the 'healing discourse' (Davies 1995) or 'survivor discourse' (Worrell 2003). It was a story in which child sexual abuse was seen to be so (inevitably) damaging that the effects, or symptoms, could be seen in adulthood, but which also allowed for the possibility of rewriting the story to have a positive and successful ending if only victims were prepared to embark on a healing journey which could take them from victim to survivor and beyond. It was also a story that could be told, not only by those who remembered being sexually abused as children but, with the correlation of symptoms with perceived abuse together with the identification of 'alternative' memories, can also be told by those with no such memories. This new orthodoxy has taken over from feminist analyses of sexual abuse whilst appropriating feminist language. In a move away from using the term victim to using that of survivor, feminists in the 1980s challenged the construction of victims as passive, vulnerable and powerless:

> In recognizing, documenting and validating the many and varied ways in which women resist sexual violence it becomes possible to move away from 'victimism' towards an understanding of the complexity of women's experiences of sexual violence.
>
> (Kelly 1988:185)

Feminists, together with those who have experienced abuse, have rightly challenged the negative implications of the term victim (Armstrong 1994, Kelly 1988, Kirkwood 1993, Lamb 1999, O'Dell 1997). However, the harm story and survivor discourses have served to reinforce abused women's past status as 'victims'. Women must first accept that they were victims, and take on the negative connotations implicit in the term, in order to claim their new identity and write themselves into the part of survivor. By the 1990s the harm story of sexual abuse and survivor story of recovery had become so firmly established that the voices of those whose accounts did not conform, or who did not progress from 'victim' to 'survivor', found themselves silenced as their stories, at least those aspects that deviated from the 'true' story, were dismissed or rendered invisible. This is the story told in much of the therapeutic literature, self-help manuals and survivor accounts and autobiographies constructed in the late twentieth and early twenty-first centuries. As abuse narratives have entered the contemporary 'symptom pool' (Showalter 1997) it is a story readily available, and appealing, to those who seek to make meaning of their lives, whether they have knowledge or memories of having been sexually abused or are simply unhappy or dissatisfied with their lives (Hacking 1995; Pendergrast 1997, 1999; Showalter 1997; Tavris 1992; Woodiwiss 2007a).

The foundations of the contemporary childhood sexual abuse story

The emergence and widespread acceptance of the contemporary CSA and recovery stories required a particular cultural moment – a moment in which such stories could be told. However, they also needed particular understandings or themes around which women could construct their own stories, and without which they would be forced to tell very different stories. In particular they required an understanding of childhood and development, sexuality, adulthood, recovery, and an expanded view of what is sexual and abusive, together with an understanding of the causes, consequences and experiences of childhood sexual abuse.

Childhood and development

Central to the harm story are models of childhood and development which lay the foundations for the creation of a narrative framework that constructs women as psychologically damaged and vulnerable to further victimisation. Over the course of the twentieth century children have come to occupy a position of increasing significance in western consciousness and psychological theory and practice (Levett 2003) within which a developmental model of childhood has come to dominate (Jenks 1996). This is a model which links biological and social development (Prout and James 1997) within an evolutionary framework of progression from innocence to knowledge. This developmental child is believed to exert considerable influence on the behaviour of the adult and this has contributed to the widespread belief in the inevitable damage caused by sexual abuse in childhood. This developmental model also feeds into the idea that very young children are more at risk of harm than older children who may have some of the emotional skills needed to deal with the experience (O'Dell 2003). Women who come to recover 'alternative' memories of childhood sexual abuse often believe that the abuse occurred when they were very young. This can be used to explain why they entered adulthood with no memories but it can also be used to explain why this unremembered abuse is believed to have had such a damaging effect on their adult lives.

More so than other forms of child abuse, the sexual abuse of children is believed to disrupt, or alter, the normal, natural path of children's development into healthy responsible adulthood (Dinsmore 1991, Parks 1990, Levenkron 2008). Sexual abuse is often referred to as an attack on childhood (Kitzinger 1997, Levenkron 2008) and this is reflected with titles such as *Stolen Tomorrows* (Levenkron 2008), *The End of Innocence* (Lalor 2001), *Childhood's Thief* (Evans 1995), *Betrayal of Innocence* (Peters 1986), *Stolen Childhood* (Huskey 1990) and *Shattered Innocence* (Weiner and Robinson-Kurplus 1995). The CSA recovery literature carries a relentlessly negative message in which sexual abuse in childhood, it is said, 'derails normal personality development, creating a variety of alternative outcomes and causing behaviours that will further damage the victim' (Levenkron 2008:15), incest 'robs children of their childhoods' (Dinsmore 1991:21) and victims are told 'they were damaged early. Something was broken at a core level' (Bass and Davis 1988:178). For the child who experiences abuse 'time was frozen' or 'stopped still' and she may 'remain fixed at that child level of emotional development' (Parks 1990:25). It is claimed that for women who were sexually abused in childhood 'adult information and knowledge are added as they grow up, but the underlying guilt, fear and inadequacy remain and govern much of their decision-making' (Parks 1990:25–26). Those who experienced such abuse are therefore positioned as qualitatively different from, or 'other' to, those who grow up without having been abused (Kitzinger 1997, Lamb 1999, O'Dell 2003, Reavey 2003). As sexual abuse is said to disrupt (healthy) development into adulthood victims do not successfully make this progression and are therefore also constructed as childlike, a state associated with weakness, powerlessness, vulnerability, sexual innocence (victims need to learn how to enjoy sex), and lack of reason, and therefore in need of looking after and educating. For the victim of CSA, childhood is said to be both lost and at the same time continuous. Unlike the non-abused child, who grows from a state of vulnerability to one of non-vulnerability, the abused child is said to remain vulnerable (O'Dell 2003) and, as an 'on-going victim' (Levenkron 2008), to remain helpless (Lamb 1999).

The powerful adult woman

The idea that sexual abuse in childhood disrupts a child's natural development to healthy adulthood helps to establish a particular norm of the healthy adult woman from which victims of CSA are said to deviate. It also helps to construct those who deviate from this norm as likely victims of sexual abuse, even if they have no memories of such abuse. The idea of a powerful, adult woman, untouched by abuse, is important to the harm story and survivor narratives as it allows for symptoms of sexual abuse to be identified in the lives of formerly abused women. Adulthood is constructed as qualitatively different from childhood and the child is thought to move from one stage to the other. This (healthy) adult (who by definition has not been abused) is strong, powerful, rational and able to look after and protect herself, and claim her right to a happy and successful future. As abuse, and particularly sexual abuse, is believed to disrupt the transition to adulthood, adult victims are often distanced from the skills, knowledge and attributes of adulthood, and therefore perceived as childlike and in need of looking after, either by a responsible adult or by the victim's adult self (Bass and Davis 1988, Dinsmore 1991).

Unlike the formerly abused woman, the woman who was not abused will grow up to thrive (Bass and Davis 1988, Dinsmore 1991). Thriving here means 'enjoying a feeling of wholeness, satisfaction in your life and work, genuine love and trust in your relationships, pleasure in your body' (Bass and Davis 1988:20). The mature, healthy, adult woman identified in the therapeutic literature can access her inner power and live a happy, fulfilled and successful life. Failure to do so is not seen as a consequence of the social, economic and political conditions which delimit their possibilities (Kitzinger 1993, Tavris 1992, Woodiwiss 2007a), but the result of abuse, which if unremembered is thought likely to have occurred in childhood. This serves to construct all women abused in childhood as damaged and in need of healing (Lamb 1999, O'Dell 1997, Reavey 2003), without which they will not be able to go 'from survivor to thriver' (Dinsmore 1991:380). It also helps to construct women who are not empowered or who are unable to claim their own inner power, often seen as unable to thrive, as victims of some form of abuse and therefore also in need of therapeutic help (Showalter 1997, Tavris 1992). Whether the effects are held by an inner child (e.g. Bass and Davis 1988) or located in the damaged, and therefore childlike, part of the adult woman (e.g. Fredrickson 1992), the identification of symptoms relies on the idea of a powerful adult woman. Located within a utopian version of reality she is said to have the right to individual happiness and success and needs only to exercise her own inner power to claim this right. In contrast, women who were sexually abused in childhood may grow up to be 'guilt-ridden, self-sabotaging, sexually dysfunctioning, on-going victims' (Parks 1990:13) who are 'not well adapted to adult life' (Herman 1992:110).

With an increased blurring of the boundaries between the self-help/self-improvement and the CSA recovery literature, women who fail to thrive are encouraged to embark on a therapeutic journey which will help them to uncover their own inner strength (see for example the works of Ainscough and Toon 1993, 2000; Ernst and Goodison 1981; Forward 1989; Hay 1984; Miller 1987, 1991; Norwood 1985, 1994; Woititz 1983). In addition to being 'an integral part of the process of revolutionary change' this healing journey is said to 'help us to reach beneath our conditioning to contact the power locked in ourselves' (Ernst and Goodison 1981:4). Although Ernst and Goodison's advice is aimed at 'ordinary women' it is not dissimilar to the advice offered to adult victims of childhood sexual abuse:

> Breaking free from your problems can release the person you are underneath...you can find your true self and live your life as you want to.
>
> (Ainscough and Toon 1993:243)

Women may not be held responsible for what caused their inability to exercise inner power but they are held responsible for the effects it has on their adult lives, said to be a result of their failure to heal.

Experiencing child sexual abuse

How a child experiences sexual abuse is an individual affair but much of the recovery literature presents a uniform experience in which the reader is presented with an account which often fails to acknowledge the (remembered) experiences of formerly abused women. It is an account which tells self-identified victims what they experienced, how they experienced it, their lack of control and inability to prevent it, and the effects it had on them at the time and later. It is also an account which enables adults who are unhappy or dissatisfied with their lives and looking for explanations to reinterpret childhood experiences as sexually abusive.

What we understand as sexual abuse has extended beyond physical contact and penetrative sex to include acts and behaviours not previously thought of as sexual abuse (Glaser and Frosh 1993, see also the Standing Committee on Sexually Abused Children, SCOSAC, 1984). The definition of child sexual abuse has expanded to include any activity or behaviour which the child (or later the adult) perceives, or might later perceive, to be sexually abusive. The way such abuse is thought to be experienced together with the perceived effects has also changed during this period, and any experience defined as sexual abuse is thought to be psychologically devastating (Lamb 1999; O'Dell 1997, 2003; Reavey 2003). Where differences are recognised, these are in the severity of the effects, and related not to what happened but to how it is perceived, both at the time and later (Renvoize 1993). The specifics of women's childhood experiences of sexual abuse are often rendered irrelevant as women are presented with an account of how they would have experienced sexual abuse. Formerly abused women are told how, as children, 'they are powerless and learn to passively accept the abuse, remain silent, and keep their feelings to themselves' (Ainscough and Toon 1993:112). In much the same way as the harm story has come to represent how women experience the effects of sexual abuse, the trauma story has come to represent how they experienced the abuse as children. This story relies on a developmental model of childhood which positions children as innocent, vulnerable and powerless. It also judges the abused child to be innocent because she was powerless, and therefore children's innocence relies on their having or exercising no power.

With an expansion in what has come to be understood as sexual abuse, some therapists have gone on to redefine other experiences as sexual and abusive. As Blume, the author of *Secret Survivors* asks, 'Must incest involve intercourse? Must incest be overtly genital? Must it involve touch at all?' (Blume 1990:5). The answer she tells us is 'No'. Incest she claims 'can occur through words, sounds or even exposure of the child to sights or acts that are sexual but do not involve her' (Blume 1990:5). A woman might only have seen her parents naked or heard them having sex to be able to claim she was sexually abused as a child. She may not have experienced any of these, but might instead be a victim of 'emotional incest' (Love 1990) or 'covert incest' (Adams 1991) wherein she is the victim of an 'emotionally abusive parent' whose love is selfish, not nurturing or giving (Adams 1991, Love 1990). Levenkron (2008) even includes in his book on understanding and treating victims of CSA, a woman who was not sexually abused in a 'straightforward' sense but who, in an attempt by her doctor to treat a urinary condition, was catheterised on a monthly basis between the ages of seven and eleven, a procedure which she experienced, or interpreted, as a sexual assault.

The contemporary story of CSA is a story that fails to acknowledge 'the other side of being a victim' and the variety of ways children may experience sexual abuse, and how some children may resist or attempt to mediate the effects of their abuse (Kitzinger 1997, Lamb 1999). As Kelly argued in the 1980s, rather than exploring women's and children's experiences of male violence most research 'has neglected, or indeed at times misread, the acts of resistance and challenge that women and girls take which display strength and determination' (Kelly 1988:185). With the trauma plot coming to dominate our contemporary storying of CSA this strength and determination has become increasingly harder to recognise as children's resistance is dismissed and their actions reinterpreted as passive acquiescence, which in the currently circulating narrative framework is a condition necessary for the victim to avoid blame. This not only constructs victims as entirely passive it also fails to recognise any attempts by them to exercise some control. In doing so it denies the lessons they may learn from resisting, albeit often in small ways, operations of power, which as Maguire points out 'is not just a negative, passive exercise. It liberates us from the constraints of an old framework and empowers us to create one better suited to our needs' (Maguire 1992:25).

Not only was this a valuable lesson learnt by feminists in the early days of second wave feminism but it has been a valuable lesson for victims of sexual abuse, one we should not deny them. Evidence of this lesson can be seen in the positive life choices victims make in adulthood as well as the negative ones. That literature which draws on the trauma and harm stories not only denies victims' own knowledge of abuse, and therefore the opportunity to create such a framework, but it replaces this understanding of power with one that equates power with health and maturity. The contemporary sexual abuse story provides an added incentive for those telling their story to exclude any exercise of power as it is only through doing so that they are able to reject an accusation of guilt and thereby claim the status of innocence. Those who did exercise some power, such as the child who 'exchanges favours' for abuse, are denied this.

Child sexual abuse as a causal narrative

Within the therapeutic and recovery literature women are encouraged to make connections between the past and present and to identify their past (childhood) histories in their adult lives. Where past histories include, or are believed to include, child sexual abuse this is elevated to prime importance (Reavey 2003). This construction of CSA not only relies on the developmental model of childhood but perhaps of more importance is the idealised version of reality in which it is located. Women are encouraged to acknowledge the negative effects of abuse and, whether or not they have memories, to identify symptoms in their adult lives. In assuming we live in a society of liberty, freedom and choice, failures experienced by victims are explained with reference to psychological damage and victims are encouraged to look to themselves and not the world in which they live (Armstrong 1994; Kitzinger 1993; Reavey 2003; Tavris 1992).

For those with no memories or knowledge of having been abused, the identification of symptoms enables the cause for their unhappiness or disaffection to be identified and, as it promises the way to a better life, provides the motivation to reinterpret their lives and rewrite their histories within a new narrative framework of healing and recovery. Those with continuous memories do not need to identify symptoms to know they were sexually abused and are instead encouraged to reinterpret their lives and attribute unhappiness to their own damaged psychologies. In order to do this they must accept the perceived wisdom of the 'incest industry' (Armstrong 1994) which promotes the idea that the healthy adult woman has the power to achieve happiness and success as well as the power to avoid falling victim to the symptoms identified in the therapeutic and self-help literature. For women with no knowledge or memories of abuse it is only through defining these 'symptoms' as psychological damage and correlating them with sexual abuse that they can (re)construct themselves as victims of CSA.

Whilst some therapists and commentators (Armstrong 1996, Herman 2000, Lamb 1999, McNally 2003, O'Dell 1997, 2003) do recognise that CSA is not inevitably damaging and that the sexual abuse of a child does 'not necessarily lead to any permanent emotional damage' (Herman 2000:33) the relentlessly overwhelming message, in both popular and recovery literature, is that psychological damage is unavoidable. Not only is sexual abuse seen as so much worse than other forms of abuse, neglect or mistreatment of children (Hacking 1995) but it is the sexual act itself (which may not be perceived as sexual at the time), rather than the circumstances surrounding that act and which inform how that act is interpreted both at the time and later, that is the focus of attention. The contemporary child sexual abuse story therefore fails to acknowledge the context in which children may have been sexually violated, or the experiences of those who only in retrospect can be claimed as sexual abuse. This context may be experienced as more traumatic or harmful than the sexual abuse itself and will lay the foundations for how all their experiences, sexually abusive or otherwise, might be interpreted or understood. The child who is neglected or made to feel worthless is likely to experience sexual abuse differently to a child who lives in an otherwise happy and supportive environment, even if the actual sexual abuse they were subjected to was the same. Their experiences beyond the sexual abuse contribute to how they understand and interpret any experience, sexually abusive or otherwise, but this is not recognised within the contemporary CSA narrative. With the focus on the 'act' itself the identification of even one brief experience that could be interpreted as sexual abuse, such as seeing a father naked or a parent having sex, can 'entitle' the child who witnessed such an event to 'claim', at the time or later in adulthood, the same identity of victim as someone raped repeatedly throughout their childhood years. With this elevation of the act itself, any sexual acts, including those not recognised as such until adulthood, are said to 'qualify' someone as a victim of CSA, and therefore how they might be experienced, interpreted, resisted or mediated, are rendered irrelevant to the telling of a CSA story.

It is fashionable within the CSA recovery movement to resist a hierarchy of abuse, in which some experiences can be recognised or identified as worse than others, and simply accept that if a woman claims to be a victim she is likely to experience the effects outlined in the literature. In some senses we are right to resist such a rating of experiences: abuse is traumatic because it is experienced as such. However, how it is experienced is also determined by how it is understood and interpreted, which is itself informed by our collective understanding and our collective refusal to recognise differences in women's or children's experiences of sexual abuse. This refusal has allowed the harm story to enter the library of currently circulating narrative frameworks available to anyone whose life is unsatisfying, unhappy or unsuccessful, or is simply looking to create a better one. Whilst it may not be helpful to look at degrees of 'harm' in relation to child sexual abuse, it is important to look at differences in children's and women's experiences and to look at where those differences originate and what informs those experiences. It may turn out to be that it is our contemporary storying of CSA, with its emphasis on perceived damage, secrecy and guilt, that is traumatic, possibly more traumatic than the abuse itself, and it is this that damages children who are sexually abused. It is certainly this which enables many adult women with no memories to tell their own sexual abuse narrative.

The inner child and evidence of psychological damage

Childhood sexual abuse is not always traumatic (McNally 2003), and neither is there evidence to suggest it inevitably results in lasting psychological harm (Finkelhor 1986, 1990; Hacking 1995; McNally 2003). A number of writers have challenged the negative construction of CSA (Armstrong 1996, Lamb 1999, McNally 2003, O'Dell 1997, 2003) which portrays it as inevitably damaging (Reavey 2003) and where it is 'the degree of suffering (not the grotesqueness of the injustice) that speaks of the wrongness of the assault' (Armstrong 1996:300). However, recognising what has happened to them and accepting they have been damaged is said to be an important step on victims' road to recovery (Bass and Davis 1988, 2002; Fredrickson 1992; Whitfield 1987,1995), and the further along this road they progress, the more healed they are said to be (Tavris 1992).

In much of the CSA recovery literature healing is centred on the concept of an inner child or damaged childlike part, as it is she who is said to influence the thoughts and behaviours of the adult woman. Readers are told that 'coming to believe that the abuse really happened and that it really hurt you is a vital part of the healing process' (Bass and Davis 1988:58). The inner child who is said to have split as a result of the abuse is said to hold the key to recovery and healing (Bass and Davis 1988, 2002; Parks 1990). It is she who is said to have been damaged and readers are encouraged to identify evidence of this damage in their adult lives. The knowledge she is thought to hold is said to be an accurate record of what happened (Bass and Davis 1988, 2002; Dinsmore 1991; Herman 1992), and more accurate than knowledge their adult selves might have. Contacting her will therefore increase their knowledge and understanding of what happened to them as children.

Whether conceptualised as an inner child or a childlike part of the adult victim, this inner self is conceptualised as vital to the journey to recovery and 'adulthood'. A constant message within this literature is the idea that:

> Inside every adult who was sexually abused are the feelings of the little child she once was. That little girl is still frightened, confused and crying – waiting to be comforted by parents who will never come for her... That child needs to be reached, needs to be comforted, needs information about what has happened to her.
>
> (Parks 1990:48)

Survivors may have difficulty with the concept of the child within:

> You may feel split, caught in a real schism. There is the 'you' that's out there in the 'real' world, and then there's the child inside you who is still a frightened victim.
>
> (Bass and Davis 1988:111)

Dinsmore advises readers to 'purchase a doll, a symbol of her inner child, to be nurtured' (Dinsmore 1991:79), but cautions women to choose carefully and take the process seriously. Not only can the search for the right doll be uplifting but it can

> Often be a catalyst for deep emotions to surface, thus giving us grist for the mill as we work on childhood trauma.
>
> (Dinsmore 1991:80)

For those who do have difficultly with the concept of an inner child, writers often support their advice with vignettes. These vignettes not only illustrate the inner child but also support the writers' own constructions of CSA and its victims as they convey the sense of 'truth' central to the recovered memory literature. In some instances the writers are themselves survivors (Parks 1990), sometimes only recognising themselves as such during the course of their work with others (see Davis 1988, Dinsmore 1991). One survivor in Parks' book says of her inner child:

> She is the living, hurt part of my subconscious, needing love and acceptance, but quite capable, unless educated, of ruining my present and future.
>
> (Parks 1990:188)

The inner child is a central figure in much of the CSA recovery literature but, not confined to this literature, populates many contemporary texts. Therefore many women who identify themselves as victims of sexual abuse and identify their own inner child have been introduced to the concept before they engaged with the CSA recovery literature. No longer confined to healing and recovery but infusing all areas of contemporary culture, the inner child can be used to help us pamper or look after ourselves, treat ourselves and negotiate a happier or more satisfying lifestyle. She can be found in the pages of popular psychology and self-help manuals, in the pages of literature, newspapers and magazines and in news and current affairs programmes, in popular television and radio soaps, in films and dramas, and in the many auto/biographies that can be found on the shelves of most book shops. So much a part of twenty-first century culture is the inner child that she even features in advertisements as a way to sell products. There are also websites devoted to contacting, healing, rescuing and playing with your own inner child, some with different sections designed to be accessed by inner children of different ages. In the therapeutic / healing literature this inner self is usually a child but elsewhere she might be an adult or some other form of inner self. She may be linked with childhood trauma or abuse but she may just be the part of ourselves who we are allowed, or are given permission, to look after or pamper. We need not have been traumatised in childhood to be able to identify our own inner self or inner child but for those who have been or believe themselves to have been, this child self can be seen to have split at the time of the traumatic event(s) and it is a child or childlike part of ourselves that we are encouraged to make contact with. Whilst adult women (and men) are encouraged to pamper their inner selves by indulging in activities such as relaxing baths, visits to health spas and indulging in 'retail therapy' or 'bibliotherapy', the traumatised woman is encouraged to indulge in childish activities such as cuddling teddy bears, listening to children's stories, and holding tea parties with her inner child (Bass and Davis 1988, Dinsmore 1991, Engel 1982).

We do not need to engage directly with recovery to become acquainted with the inner child but are likely to meet her in the pages of contemporary literature such as the novels of Margaret Atwood (1994) and Fay Weldon (1994), and in films such as *Sybil* and *The Three Faces of Eve*. She might make an appearance in celebrity biographies (see Roseanne Arnold 1994) and in light entertainment programmes on radio and television (such as The Bill). She has also featured in docudramas and documentaries such as *The Woman with Seven Personalities*. We are also likely to come across this inner child in survivor's stories, such as Fraser's *My Father's House* (1987) and Spring's *Cry Hard and Swim* (1987), which are no longer confined to the self-help/popular psychology sections of bookstores. Stories about overcoming childhood trauma are now so popular that they are not confined to the self-help/popular psychology sections of bookshops but have entered the mainstream and are even sold as holiday reading at airports. The twenty-first century shelves are filled with titles such as *Out of the Dark* (Caine and Royston 2004), the Dave Pelzer trilogy *A Child Called It* (1995, 2000), *The Lost Boy* (1997, 2003) and *A Man Named Dave* (1999, 2001) and *Don't Tell Mummy: A True Story of the Ultimate Betrayal* (Maguire 2007).

The symptoms

Central to the contemporary story of CSA is the promotion of an idealised version of reality which is itself located within a therapeutic ideology which embraces the idea that 'feeling bad is something to be got rid' and 'if we're unhappy there must be something wrong' (Kitzinger and Perkins 1993:83). In this reality women are not limited by external constraints (Faludi 1991, Tavris 1992) and, as long as they are healthy and therefore able to exercise their own inner power, they can achieve happiness, success and satisfaction in their lives. This allows for the identification of 'symptoms' in women's lives which, in the absence of explanations which recognise external factors, can only be attributed to a damaged inner child or childlike psychology.

According to Davis (2005) the main self-help books aimed at adult victims of CSA including *The Right to Innocence* by Engel (1982), *Repressed*

Memories by Fredrickson (1992), *Secret Survivors* by Blume (1990) and *The Courage to Heal* by Bass and Davis (1988) have all been popular with adult survivors, with *The Courage to Heal* going on to become a major bestseller. The latter text is one of the most popular self-help books aimed at adult victims of CSA and published a twentieth anniversary edition in 2008. In this text, Bass and Davis list over seventy symptoms, many of which take the form of 'adult behaviour patterns', 'acquired survival skills' or 'compulsive self-abuse'. They are grouped under a number of themes or headings such as self-esteem and personal power; feelings; your body; intimacy; sexuality; children and parenting, and families of origin. Often presented in the form of checklists of 'symptoms' they include

- Do you have a full range of feelings in your body? Or do you sometimes go numb?
- Are you aware of the messages your body gives you (hunger, fear, tiredness, pain)?
- Do you respond to them?
- Do you feel powerless like a victim?
- Do you have a hard time nurturing and taking care of yourself?
- Are you able to enjoy feeling good?
- Do you feel unable to protect yourself in dangerous situations?
- Have you ever experienced repeated victimization (rape, assault, battery) as an adult?
- Do you have trouble feeling motivated?
- Can you accomplish things you set out to achieve?
- Do you feel you have to be perfect?
- Are you comfortable with anger? Sadness? Happiness? Calm?
- Do you have a hard time loving and accepting you body? Do you feel at home in it?
- Do you often feel taken advantage of?
- Do you find your relationships just don't work out?
- Can you say no?
- Do you often have sex because you want to, or only because your partner wants it?
- Do you find it hard to set clear boundaries with children? To balance their needs with your own?
- Have you had trouble protecting the children in your care?
- Are you overprotective?
- Are you satisfied with your family relationships? Or are they strained and difficult?

- Do you feel crazy, invalidated, or depressed whenever you see your family?
- Have you ever been rejected by your family?

(Bass and Davis 1988:35–39)

Women find these symptoms listed elsewhere in the recovery literature, which not only reinforces the messages but also underscores their authority. Parks, for example, suggests that adult victims are 'guilt ridden, self-sabotaging, sexually dysfunctioning on-going victims' (Parks 1990:13). Herman believes the adult victim to be at 'great risk of repeated victimization' who 'finds it difficult to form conscious and accurate assessments of danger' (Herman 1992:111) and Bass and Davis suggest that 'Survivors were programmed to self destruct' (Bass and Davis 1988:179). Dinsmore includes in her list of possible symptoms chronic depression, drug and alcohol abuse, anxiety, suicide attempts and a history of revictimization (Dinsmore 1991:114). Blume includes depression, phobias, low self-esteem, fear of the dark, wearing baggy clothes and a pattern of ambivalent or intensely conflictive relationships (Blume 1990), and Engel includes an inability to complete tasks and difficulty in receiving from others (Engel 1982). The idea of revictimisation is also a pervasive theme running through the literature. The adult victim is said to be at 'great risk of repeated victimization in adult life' as she 'finds it difficult to form conscious and accurate assessments of danger' (Herman 1992:111). She is likely to find herself in abusive or exploitative relationships (Levenkron 2008) and to find healthy sexual and intimate relationships difficult (Dinsmore 1991, Levenkron 2008, Parks 1990). In the words of Bass and Davis, 'Survivors were programmed to self destruct' (Bass and Davis 1988:179).

These checklists are 'general enough to include everybody' (Tavris 1992:323), and can apply to most women at some time in their lives, whether or not they have been victimised in childhood (Haaken 1999, Showalter 1997, Tavris 1992). Their central premise is that the cause of the symptoms readers are encouraged to identify is likely to be located within the psychology of the reader who is then encouraged to dismiss external factors and look to themselves for explanations and solutions. These symptom lists also suggest to the reader what is appropriate and inappropriate in terms of thoughts, feelings and behaviours, both in adulthood and in childhood. Much of this literature not only 'gives a clear story of what a good/normal woman should be' (Warner 1996:47), but also constructs the victim of sexual abuse as both long suffering (Lamb 1999) and 'other' (Haaken 1998b, O'Dell 2003, Reavey 2003). It is therefore not only women who are unhappy or disaffected with their lives and looking for answers who could be seen to carry 'evidence' of past trauma but so too can those who deviate from prescribed norms of healthy female adulthood.

The readers of self-help texts are not only encouraged to listen to the 'experts' who write them, but also to the stories and testimonies of other victims, and find themselves in the stories of those others. Many writers also attempt to add validity to their arguments by drawing on the words of survivors themselves to help the reader 'recognize the damage' and encourage them on their journey to recovery:

> It has controlled every facet of my life. It has damaged me in every possible way. It has destroyed everything in my life that has been of value. It has prevented me from living a comfortable emotional life. It's prevented me from being able to love clearly.
>
> (Jennierose quoted in Bass and Davis 1988:33)

Levenkron not only uses victims' experiences to illustrate the harm story but the examples he uses can also be read as a warning as they illustrate how victims can be blamed for the actions of others. Jen, for example, 'cuts herself and dresses seductively. In her relationships with men, she is dependent and they treat her sadistically' (Levenkron 2008:17), and June 'is only attracted to abusive men, some of whom exploit her financially. She is in the process of divorcing her husband. Kind men do not arouse her sexually' (Levenkron 2008:17). Not only do these vignettes help to reinforce the story of the sexual abuse victim as psychologically damaged and likely to live an unhappy life in which she is vulnerable to further abuse but, in an additional twist to this plot line, she is held responsible for the behaviour of others. In a further twist, the abusive actions of these men can also be interpreted as evidence of sexual abuse in their childhoods.

Those who read the self-help literature aimed at victims of CSA are likely to combine this with reading survivor auto/biographies, which draw on the same narrative framework and reinforce the messages conveyed in self-help and recovery texts. This message is further reinforced through other cultural texts including soaps, docudramas and films, in the pages of contemporary novels, and in newspapers and magazines. Many of these also contain checklists of symptoms for the reader to identify with. For many reading is also combined with seeing a counsellor or therapist, who are also likely to make use self-help books, as diagnostic tools and sometimes or as part of a recovery programme, often setting the exercises as homework. Not all the 'self-help' literature is therefore aimed solely at survivors. *The Courage to Heal* (Bass and Davis 1988) for example, in addition to sections for family members and partners, has a section aimed at counsellors. Here counsellors are told to educate themselves about sexual abuse as they are likely to see women who have been abused, to recognise the symptoms of early sexual abuse and, for those who suspect a history of sexual abuse in clients who have denied it, to ask again later. For these clients, the counsellor is told, ' "No I wasn't" may mean "No I don't remember yet" ' (Bass and Davis 1988:350). Dinsmore also includes a section for therapists where she suggests 'therapists need to learn the symptoms and effects of childhood sexual abuse' (Dinsmore 1991:114). This literature is therefore an important resource not only for those in the process of making sense of their lives and for whom a sexual abuse story line offers them a coherent and logical narrative, but also for those therapists helping them to do so.

Sex and the contemporary sexual abuse story

Women's relationship with sex and sexuality is an area that receives particular attention within the CSA recovery literature. As with other aspects of this literature there are two stories that run in parallel. The first is the story of the healthy adult woman who, by definition, is sexually active, desirous and engages with sex in just the right way, for the right amount of time, for the right reasons and with the right partner. In contrast, the victim of CSA is constructed as someone who does not and cannot measure up to this ideal. Not only does this help to construct the victim of sexual abuse as someone for whom sex and sexuality is a problematic area but also serves to construct any woman who does not conform to this particular understanding of adult sexuality as problematic and, as they display some of the symptoms of CSA in their adult lives, as someone who is likely to have been sexually abused in their childhood.

Most of the therapeutic and recovery literature includes sections on sex and relationships and like other areas of the recovery literature, women are presented with lists of 'symptoms' or problems which they are encouraged to identify in their own lives. Within this therapeutically infused world of sexuality inhabited by self-identified survivors, women are not only said to have the right to a happy and fulfilling sex life but the desire for this is a sign of healthy adult womanhood (Kitzinger 1997, Woodiwiss 2008). It is not only failure to exercise these rights that positions women as unhealthy but so too is a lack of desire. Lack of a sexual partner is no excuse as women are encouraged to develop a healthy and active sexual relationship with themselves as well as, eventually, a partner. Failure to do so is seen as evidence of psychological damage and within the context of recovery is seen as evidence of CSA. A central premise of the recovery literature, which enables evidence of sexual abuse to be identified in the lives of children and adult women, is the distinction between childhood innocence and adult knowledge (Kitzinger 1997, Reavey 2003). Whereas the non-abused child is defined as sexually innocent and the healthy adult woman is defined as sexually knowledgeable, active and desirous. This allows for sexual knowledge, desire or activity in a child and the lack of such knowledge, desire or activity in the adult woman both to be defined as evidence of sexual abuse. Among the symptoms found in the pages of the recovery literature and self-help manuals are 'symptoms' associated with sex, which include an inability to stay present during sex, an inability to experience sexual pleasure and feeling ones worth as primarily sexual.

There are, Dinsmore suggests, 'several ways a survivor may relate sexually' (Dinsmore 1991:92) which are by definition seen as unhealthy and problematic within therapeutic discourses:

> She may be asexual, having no sexual contact with anyone... she may be very sexual with numerous partners but not feel emotional or physical pleasure. She may feel obligated to be sexual in a primary committed relationship but not feel any pleasure.
>
> (Dinsmore 1991:92–93)

Elsewhere readers are told that victims might avoid 'romantic and sexual encounters', feel 'guilty over sexual arousal' (Levenkron 2008), and have difficulties with 'vaginal entry and reaching orgasm' (Renvoize 1993:147). She might also suffer similar consequences to those whose stories are included in the literature such as Rose who says 'I find sex so disgusting and can't even bear to see my own body naked' (Rose quoted in Baker 2002:13), Judy who 'was uncomfortable having sex, but... never knew why' (quoted in Bass and Davis (1988:360), and Olivia who is 'married, thirty-two, and incapable of being sexually aroused' (Levenkron 2008:17).

Within the narrative framework of CSA recovery, finding 'evidence' in their child or adult lives provides women with a story line they can use to make sense of their lives. It can also be used to write the story they want to live by, which may or may not involve being sexually active. Whilst this might enable some women to construct a future biography to exclude sexual activity they must, in doing so, identify themselves as damaged. Not only does this help to construct women who do not conform to a particular construction of healthy adult sexuality as victims of sexual abuse, it also helps to reinforce this construction as the norm against which all women can be measured. As such it could also be seen to encourage victims to become sexually active, even if not sexual desirous, as a way to demonstrate, to themselves as well as others, that they are healthy, healed and recovered. It is however, a storyline that does not allow women to construct a life story involving a self who is healthy but at the same time either not sexually active or desirous or not willing to conform to this ideal of sexual well-being presented in the CSA recovery literature.

The healing discourse

Women engage within self-help and therapeutic literature, including that aimed at victims of CSA, for a variety of reasons but primarily because they want to improve their lives. Whilst many women construct a sexual abuse narrative, often based only on the correlation of perceived symptoms with past abuse, they do so because they believe this story will lead them, through its therapeutic corollary the healing discourse, to a happy and successful life. The telling of a sexual abuse story reflects the 'first stage of therapy' identified by Davis in which the client is encouraged 'to give an account that emphasized vulnerability, powerlessness, a false identity, and psychological defenses and coping mechanisms that have blocked genuine self-awareness' (Davis 2005:193). Whilst in this first account 'the client is a victim', in the next account, produced during 'the second stage of therapy' (Davis 2005), the writer is encouraged to reconstruct herself as a survivor. It is the healing discourse that enables such an account to be written.

Readers of CSA recovery literature are presented with a catalogue of possible symptoms which are likely to have a devastating effect on their adult lives. It is therefore important that they are also given hope that they can improve their lives and write their own 'survivor account' as identified by Davis (2005). Survivor testimonies are particularly important when it comes to 'victims' overcoming trauma, healing and recovery, and going on to lead happy, successful and fulfilled lives. It is the words of survivors, rather than the words of therapists or writers of self-help manuals, that carry the message of optimism to greatest effect and it is in their stories that readers can try and identify not only with the past and the present, but also the future. Writers can offer advice as to how to move from victim to survivor but in the words of other survivors they can see that it might be achieved:

> With incest you are powerless. You have no self-worth. My greatest accomplishment is that I took my power back. And I never give it away to bosses, authorities, my own family. No one can make me feel unworthy again.
>
> (Nyla, quoted in Cameron 2000:302)

The appeal of the harm story can best be understood when it is viewed as part one of a narrative that enables the writer to construct a new chapter in which they can contact their inner (child) self, access their inner power, and thereby find happiness, success and fulfilment. The healing or survivor discourse might provide such a narrative framework to some but the happy, successful, fulfilled life is not a story that all women are able to write themselves into.

Alternative endings: False memory syndrome

Not all those whose biographies feature sexual abuse based on the harm story and recovered memories are able to write a happy ending or new beginning. Some are able to employ this narrative framework to identify 'symptoms' in their adult lives but are not able to move beyond this identification to write themselves into a storyline that, drawing on the healing discourse, sees them access their inner power and claim their right to a happy, fulfilling and successful life. For these women there are a number of narrative frameworks available to them which, although appearing to take them in very different directions, do not completely reject the framework of an abuse narrative within which to make sense of their lives.

One such direction might take the narrator deeper into the world of abuse narratives and recovered memories and whilst the other would appear to lead them away from this world that is not quite the case. This latter direction involves claiming an identity as a victim of false memory syndrome (FMS), whereby the teller rejects the abuse narrative they previously told and construct for themselves instead a story in which they cast themselves as 'victims', not of sexual abuse but of false memories of sexual abuse. Those on the other side of the 'recovered memory wars' led by the False Memory Syndrome Foundation (FMSF) and the British False

Memory Foundation (bfms) have challenged the veracity and truthfulness of sexual abuse claims based on 'recovered memories' and believe those who construct such narratives are victims of misguided or possibly malicious therapists who implant 'false' memories of sexual abuse in the minds of weak and vulnerable victims (de Rivera 1998a, 1998b; Loftus and Ketcham 1994; Ofshe and Watters 1995). These women, it is argued are the victims, not of sexual abuse in childhood, but of false memory syndrome in adulthood. This new story would appear to be based on the storyteller coming to recognise as 'false' the story they had previously told and invested in, but this is too simplistic an understanding. Claiming a history of false memory syndrome is no more tied to believing in the falsity of their former abuse narrative than a history of CSA is tied to believing in the truth of that narrative.

We are all involved in an ongoing process of storying our lives, of telling stories to make sense of who and what we are and the circumstances we find ourselves in. In doing so we are also writing a script by which we might engage with the world and live our lives in a way we hope will bring us among other things, happiness, success and fulfilment. In telling their story of CSA some are able to write such a script but others cannot. These writers are faced with a new problem: how to write a new script, that might lead to such an ending, whilst at the same time explaining how and why they came to write a story that they now claim to be untrue. Rewriting their story within a narrative framework of FMS offers the possibility of writing a happier ending and a new character for themselves and a new cast to populate their story. Very often, stories of sexual abuse involved accusations against family members and family break-ups and those who identify themselves as victims of FMS are likely to have removed themselves from their families. This new storyline offers a way to mend those bridges and possibly unite families against a different 'abuser'. For those who invested in their character as 'victim', this new story also allows them to keep this identity, at least until they no longer need or want it. This story line is not, however, limited to those who reject their memories of sexual abuse but could also be employed by those who, without necessarily rejecting their memories, want to establish closer contact with their families. This 'new' story is, like the story of CSA, a story of, or for, our time.

Alternative endings: Multiplicity

Narratives of sexual abuse based on recovered memories rely to some extent on an inner child or children and it is therefore of little surprise to discover that multiple personality syndrome (MPS) and the emergence of tens, and sometimes hundreds, of 'alters' is also associated with stories of childhood sexual abuse. There is some consensus among the majority of those working within the field of multiple personalities that hypnosis is significant for the emergence of these personalities either because hypnosis is thought to encourage an alter personality to surface (Bliss 1986, Putnam 1989) or because it is thought to be central to the creation and acting out of alter personalities (Ofshe and Watters 1995). Whilst there is evidence to suggest that hypnosis is significant for the emergence of multiple personalities in some cases, there is also evidence to suggest other routes by which these personalities might come to life. If we look at the emergence of multiple personalities within a narrative framework of contemporary storytelling we can see that their emergence or creation can be understood as part of the ongoing process of storying our lives, and refining or developing our characters, that we all engage in.

Rewriting their life story within a framework that rejects previously held memories is not the only option available to those unable to write themselves into a happy, successful, fulfilling narrative. Another alternative plot line is available, particularly to those who have invested heavily in an abuse narrative. The sexual abuse narrative, particularly for those who story relies on alternative memories, is based on some form of inner child or child self. It is this 'child' who holds the key to knowledge and it is she who is said to be in need of healing. For those who have invested in this narrative and the idea of an inner child a continuation of their storyline might lead them to discover, or search for, additional inner children who also hold knowledge of previous abuse. Not all those who engage with the recovery literature identify more than one inner child, but the sexual abuse narrative does allow for the existence of additional children, and a way to contact them. For those who have invested in the idea that the difficulties they experience in adulthood are caused in some way by a damaged inner child, it is only a small step to attributing ongoing difficulties to an additional inner child or children, who has yet to be contacted and healed, and from here it is possible to contact many. As the shelves of bookshops testify, with titles such as *When Rabbit Howls* (Chase 1987) and *37 to One: Living as an Integrated Multiple* (Hocking 1996), there are many auto/biographies written by women who believe themselves to share their lives, not with one inner child, but with many. These texts do not provide the reader with a ready-made script to follow, but they do offer a framework through which they can make meaning of their lives.

Beyond the harm story

The contemporary story of childhood sexual abuse views it as an entirely traumatic experience with inevitable and devastating long-term effects, as if we can only acknowledge the wrongfulness of child sexual abuse if we can equate it with inevitable psychological damage. This relentlessly negative construction of child sexual abuse and its consequences is also a pervasive theme underpinning the CSA recovery and recovered memory literature. However there are some dissenting voices. As Finkelhor and Browne point out, although there is widespread acceptance that sexual abuse will have negative consequences for a child's development 'the search for scientific proof is not doing very well (Browne and Finkelhor (1986) cited in Hacking 1995:64). There is they argue:

> An unfortunate tendency in interpreting the effects of sexual abuse... to overemphasize long-term impact as the ultimate criterion... child sexual abuse needs to be recognised as a serious problem of childhood, if only for the immediate pain, confusion and upset.
>
> (Browne and Finkelhor (1986) cited in Hacking 1995:64–65)

Hacking also questions the focus on sexual abuse, to the exclusion of other forms of child abuse. As he rightly identifies it is this construction of CSA that is central to the emergence of the contemporary abuse narrative as an explanation for many of society's ills:

> If we had been content to intervene in child abuse just because it is bad, we would not have our present set of beliefs about the consequences of child abuse.
>
> (Hacking 1995:66)

It is this set of beliefs that allows for 'knowledge' or 'memories' to be uncovered from the minds and bodies of victims and enables women with no memories to rewrite their biographies around an organising framework of sexual abuse. It is also this set of beliefs that forces those with continuous memories to deny aspects of their biographies and tell a particular version that conforms to our collective understanding of sexual abuse. It is no longer adequate to look simply at whether women's stories of CSA based on recovered memories are true or not. Instead we need to look at the process through which they have constructed such stories, and what other stories might also make sense of (and improve) their lives. In doing so it is also necessary to join those who challenge the relentlessly negative understanding of CSA that is encapsulated in our present set of beliefs about the causes and consequences of child abuse. To do so is not to deny the wrongfulness of child sexual abuse but to recognise the varied ways that women make sense of their lives, whether or not they were victims of sexual abuse as children.

Giving voice

Our bookshops are full of stories and self-help texts aimed at adult victims of childhood traumas. Among these contemporary stories are recovery tales, tales of surviving family dysfunction and childhood sexual abuse. There are even stories of surviving the stories told publicly by family members of surviving abuse. However, as Armstrong noted in the 1990s, in the cacophony that is the contemporary telling of sexual abuse recovery stories 'children's voices, women's voices, are once more not, in any purposeful sense, being heard' (Armstrong 1994:7–8). Women can tell of how they have been damaged by abuse, which they do not remember, but they cannot easily tell of how they resisted and challenged, coped with and learnt from, a sexually abusive childhood that they do remember. This alternative is a story that has been shunted from the library of contemporary storytelling. It is a storyline which we must reintroduce if women are to be free to tell, or not, of having been sexually abused as children.

Not all the women whose stories feature in the following pages remember being sexually abuse as children but they have all, at some point in their lives, constructed their biographies around an organising framework of such abuse. Whilst for some this involved drawing on the current orthodoxy to construct a sexual abuse narrative that made sense of their lives and could act as a guide for living, for others that orthodoxy has forced them to deny important aspects of a life story they could once have told but which they must now reject in favour of the harm story and healing discourse of contemporary sexual abuse survivorship.

3
Beyond the Recovered Memory Wars

Almost any problem or behaviour can be seen as a symptom of abuse, just as most any problem, behaviour, or perception can be said to be a memory of abuse.

(Ofshe and Watters 1995:85)

Introduction: The main debate

The childhood sexual abuse narrative that is currently available to those looking to make sense of, understand or improve their lives is based largely on an understanding of CSA which allows for evidence or symptoms, in the form of 'recovered' or 'alternative' memories, to be identified in the lives of formerly abused women. This book explores how women construct and make use of their own life stories or narratives of CSA, the majority of which are based on recovered or alternative memories of having been sexually abused in childhood. However, in order to explore women's narratives of CSA it is necessary to look first at what has come to be known as the 'recovered memory wars'. This is not because I wish to establish the 'truth' or 'falsity' of women's stories but rather to illustrate how the telling of such stories might come about and how the emergence of stories based on recovered memories have influenced the telling of other CSA recovery stories.

Recovered memories

The recovered memory wars appear to be about the validity of memories of CSA and participants often wrongly assume that the memories under debate are always 'recall memories' whereby individuals remember, or falsely remember, past experiences of sexual abuse in childhood.

The dispute therefore centres on whether memories are 'true' or not and, if 'untrue' or false, where these memories come from. The focus is largely on the role therapists and writers of CSA recovery literature play in the recovery or creation of previously unknown, inaccessible or, as some would argue, false memories of CSA, rather than on the women whose memories are at the centre of the debate. For many whose life story is based on 'recovered memories' of CSA, it is not 'recall memories' that they recover, but 'alternative memories' which can include a range of perceived 'symptoms', reinterpreted as alternative memories, and believed to be stored in, and recoverable from, the minds and bodies of victims. It is these alternative memories, rather than recall memories, that much of the CSA recovery and recovered memory literature aims to help those who believe themselves to be victims to uncover.

The concept of 'alternative' or 'recovered' memories is not based simply on the wrongfulness of CSA but on the belief that CSA is a devastating experience that inevitably has deep and long-term effects on victims, combined with a failure to recognise a range of external factors which might equally be the cause of women's unhappiness or dissatisfaction. Traumatic memories, such as those relating to CSA, it is argued, are not encoded and stored in the same way as non-traumatic memories and can take the form of imagistic memory, body memory, feeling memory and acting-out memory (Fredrickson 1992, Herman 1992, Whitfield 1995). As discussed in the previous chapter, they are often shown as lists of symptoms but can also take the form of dreams and flashbacks, physical or bodily experiences such as pain and nausea, feelings such as sadness, depression, anxiety or fear and other (common) events or difficulties experienced in the lives of adult women (Bass and Davis 1988, Blume 1990, Fredrickson 1992, Herman 1992). These memories are seen as the influence of a damaged 'inner child' or child like part of the adult who is thought to exert an unhealthy influence on the former victim. Within much of the CSA recovery literature these memories are also viewed as unmediated (and therefore 'true') versions of past events (Bass and Davis 1988, Blume 1990, Courtois 1992, Fredrickson 1992, Herman 1992, Olio 1989, Whitfield 1995), and as such should not be challenged or subjected to (re)interpretation.

The surfacing of these memories is said to be spontaneous and inevitable and therefore neither the individual who remembers or, if she has one, her therapist, are thought to be responsible for the emergence or construction of such memories. Proponents of 'alternative memories' often make connections between attempts to silence women's accounts and feminist struggles to have women's stories of rape and abuse heard, making it particularly difficult for feminists to question such memories (Haaken 1998b, 2003, Showalter 1997). An alternative position is taken by those who claim that false memories of abuse are implanted in the minds of weak and vulnerable victims by malicious or misguided therapists (de Rivera 1998a, 1998b, Dineen 1999, Ofshe and Watters 1995, Pendergrast 1997, Yapko 1994a, 1994b). Although Multiple personality disorder or syndrome (MPD/S), or Dissociative identity disorder (DID), is not central to the memory wars, similar arguments have also been applied to the emergence or creation of multiple personalities (see for example Putnam 1989 for the emergence of alter personalities, Ofshe and Watters 1995 for the creation of alter personalities and Showalter 1997, Hacking 1995 for women's use of alter personalities). These arguments not only fail to recognise that most recovered memories are not recall memories they also fail to acknowledge the active role played by those who tell their own stories of CSA, which for some might involve making a break with a (familial) past (Haaken 1999).

The CSA recovery literature is aimed at those with continuous memories as well as those who simply feel that they are victims of CSA but much of it is written with the aim of helping to uncover evidence of abuse. Whilst those with continuous memories are encouraged to make connections between past abuse and adult difficulties, those with no memories are encouraged to look for evidence, in the form of symptoms, in their adult lives. These symptoms can be seen as the result of psychological damage (Fredrickson 1992, Herman 1992) or the influence of an 'inner child' on the thoughts, feelings and behaviour of the adult victim (Bass and Davis 1988, Cameron 2000, Dinsmore 1991, Parks 1990, Hall and Lloyd 1989, Whitfield 1995). Symptoms can be used to identify the effects of CSA. However, for many, coming to 'know' they were abused relies on a redefinition of memory to include 'alternative memories' such as imagistic memory, body memory, acting-out memory and feeling memory (Fredrickson 1992, Herman 1992, Whitfield 1995). These can take the form of dreams and flashbacks, physical or bodily experiences, such as pain and nausea, and feelings such as sadness, depression, anxiety or fear. Although proponents of recovered memories recognise the limitations of normal recall memory in recording past events, they argue that traumatic memories are different and the processes by which trauma is stored in the mind or body allows them to remain intact as an accurate and true record of past events. Trauma is believed to affect the way events are encoded into memory and the way those 'memories' return (Bass and Davis 1988, Cameron 2000, Dinsmore 1991, Fredrickson 1992, Herman 1992, Miller 1987, 1991). These memories, it is claimed:

> Were never encoded linguistically, thus traumatic memories reappear implicitly via the sensorimotor systems as kinaesthetic sensations, smells or tastes, or visual images, flashbacks and nightmares.
>
> (Hovdestad and Kristiansen 1996:38)

More significantly, although explicit memory improves with age, these implicit memories, it is argued, do not, 'indicating that the implicit memory system is age-independent' and thus 'it is neurobiologically possible to recover implicit memories of trauma experienced during infancy' (Hovdestad and Kristiansen 1996:33), a time from which explicit memories would not be expected. The very young child together with the child who does not understand are not at a disadvantage in storing traumatic memories which then can be recovered from a time when other memories do not exist.

These alternative memories are said to provide more solid knowledge and enable victims to 'validate concretely what they know intuitively' (Dinsmore 1991:65). For those whose mind 'chooses to forget', the 'body remembers'. These memories 'are stored in our bodies, and it is 'possible to physically reexperience the terror of the abuse' (Bass and Davis 1988:74–75). Victims are told, 'everyone has a child within her' (Hall and Lloyd 1989) and 'within all of us there is an inner voice telling us how we feel' (Bass and Davis 1988:117). This voice may be experienced in a variety of ways – dreams, headaches, exhaustion, obsessive cleaning – 'the important thing is not what you experience, but that you recognise it as a message' (Bass and Davis 1988:117). For those with no conscious knowledge their unconscious:

> Had for years been speaking to them in a variety of languages – bodily symptoms, emotions, sexual problems, compulsive self-abuse, and strange dreams and fantasies.
>
> (Cameron 2000:158)

Repressed memories, acknowledges Fredrickson, 'never feel the same as recall memories' and victims 'will not have the sense of having experienced the abuse' (Fredrickson 1992:99) she is remembering. Validation of this newly uncovered knowledge is said to take the form of 'sense memories, childhood coping skills, childhood and adult behaviour patterns and acquired survival skills' (Dinsmore 1991:64), and the victim will 'gradually come to know that they [the memories] are real, but not in the same way that you will remember something that was never repressed' (Fredrickson 1992:99–100). These 'implicit memories of trauma have a life of their own' (Hovdestad and Kristiansen 1996:43). They are seen as a spontaneous and inevitable display of the effects of past trauma and neither therapist nor victim are believed responsible for their emergence.

The inner child

The inner child is a central character within much of the CSA recovery literature but she can take a variety of forms. She is the inner child, the child within, the damaged child-like part of the adult and the inner or core self. She might also be a discrete personality or a personality fragment. She is the holder of memories and information that the adult woman may or may not have knowledge of. For some she is not alone but may be one of a group of 'alters' or multiple personalities (male or female, of different ages and even animals), who split during years of abuse in childhood but continue to share the adult victim's world and protect the 'first person' from harm. She can be, based on the idea of the innocent child, the undamaged part of the adult victim, the core to which they can return. The inner self who, once rid of the experiences and effects of abuse, can go on to become the woman she would have been (Ainscough and Toon 1993, 2000; Bass and Davis 1988, 2002; Parks 1990). Alternatively, she is said to be the abused and damaged part of the adult woman (Fredrickson 1992). Some writers use both terms wherein the 'inner self' is also seen as 'the child within' (Whitfield 1995). Thought to be created at the point of trauma, when the innocent child is unable to cope with the experience and splits, the inner child is said to be stuck at the time of the abuse and is therefore seen as the key to both knowledge and healing (Bass and Davis 1988, 2002; Parks 1990). Trapped with feelings and emotions from the time of the abuse and the holder of memories, she is believed to have access to the knowledge or truth of past events (Bass and Davis 1988, 2002; Dinsmore 1991; Fredrickson 1992; Herman 1992; Whitfield 1995).

The accuracy of this knowledge and the view of the 'inner child' as an 'objective observer' or recorder of events is reinforced by the idea that for her 'time was frozen' or 'stopped at the moment of trauma' (Dinsmore 1991:59). By contacting their inner child the survivor gains access to knowledge which she either 'sees' or 'experiences', and so 'startle reactions, flashbacks, and sleep disorders, such as nightmares, occur, replicating the experience as if it were happening at that moment' (Dinsmore 1991:59). The victim is said to 'reexperience the original abuse' (Bass and Davis 1988:73), which is seen 'through the child's eyes' (Cameron 2000:195). Flashbacks are seen to be involuntary, spontaneous and, for the majority of victims, inevitable, but some claim they can also 'provide a context for previously denied memories laid down during similar dissociated states years before' (Cameron 2000:183) thereby enabling the victim to gain additional knowledge. The victim can 'record and use the flashback as a way of going deeper into childhood memory' or can later 'relive the flashback with congruent effect and gain access to further events of her childhood' (Dinsmore 1991:66). Whether acquired from the original flashback or a result of going deeper into memory, this knowledge is seen as ever present and waiting to be viewed. As Cameron argues of such memories, 'reality had broken through' (Cameron 2000:178).

In the literature that plays host to a damaged inner child, it is she who is said to influence the thoughts, feelings and behaviours of adult women, evidenced by the array of 'symptoms'. It is in identifying symptoms that women not only begin their journey to recovery but also first make the acquaintance of the inner child. In attempting to make sense of and improve their lives it is the aspect of the inner child who is thought to influence their adult selves that women are likely to come across first. Therefore, before they acknowledge their own inner child and develop a relationship with her, women may have already accepted the idea of an inner child, and in doing so brought their own inner child a step closer to 'reality'. This is perhaps all the more imperative for those whose only knowledge comes from identifying her influence, and they are encouraged to let their inner child play a significant role in their lives, in terms of healing and memory retrieval (Bass and Davis 1988, Engel 1982, Parks 1990). The need to validate abuse claims may provide an initial impetus for some to contact an inner child but many go on to develop relationships which are not limited to retrieving memories. Readers are encouraged to indulge their inner child, to hold birthday parties for her, read children's stories, watch children's television and buy her dolls, teddy bears and other presents. For some, it may simply offer a way to treat themselves.

The role of therapists and self-help literature in the creation or surfacing of the inner child is a central question within the recovered memory wars, within which women are often constructed as passive victims of sexual abuse or therapists. However, the relationships women develop with an inner child are not as simplistic or as static as the debate would suggest. Whilst she has a certain uniformity within the literature, the inner child, or childlike part, of women's accounts is more fluid and women's engagement with her more critical, complex and pragmatic. She may be more or less real, more or less childlike, more or less in control, depending on the (changing) needs, wishes and circumstances of those who engage with her. For some she may not exist at all whilst for others she may be a useful tool or companion on their journey through life or to recovery. For others she may be the product of therapeutic techniques, such as inner child work, which can be perceived as both useful and dangerous. Whatever she is, she is not and cannot be taken straight from the pages of the CSA recovery literature or imposed on women by external agencies, but neither does she emerge fully formed from women's subconscious.

Not all proponents of recovered memories embrace the inner child and whilst this appears to have little impact on the memories themselves, it does inform the role of therapists. Fredrickson (1992) a psychotherapist and Herman (1992) a feminist therapist, both believe therapists need to take an active role in helping their patients uncover and interpret hidden knowledge. In her widely cited book *Repressed Memories* (1992) Fredrickson claims that both the conscious and unconscious 'have the capability to record and access events and information' (Fredrickson 1992:88). People, she argues, have five kinds of memory: recall memory is consciously retained whilst imagistic, feeling, body and acting-out are the memory processes of the unconscious mind. These 'repressed' memories 'stalk your unconscious and hamper your life with their aftermath' (Fredrickson 1992:24) as the victim 'continues to register the effects in her body' (Herman 1992:108) and believes the therapist must help victims retrieve these memories. Herman (1992) also identifies a central role for the therapist. Together patient and therapist must recreate the story and in this process the therapist 'normalizes the patients' responses, facilitates naming and the use of language, and shares the emotional burden of the trauma' (Herman 1992:178). The creation and telling of the trauma story is for therapists such as Fredrickson and Herman a joint effort between patient and therapist.

The emergence of stored traumatic memories is said to be inevitable and spontaneous, but without the concept of an inner child the meaning attached to them may require interpretation (Fredrickson 1992, Herman 1992). The symptoms 'speak in a disguised language of secrets too terrible to remember' (Herman 1992:96). A professional therapist can help the victim with what Fredrickson (1992) identifies as one of the seven methods of memory retrieval: imagistic work; dream work; journal writing; body work; hypnosis; feelings work; art therapy (Fredrickson 1992:97–99). These memories 'will tell you a story if you know how to listen to them' (Fredrickson 1992:24), and victims are advised to seek professional help not only for support and validation but also in the process of uncovering and interpreting their sometimes hidden knowledge of abuse (Fredrickson 1992, Herman 1992). The process of discovery and healing is 'an internal journey in which you must piece together mind and body clues to find out what you have forgotten' (Fredrickson 1992:25) and whilst the clues are ever present the victim may need the help of a therapist to piece them together. This can take the form of 'imagistic memory work', a therapeutic technique advocated by a number of leading exponents of the recovered memory movement including Bass and Davis (1988), Fredrickson (1992), Maltz (1991) and Prozan (1993). The client is encouraged to spend time 'imagining that you were sexually abused, without worry about accuracy, proving anything or having your ideas make sense' and to 'give rein to your imagination' (Maltz 1991:50–51). This technique draws on the idea that 'bad' thoughts, including sexual thoughts and fantasies, are improper, incorrect and sick and so women feel they must disown them (Showalter 1997). For those who, in giving rein to their imagination, describe sexual or disturbing thoughts and feelings, the belief in buried knowledge provides an explanation for such imagery. We should not be surprised, argues Showalter, that women still find it 'difficult or impossible to acknowledge erotic, antisocial, unfaithful aspects of their own psyches' (Showalter 1997:165). One way of doing so is to attribute them to a damaged (child) self.

At one level the 'recovered memory movement' is about retrieving buried memories but not all agree on the need to recover memories, and some recognise that recall memories are rarely recovered. Far from being problematic, a lack of memories can be seen as evidence of CSA. In the incest survivors' after-effects checklist in *Secret Survivors* (1990) Blume lists at number twenty-six the symptom 'Denial: no awareness at all' (Blume 1990). In a similar vein Fredrickson suggests that 'profound disbelief is an indication that memories are real' (Fredrickson 1992:171). Forgetting, or amnesia, is one of the most common symptoms of CSA and therefore remembering or recovering memories is thought by some to play a central role in a victim's journey to recovery (Olio 1989, Courtois 1992, Herman 1992). Recovering memories is, exhorts Olio, 'crucial to successful resolution of the trauma' (Olio

1989:99). To avoid them leads to 'stagnation in the recovery process' (Herman 1992:176). Recognising that gaps in the story can sometimes remain even after painstaking exploration, Herman advocates the 'judicious use of powerful techniques such as hypnotherapy', psychodrama and 'the use of sodium amytal' (Herman 1992:185–186). More important than retrieving memories is recognising the damage and dealing with the effects of sexual abuse (Bass and Davis 1988, 2002, Dinsmore 1991). Memory, counsels Dinsmore, is 'not needed for survivors to begin the acknowledgement process' (Dinsmore 1991:56) or even the healing process as 'one does not need memory to heal from abuse' (Dinsmore 1991:65). Whereas some recovered memory advocates believe memories are crucial, others acknowledge that:

> Instances of regaining such memories are rare.
>
> (Dinsmore 1991:64)

> Many women don't have memories, and some never get memories. This doesn't mean they weren't abused.
>
> (Bass and Davis 1988:81)

As these writers go on to acknowledge:

> If you don't have any memory of it, it can be hard to believe the abuse really happened.
>
> (Bass and Davis 1988:82)

There is an alternative for those who find it hard to believe the abuse really happened and begin to doubt their once believed in memories, and question whether they provide an adequate explanation for unhappiness or offer a way to future happiness. Those who wish to turn their back on a CSA storyline, can draw on an alternative framework of the FMS in which they are able to rewrite their life story and construct themselves, not as victims of CSA, but victims of false memories.

False memories

The sexual abuse narrative may have entered the stockpile of available stories but it is not without its critics, many of whom believe that recovered memories are created in therapy by misguided or malicious (often feminist) therapists. Much of the criticism has been institutionalised in the American False Memory Syndrome Foundation (FMSF) and the British False Memory Society (bfms). These are largely action groups established to help 'falsely accused parents', to publicize the dangers of irresponsible therapists and to support those who retract their memories and their allegations. Members of the FMSF and bfms have themselves created a new disorder in the form of false memory syndrome (FMS), to support the view that false memories are implanted in the minds of (often) weak and vulnerable patients. As they rightly point out, the symptoms identified in the recovered memory literature do not necessarily indicate a history of CSA. Although focussing on what they understand to be FMS, both the FMSF and the bfms are also critical of MPD, and claim both conditions are created by therapists. Which one emerges first depends on 'whether the therapist first hunts for alter personalities or for repressed memories' (Ofshe and Watters 1995:205). Proponents of FMS still construct those whose biographies are based on recovered memories as victims, but victims of FMS, at the hands of therapists, rather than victims of CSA. FMS refers to 'a distinctive iatrogenic pattern of beliefs/behaviours that appears to develop in the course of iatrogenic therapy' (de Rivera 1997:271). This involves the development of a contra factual belief system and a transformation of personal identity (de Rivera 1997). Although proponents of FMS agree that it is a condition created in therapy there is no consensus as to how this 'contra factual belief system' and the 'transformation of identity' are achieved and what role, if any, the patients themselves play. This disagreement is largely centred around two models. The mind control model promoted by Ofshe and Watters (1995) and the FMSF, and the self-narrative model as outlined by Sarbin (1998).

In the mind control model the therapist is said to undermine the ability of patients to make decisions. As a result they relinquish control to the therapist who then provides them with a story that gives meaning to their lives. Therapists, working on the premise that the effects of sexual abuse in childhood can be seen in the lives of adult victims are said to search for non-existent hidden memories. The central premise of this model is that the therapist is the author of the story and convinces, or persuades, the patient of its validity. The patient is often isolated from those who might challenge this new story – either because they are sceptical or because, as might be the case with the accused and their families, they have knowledge which contradicts the new story. At the same time the patient might be encouraged to immerse themselves in the culture of repressed memories and gain additional support for their story. This is the model favoured by the American FMSF and exemplified by Ofshe and Watters in their widely cited book *Making Monsters* (1995). They acknowledge that many who enter therapy have been:

> Exposed to the theories of the recovered memory movement – ideas that might be sufficient to predispose them to the belief that sexual abuse is at the bottom of their problems.
>
> (Ofshe and Watters 1995:84)

However, they do not interpret this awareness as contributing to the construction of abuse narratives except that it makes patients more open to manipulation by therapists. As they believe therapists take an active role in the telling of an abuse story, with patients relegated to a minor role of passive acceptance, their focus is on therapists and writers of CSA recovery literature. Ofshe and Watters suggest that a client's acceptance of an abuse history is often a two-stage process. Therapists, they argue, can convince patients to relabel feelings and symptoms as memories in only a few sessions but 'helping the client to create a detailed pseudomemory of abuse can take much longer' (Ofshe and Watters 1995:87). The first stage involves convincing clients that their symptoms indicate past abuse and then changing their understanding of memory so that these symptoms can be reinterpreted as memory. As they point out:

> Almost any problem or behaviour can be seen as a symptom of abuse, just as most any problem, behaviour, or perception can be said to be a memory of abuse.
>
> (Ofshe and Watters 1995:85)

The second stage, the creation of pseudomemories and the construction of an abuse narrative, is they believe more difficult. The focus in much of their writing is on those aspects of therapy said to create false or pseudomemories. Drawing directly on the work of therapists they highlight some of the advice offered to patients:

> Spend time imagining you were sexually abused, without worrying about accuracy, proving anything or having your ideas make sense. As you give rein to your imagination, let your intuition guide your thoughts.
>
> (Maltz 1991 cited in Ofshe and Watters 1995:92)

They draw on examples from the literature to illustrate the role therapists and the therapeutic encounter can play in the construction of 'false' memories. Maltz, for example, recommends the therapist ask the patient questions such as 'Who would have been likely perpetrators?' and 'Why would it have been important for you to forget what happened?' (Maltz 1991). Another example of 'imagistic memory work' used to reinforce their argument is taken from Fredrickson who includes the advice 'whether what is remembered... is made up or real is of no concern at the beginning of the process' (Fredrickson 1992 cited in Ofshe and Watters 1995:93). The bfms is also critical of Fredrickson who they argue provides:

> The building blocks of an action-packed visual narrative, including the suggestion that the therapist provide scene prompts to cue the sluggish 'memory'.
>
> (bfms1999)

Advocates of the mind control model of FMS have shown that therapy can play a central role in the construction of false memories of abuse but this is not the same as demonstrating that it does. Missing are the voices of those whose memories are said to have been recovered or implanted, those who continue to believe in their memories as well as those who have retracted them.

The self-narrative model does appear to acknowledge the teller who is seen to be 'the first author of the story' (de Rivera 1998a), at least in making the original suggestion. This is located within a framework of FMS and therefore not only assumes the memory to be false but allocates ultimate responsibility with the therapist. In this model the patient, drawing on readily available ideas on child abuse and repressed memories, begins to construct a story which makes sense of her life. The therapist is responsible in that s/he does not challenge this story but instead gives it credibility and encourages, or initiates, the search for memories to support the new story. Whilst the patient may be responsible for the original idea, the details and the patient's conviction in its truth are seen as the responsibility of the therapist. Within this model the patient is seen to be unhappy and disaffected with her life and vulnerable to the manipulations of misguided, or malicious, therapists. The principle of this model is the 'readiness of human beings both to organize their experience and to interpret their social lives according to narrative plots' (Sarbin 1998:15), which in the context of recovered memories are assumed to be false. As Sarbin argues, 'the content of experiences identified as believings' (based on phenomena) 'cannot be differentiated from the content of experiences identified as imaginings'

(Sarbin 1998:22). The assumption is that the experiences on which these narratives are based are false but we cannot prove them to be. Within this model there is an assumption that at some level the story is initially known to be false but, under the right conditions, gains credibility and comes to be believed. The story is not constructed over a period of time during which the teller comes to reinterpret her life but rather she is said to adopt a ready made story, albeit lacking some details, which makes sense of her life and which she then comes to believe. Although this model evades to some extent the question of truth, it is based on a true/false dichotomy in which the story, and the memories, can only be either true or false.

Evading the issue of truth, albeit by assuming indemonstrable falsity, the question then becomes how do 'some imaginings become believings, that is, serve as guides to conduct' (Sarbin 1998:22). Identifying the patient as the first author could imply responsibility but if the patient is a victim of FMS then at least some of that responsibility must lie with the therapist. The central question identified by Sarbin allows for this shift in the allocation of responsibility. The story is only believed with any degree of certainty when it is given credibility and therefore we need to ask:

> What are the antecedent and current conditions that account for the credibility a person assigns to the propositions arising from poetic imaginings?
>
> (Sarbin 1998:24)

This does allow for some acknowledgement of the wider context within which abuse narratives are constructed but the focus is on the therapeutic encounter and therapeutic 'conditions' under which the story gains credibility and attention is directed away from those who believe themselves to have been abused. However, according to McNally the proportion of those who report having recovered memories during psychotherapy is between 14 and 68 percent (McNally 2003). As McNally observes 'the fact that a trauma memory surfaces outside therapy does not guarantee its accuracy' (McNally 2003:259), but it does suggest that we should look beyond the confines of the traditional therapeutic relationship. Indeed, not only can we see the influence of therapy infusing our everyday lives but therapy itself can now increasingly be accessed outside of the traditional therapeutic relationship. Therapy can be accessed, along with the views, and experiences of other 'victims' and survivors, from the privacy of our own homes. Not only can we obverse therapeutic culture in operation on television and radio but we can also participate more directly through interactive technology such as chat rooms, blogs and support groups found on the Internet, and which connect us with communities of people seeking answers to similar questions across the globe. Those who tell their stories to such communities are likely to find their stories validated as they are listened to by people already predisposed to believing them. They are also likely to find validation for their story in the stories told by other members of such communities.

Beyond the main debate

The main debates within the recovered memory wars have focussed on the role of therapists and the truth or falsity of abuse narratives. Within these debates the FMSF, the bfms, and those who question recovered memories of CSA are seen as anti-feminists who silence the voices of women and deny the sexual abuse of children. This has made it difficult for those, particularly feminists, concerned about recovered memories to enter the discussion and has led some to call for a reframing of the debate. Whilst some argue for a redefining of meanings so as to identify some truth in women's stories of sexual abuse (Brown 1996, Enns et al 1995, Haaken 1998b, Park 1997), others start with an assumption of falsity but look at the role women themselves play in knowingly adopting false narratives of CSA (Hacking 1995, Showalter 1997, Spence 1998). Within this approach some agency is accorded to the 'victim' or storyteller but she is constructed as someone who makes use of ready-made narratives to explain unhappiness and failure (Hacking 1995, Showalter 1997, Spence 1998). Recognition of the widespread availability of ideas around CSA, repressed memories and recovery, together with the view that women knowingly tell false stories of sexual abuse, has led to a focus on the problematic psychologies of those who come to tell these stories. This has led to a reframing of questions to include: why do people knowingly adopt a narrative that is untrue? (Spence 1998) or 'what needs are women attempting to meet through these therapeutic investments, sickness lifestyles, and emotional histories?' (Showalter 1997:11).

Although critical of the CSA recovery, self-help and recovered memory literature those who take up this position to some extent reinforce the premise that satisfaction and fulfilment is a matter of self-actualisation. Spence (1998) argues that those who construct false stories of abuse have a 'low tolerance to modern day hassles' (Spence 1998) but in doing so dismisses or minimises the variety of ways that women's lives are constrained, and identifies a failure to cope with modern living as a failing in individual women. Spence suggests three reasons for the adoption of a false abuse narrative: (1) it explains and excuses the teller's failure to cope with life, (2) it provides the sufferer with an 'all consuming personal narrative – a new identity', (3) it is a means to achieve a position of authority. This new 'identity-explanation-narrative' he argues 'is remarkably successful – almost invulnerable – as a piece of causal reasoning to explain present unhappiness' (Spence 1998:221–222). As it is a narrative that 'stands almost entirely on first-person testimony' it 'becomes very hard to validate' (Spence 1998:222) and therefore elevates the teller to a position of authority. Any role played by the therapist is seen by Spence to result either from manipulation or a 'disturbing unspoken pact' in which the therapist is paid for services in return for supporting the false story. A similar understanding underpins Showalter's argument wherein she identifies both abuse narratives and multiplicity as hysterical epidemics to which unhappy or discontented women succumb (Showalter 1997). Although she recognises that women can use a sexual abuse narrative to make sense of and improve their lives, express feelings and act out otherwise difficult behaviour, she too focuses on perceived inadequacies of those who do so, but does not share Spence's view of their intent. They do not, she argues, 'generate these confabulations out of an intention to deceive. They may need to define an identity, work out anger toward the accused, or respond to cultural pressure' (Showalter 1997:147). Central to arguments which claim women knowingly use false narratives of CSA is an acknowledgement that through doing so they may improve their lives. Whilst this recognises that external factors contribute to unhappiness and dissatisfaction, and allows for the possibility that a CSA narrative, even if untrue, might offer a reasonable explanation for such unhappiness, the focus remains on the problematic psychologies of those who make use of these narratives.

The process of constructing an identity based on recovered memories of CSA is often assumed to be traumatic but as Showalter (1997) points out this is not always the case. Using the example of Marion, a woman whose story she read in an alumni magazine, Showalter suggests that:

> When she began to think of herself as a survivor, Marion could explain many of the disappointments and failures in her professional life.
>
> (Showalter 1997:152)

It is not only for Marion that Showalter believes the experience has 'been a good one ... both socially and professionally'. Showalter is also

> Certain that many professional women besides Marion have found comfort and community through the process of recovered memory.
> (Showalter 1997:153)

Showalter is right to believe that many women have found comfort and community in the telling of a sexual abuse narrative, but this is because our contemporary storying of CSA helps them make sense of their lives, whether or not they were sexually abused. It is no surprise that women then want, or need, to tell their story to a community who will validate it. Although Showalter looks for an explanation for why these 'hysterical epidemics' have gained currency and entered the 'symptom pool' she looks to the psychologies of individual women, rather than society and the conditions in which they live, for the answer. Like Spence, she accords some agency to the storytellers and rejects the idea that they are simply manipulated by therapists but Showalter also sees the adoption of an abuse narrative as a way to mediate or excuse individual failure.

The view that the narrators of these stories take ready-made fictions and use them to explain present unhappiness or failure appears to be supported by Hacking when he suggests, 'we grasp at whatever picture is floating by and put our past into its frame' (Hacking 1995:88–89). However, he does allow for the possibility that the construction of an abuse narrative may involve the reinterpretation of a life in which, from the vantage point of the present, childhood experiences can be reinterpreted as sexually abusive (Hacking 1991, 1995). The expanded definition of sexual abuse in western culture enables the construction of an abuse narrative that can be true *of the past* even when it was not true *in the past* (Hacking 1995). The construction of such a narrative, he suggests, is a 'way of explaining oneself, not by recovering the past, but by redescribing it, rethinking it, refeeling it' (Hacking 1995:94). However, there is the implication in Hacking's work that, even where victims come to reinterpret their lives and construct a 'true' history of abuse, this is done by taking a ready made narrative and tailoring it to meet their individual needs. Past experiences are reinterpreted within this new, adopted narrative framework. Hacking accepts there may be an element of truth in some child abuse narratives, at least in the present, but he shares with Spence and Showalter the view that the initial motivation for their adoption is to excuse failure and blame unhappiness on an external cause.

Finding a truth

Looking for truth in accounts based on recovered memories has led some to ask different questions such as 'In what sense, then, might these memories be true?' (Parks 1997:15). Whilst not disputing that some recovered memories might be true in the sense that they relate to lived experiences, those who take up this position also believe that they may reflect women's adaptations to their 'sexual, emotional, physical, social and economic, or even therapeutic circumstances' (Parks 1997:34). Brown also argues that on hearing women's claims to have recovered memories of CSA, therapists should respect and accord authority to that knowing, but goes on to argue that the distress and shame caused by this 'knowing' 'need not have derived from direct encounters with sexual or physical violation' (Brown 1996:14). It may result from sexism, racism, heterosexism and other forms of oppression. As this suggests, not only childhood abuse but also women's everyday lives can have damaging psychological effects. Whereas in the recovered memory literature 'symptoms' are seen as evidence of abuse in childhood, here they are recognised (or interpreted) as abusive but this 'abuse' may have occurred in adulthood. This constructs women as psychologically weaker and less able to cope with the stresses and strains of everyday life than men, an argument found in other self-help literature. In identifying psychological damage and a need for healing the question of truth becomes irrelevant, as the focus is on the effects of 'abuse', whether suffered in childhood or later life. Whatever the cause, it seems women are in need of healing.

There are some including Tavris (1992) and Kitzinger (1993) who, whilst identifying negative effects of women's subordinate position in society, do not look to women's psychologies to explain their engagement with CSA narratives but look instead to the therapeutic culture in which this takes place. Tavris acknowledges the sexual abuse victim story 'draws like a magnet those who feel vulnerable and victimized' (Tavris 1992:321). She argues that CSA has become 'a metaphor for all that is wrong in women's lives' and suggests women use repression and narratives of CSA as 'a way to participate in this metaphor' (Tavris 1992:321). Within our therapeutically informed culture, where political action has been replaced by an individualising mental health movement (Kitzinger 1993), the sexual victim identity is for some women 'a lightening rod for the inchoate feelings of victimization they have as a result of their status in society at large' which provides a 'clearer focus than such vague enemies as "the system", sexism, deadening work, welfare or boredom' (Tavris 1992:321). Tavris believes the victim identity enables women to recognise 'a truth' in their lives. Linking that identity with CSA provides a way to participate in the airing of grievances within a culture that offers women few alternatives. The problem with recovered memories is not that some women construct false histories, but that constructing these histories and focussing on an abusive event in the past, whether true or not, does not ultimately help them to improve their lives or challenge the structures and practices which cause those grievances. Identifying a history of abuse can help a woman make sense of her life but it does so by identifying abuse as the cause of her problems and encourages her to focus on her own personal healing in order to alleviate or cope with problems rather than address the cause of those problems.

An element of truth can be seen in the stories of women who infer a history of CSA even if they were not sexually abused as children. As Haaken says of those reading *The Courage To Heal* (Bass and Davis 1988),

> While many self-diagnosed survivors who recover new memories of sexual abuse may not have been literally abused by their fathers, they are likely to find some of the truth of their experiences embedded in the narratives of this lengthy text.
>
> (Haaken 1998b:180)

Haaken criticises the claims in Bass and Davis' text that recovered memories are a message coming directly from the unconscious, arguing that they fail to 'appreciate the rich, textured nature of memory or the multiple meanings and interpretations of representations of the past' (Haaken 1998b:183). For Haaken 'There is a dynamic, motivational aspect to remembering' (Haaken 1998b:253) which the literature on recovered memory fails to recognise. The motivation is not simply to make use of a ready-made narrative to excuse failures, as suggested by Showalter (1997), but involves the desire to articulate a range of thoughts and feelings in the process of understanding and improving ones life and achieving desired goals. The truth of memory, Haaken suggests, 'may reside in underlying themes... rather than its factual content' (Haaken 1998b:251). Women might, in constructing an abuse narrative, be reconstructing themselves as victims but they might be able to do so because they have already constructed themselves as victims, albeit not necessarily of CSA.

The context and women's motivation are central to the creation, shaping and organisation of (emerging) memories of CSA (Haaken 1998b). For Haaken the significant context is the position of women within the family and their role as caregivers, which delimits their opportunities for independence and self-identity (Haaken 1998b). She believes that for many women, recovered memories of CSA 'are an effort to disengage from familial entrapments, to fortify the blurry boundary between self and others, and to sever binding ties' (Haaken 1998b:247). Central to this argument is the idea that a motivating and organising theme in women's lives is in the need to break from parental constraints. Sexual abuse as a social script is 'readily mobilized in various memory-making contexts' (Haaken 1998b:186). When this context is the desire to break free from family ties, to reject parental influences and constraints, the memories that emerge, reinterpreted or re-felt as abusive, can provide justification for breaking those ties. Although she believes the family is significant, it is the therapeutic encounter which Haaken claims can contribute to the creation of new memories (Haaken 2003). Not through a powerful authority figure implanting false memories but in the creation of an atmosphere that facilitates the expression of thoughts and feelings which can be articulated through an abuse narrative. The memories that form the basis of this narrative need not be literally true but may still be true to the woman's feelings.

Haaken recognises the CSA narrative as a readily mobilised social script but, like Tavris, links its widespread use with a lack of alternatives (Haaken 2003, Tavris 1992). This lack relates not only to available discourses and narrative frameworks but also the cultural invisibility of many of the 'subtle or ambiguous forms of bad treatment girls and women endure' (Haaken 1998b:127). For some, therefore, 'dramatizing abuse is the strategy of resistance most readily available' (Haaken 1998b:127). The expanded definition of sexual abuse together with the collapse of the meanings of these experiences in the unifying appeal of survivorship, Haaken claims, renders the CSA narrative the more appealing (Haaken 1999, 2003). It enables a reinterpretation of past experiences, viewed through a lens of sexual abuse, to be understood in the present as sexual abuse. This, together with the contemporary focus on CSA, Haaken argues, encourages women to draw on a sexual abuse narrative as a legitimate, and possibly only, means to articulate otherwise neglected or invisible aspects of the 'bad treatment' they endure (Haaken 2003). Women do not create a new identity as victim, but reinforce an identity (which includes victim), as they incorporate a history of CSA into the ongoing process of recreating their identity and sense of self.

This view of women's pragmatic use of abuse narratives is shared by Tietjens-Meyers, although she is more sceptical as to its value and suggests we should 'regard the sadistic incest scenario as a figurative window onto ones present and to remain agnostic about its relation to ones past' (Tietjens-Meyers 1997:244). We all draw on culturally furnished figurations to make sense of our lives and who we are and then 'elaborate these figurations into autobiographical narratives' (Tietjens-Meyers 1997:244). The sexual abuse narrative has become widespread amongst women, she argues, because many of the complaints widespread among women are 'amenable to this figuration' (Tietjens-Meyers 1997:244). However, she cautions against relying on these narratives to construct a sense of self and suggests that 'where the past is epistemically opaque, self-definition must be insulated from memory' (Tietjens-Meyers 1997:244). The issue for Tietjens-Meyers is not the truth or falsity of women's abuse claims but the value of using recovered memories to construct autobiographical narratives based on the sadistic incest scenario. It is rarely possible to establish the accuracy or truth of recovered memories and therefore the narrator of such a story may be 'doomed to a tormenting state of autobiographical limbo' (Tietjens-Meyers 1997:246). Tietjens-Meyers also questions whether the sadistic incest scenario helps women improve their lives and asks whether it might 'stifle women's potential and divert them into a cramped, subordinate social niche?' (Tietjens-Meyers 1997:245). Calling directly on feminists Tietjens-Meyers urges, 'since other figurations could be devised to represent the miseries and sorrows that the sadistic incest scenario is presently being used to represent, feminists have every reason to oppose it and to champion alternative figurations' (Tietjens-Meyers 1997:246). However, she believes alternatives are necessary for those with no memories of abuse, but not necessarily for those who have memories, for whom CSA is 'a shattering experience that often leads to a shattered condition' (Tietjens-Meyers 1997:248). It is this commonplace but problematic view of the inevitable consequences of childhood sexual abuse that has enabled the sadistic incest scenario to gain currency as a way to explain the 'miseries and sorrows' of many women's lives.

Within this model the identity of victim can be constructed in response to lived experiences rather than seen as the adoption of a role. This may provide 'victims' with a more secure identity, where they do not need to search for hidden memories, but it also raises the question of why women choose to construct themselves as psychologically damaged and responsible for their future happiness and well-being. This redefinition of recovered memories has developed in part in response to the recovered memory debate but it shares many commonalities with other elements of the recovery, self-help and self-improvement literature, bringing us full circle within which 'incest has crossed the boundary... into metaphor' (Armstrong 1994:213). Whether they are the victims of CSA, patriarchy or modernity, of toxic parents or a toxic world, women are encouraged to engage with the discourses of therapy, self-help and recovery and embark on a journey of self-improvement and self-development in which the self is seen as a project on which to be worked, but where women are seen to have more work to do than men.

False memories of sexual abuse

Opponents of recovered memories who rally behind the banner of FMS concentrate their efforts almost exclusively on the role of therapists and in doing so fail to explore the role of self identified victims in the construction of a sexual abuse narrative based on 'recovered memories'. de Rivera (1998b) did go some way towards addressing this omission when he looked at the mind control, self-narrative and role enactment models. The role enactment model is similar to the model outlined by Spence (above), except that the person enacting this role, suffering from FMS, does not know it to be false and is not responsible for believing in its validity. This model draws on the theory that in our everyday lives we all enact a variety of roles, at different times and in different situations, which are consistent with those times and situations. The distinction between the three models offered by de Rivera lies in the level of responsibility accorded to the therapist. In the mind control model patients are subjects of the therapists story, the self-narrative model sees patients as subjects of their own story and in the role enactment model they are actors in a drama played out in society (de Rivera 1998b:172). All three models rely on the presence of an authority figure in the form of a therapist who exerts undue influence on the patient and 'asserts that the narrative explains the person's problems or supports the validity of the narrative' (de Rivera 1998b:186). When constrained by a discourse of FMS, all three models allocate ultimate responsibility, and blame, to the therapist. The different models illustrate the different levels of influence exerted by the therapist.

de Rivera did not attempt to explore his respondents' experiences, but instead asked them which of the three models accounted for 'what happened to them'. Of the fifty-six respondents who participated twenty-three endorsed the mind control model, ten the self-narrative model, seven a combination of mind control and role enactment and four a combination of all three. Six felt that none of the accounts 'did justice to their experience' (de Rivera 1998b:173). The participants were self-selected out of a group of one hundred and fifty-nine who agreed to be involved after being sent the three accounts. All the respondents had retracted their claims of abuse and identified themselves as having suffered from FMS prior to their participation in the research and were members of the FMSF foundation. Although de Rivera's research only looks at how self-identified FMS victims come to construct a 'false CSA narrative' it does raise some interesting issues around the construction of abuse narratives, including the retractor accounts in which the respondents had invested. The reasons most respondents gave for their certainty that their memories were false were related to the benefits they gained when they rejected these memories. FMS appears to challenge the validity of recovered memories but it is no more dependent on the falsity of recovered memories than the construction of a CSA narrative is reliant on the truth of those memories. The respondents in de Rivera's research it would appear rejected their recovered memories and their sexual abuse narratives because, as a guide for living, they did not ultimately make them happy or improve their lives. This was only achieved with the rejection of one narrative in favour of an alternative abuse narrative in which victims suffered from false memory syndrome. It is therefore important to look at the role of those who construct an abuse narrative whether based on 'recovered' memories and a narrative framework of CSA or on 'false' memories and a narrative framework of FMS.

Trauma and the creation of identities

The concept of multiple personalities, or alters, does not feature in all the CSA recovery and recovered memory literature and where it does this is typically restricted to the identification of only one alter personality, which usually takes the form of an inner child. For others however, sexual abuse in childhood is thought to result in a more extreme form of multiplicity (Putnam 1989, Ross 1995) in which the (typically female) victim is believed to have an average of 15 personalities. The majority of those who develop MPD or MPS are said to have been sexually abused in childhood, usually before they reach the age of five (Bass and Davis 1988), or to have been victims of more extreme forms of trauma such as ritual or satanic abuse (Bloom 1994, Ross 1995). Recovered memories of CSA are often reliant on a form of multiple personality (whether understood as MPD, MPS or DID), albeit usually involving only one alter, who takes the form of an inner child. This is because CSA is believed to cause the abused child to 'split' at the time of the abuse and to be 'stuck' holding the knowledge of that abuse, at the time the abuse took place. Whilst the majority of the CSA recovery literature relies on a single 'alter', or inner child, much of the MPS literature assumes populations of alters, thought to be created during more extreme forms of abuse, including ritual and satanic abuse, and abuse involving a number of abusers (Bloom 1994, Putnam 1989, Ross 1995). No causal connection has been established between CSA and multiplicity (Ganway 1989, Hacking 1995) but this has become a matter of common perception, and has been used as an explanation for repressed memories of CSA (Showalter 1997). Multiplicity has also been connected with concerns over CSA (Hacking 1995) and, it has been suggested, offers women 'a way to express forbidden aspects of the self' (Showalter 1997:164). Showalter links the increasing number of 'alters' a multiple displays with 'the increased number and complexity of social roles women are expected to fill' (Showalter 1997:163). Like Showalter, Hacking links multiplicity with earlier hysterias, and suggests that 'dissociative behaviour is a language of distress' (Hacking 1995) which provides women with a way to express inadmissible emotions. As MPS is more common in women than men, this suggests that women are not only less able to cope with their changing social roles but are also more in need of a 'language of distress'.

MPS is said to refer to autonomous personalities, but the official heading of Dissociative Identity disorder (DID) in the fourth edition of the Diagnostic and Statistical Manual (DSM IV) (American Psychiatric Association 1994), allows for this condition to be seen in terms of personality fragments rather than discrete personalities. However, neither the change in definition nor the shift in understanding has been universally accepted within the field of dissociative conditions. Coons (1980), for example, had argued, before the official change in definition, against considering these alters as separate or autonomous personalities suggesting that they should be seen as 'personality states, other selves, or personality fragments' (Coons 1980). True MPD, diagnosed as amnesia between alters and the host, is more reliant on witnesses than recovered memories of abuse as the host is said to be unaware of her alter personalities, at least until an external source brings them to her attention. DID, on the other hand, is less reliant on external witnesses as these personality states can be seen as the expression of different aspects of the victim's personality. As such, they are also less reliant on formal diagnoses. The field of multiple personalities has also seen the emergence of alters who themselves have alters or multiple personalities such as *When Rabbit Howls* (Chase 1987), *37 to One* (Hocking 1996).

Unlike the literature on recovered memory there appears to be agreement amongst both proponents and critics of MPD that hypnosis plays a significant role in the 'diagnosis' and 'treatment' of MPD. Whilst supporters of MPD believe hypnosis can be useful in encouraging an alter personality to come forward and take control of the patient's consciousness (Bliss 1986, Putnam 1989) those on the other side believe hypnosis is central to the creation of MPD and the acting out of multiple personality behaviour (Ofshe and Watters 1995). However, as will be seen in the account of Anne, one of the women who participated in this research, this is not the only route by which multiple personalities might come to life. It is possible that at least some alters may enter the world with no help from hypnosis, and very much under the direction of their 'host', the adult self. The concept of the inner child, although central in much of the recovered memory literature and itself a form of MPD, albeit usually with only one alter, does not feature in the debates around MPD. This is surprising, especially given the shift from MPD to DID. Within the recovered memory debates the argument centres on whether memories are true or false. In the MPD debate the argument is whether hypnosis is used to create multiples or to facilitate the emergence of already existing personalities. Ofshe and Watters clearly believe the former. Although critics acknowledge that some patients may be motivated to accept a diagnosis of MPD, for example to absolve themselves of responsibility for thoughts and actions they are unhappy or uncomfortable with, they believe that:

> To fully understand how and why patients first begin to act out their hidden selves, we must explore the close relationship between MPD treatment and the use of hypnosis.
>
> (Ofshe and Watters 1995:215)

The therapist who suspects MPD might 'directly ask for a personality to step forward and take control of the clients' consciousness' which can be done 'with or without hypnosis or trance-inducing drugs' (Putnam 1989 cited in Ofshe and Watters 1995:213). As with abuse narratives, Ofshe and Watters acknowledge that modern patients know how MPD patients would act and the 'type of behaviour that would confirm the diagnosis' (Ofshe and Watters 1995:212). This is then used to support the view that these patients are in some way inadequate. For the patient who 'abuses alcohol or hits her child', confirming the therapist's diagnosis 'would not only be a step toward an explanation for those actions but would also give the client some sense of absolution for their consequences' (Ofshe and Watters 1995:212).

The mind control model used to explain the emergence of recovered memories, endorsed by the FMSF and the bfms, is also used to explain the emergence of MPD. Like recovered memories of abuse, MPD is said to be a condition constructed during the course of therapy (Aldridge-Morris 2000, McHugh 1993, Ofshe and Watters 1995) and 'never occurs as a spontaneous natural event in adults' (Merskey 1992 cited in Ofshe and Watters 1995:222). Patients are said to be unaware of having the condition before treatment and develop 'their most dramatic and debilitating symptoms only in the course of therapy' (Ofshe and Watters 1995:207). Whereas proponents of MPD believe it is the result of sexual abuse in childhood, Dr Aldridge-Morris, a consultant clinical psychologist and member of the advisory board of the bfms, suggests that:

> The place to look for MPD is not in the brain, but in the culture, the practice of a sub-group of clinicians and a host of poorly qualified acolytes, and the hypnotic suggestibility of a patient group.
>
> (Aldridge-Morris 2000:11)

Although Aldridge-Morris allocates responsibility and blame for the emergence of MPD with clinicians, he also identifies aspects of a patient's psychology as a contributing factor. He identifies victims as weak, vulnerable and at the mercy of traumatic experiences or misguided therapists, rather than fully engaged responsible adults. Whilst he argues that we should look for multiple personalities 'in the culture', he does not fully acknowledge the extent to which that culture has permeated all aspects of our everyday lives and is engaged with by responsible adults who may well play a part in the identification or creation of multiple personalities in their own lives in the process of constructing a life story that makes sense to them.

The change in terminology from MPD to DID in the DSM IV (1994) indicates a broadening in the understanding of multiplicity and as such has had a major impact on the debate, although not necessarily on the lives of those who believe themselves to play host to numerous personalities. This has enabled sceptics to engage in discussions around MPD without rejecting the condition outright. However, the change in definition does maintain the belief that MPD or DID is a psychiatric disorder together with the view that sexual abuse in childhood has long-term negative psychological effects that may well manifest themselves as multiple or dissociated personalities. Although some in the MPD movement still claim that multiplicity, caused by trauma, results in splitting and therefore autonomous personalities, this shift in terminology has also led to an expansion of the condition which in turn has led to more women being diagnosed, or diagnosing themselves, as suffering from DID. Whilst this might be seen to construct more women as psychologically damaged it can also be seen as enabling women to actively engage with some of the ideas of DID, such as exploring or articulating different aspects of their identities, in a way that they were perhaps unable to within a more rigid discourse of MPD. Perhaps more significantly, it also blurs the boundaries between MPD and the inner child or children of the CSA recovery and recovered memory literature.

The recovered memory wars have been constructed as a debate over the truth or falsity of memories of childhood sexual abuse. Within this debate, and to those who observe it from the sidelines, there is an assumption that the memories in question are recall memories in which the rememberer recalls actual memories of sexual abuse in childhood. However, this is far from the case and even those working in the field of 'recovered memories' acknowledge that such memories are unlikely to be recovered. Within the debate the overriding image of 'victims', of CSA or therapists, is of women who, lacking agency, are weak, vulnerable and at the mercy of their damaged psychologies. Although they are in some respects at the centre of the debate, the voices of women who have drawn on our contemporary storying of childhood sexual abuse to construct their own sexual abuse narrative are largely absent. This is particularly surprising given that the tellers of these stories do not base them on 'recovered recall memories' but on the piecing together of 'symptoms' in an attempt to make sense of their lives, and this is not something that can successfully be forced upon them.

4
Choosing a Story: Making Sense, Finding Evidence

So the main thing for me was to learn that I could forget

(Beccy)

That would really completely make sense but I still didn't have any memories

(Beccy)

Introduction

We live in a society of story telling in which we constantly tell and retell our life stories. We tell stories to make sense of our lives and who we are, to justify or explain our actions, and to guide us through life. Telling stories enables us to maintain or make, and sometimes sever, connections with a past and lay foundations for the future. It is through our story telling that we construct a sense of place, a sense of self and a sense of purpose. In telling our stories we draw on currently circulating narrative frameworks which, in the late twentieth and twenty-first centuries, are infused with a therapeutic culture of self-help and self-development. One such narrative framework is based on childhood sexual abuse and is increasingly available to women whether or not they have concrete memories of such abuse. However, we do not simply pick and choose from lists of ready made plots and subplots, before going on to select from a cast of possible characters that includes both victims and villains. In telling our stories we all continually re-construct our selves and our life stories in an ongoing process of re-interpreting our lives, both in the past and the present, but whatever stories we tell of ourselves, they must make sense to us and make sense of us. In order to have confidence in the stories we tell, we must believe in them and to do this we need some supporting evidence, but not all those who tell stories of sexual abuse in childhood have knowledge or memories of having been abused. For those whose biographies featured sexual abuse in childhood, particularly those with no knowledge or memories of such abuse, this involved identifying 'symptoms', reinterpreted as 'alternative memories', which could support their story.

In this chapter I look at how women were introduced to the contemporary childhood sexual abuse narrative and began to identify it as a story that made sense of their lives and promised a brighter future. I also look at some alternative narrative frameworks for those for whom this story no longer adequately explained, made sense of or improved their lives. I also show that the women whose stories feature in this book told stories of sexual abuse because they helped give meaning to their lives. Those for whom this did not ultimately work did not cling to those stories but constructed new ones with some rejecting the story outright whilst others reworked it to suit the needs and circumstances in which they found themselves.

The participants and their stories

Those who contributed their stories to this book had at some point constructed, and invested in, a sexual abuse narrative in which they identified CSA as a principle or organising factor in their adult lives. Whilst these stories drew on the same narrative frameworks, they were at the same time unique: each written to make sense of and explain different lives. In constructing their stories women were informed by a range of widely circulating cultural texts where they first heard the contemporary story of childhood sexual abuse. It was in these cultural texts that some women witnessed the playing out of the 'recovered memory wars', and others learned of a different narrative framework, in the form of false memory syndrome, which offered those who lost confidence in their narratives a way to rewrite their biographies and construct themselves, not as victims of CSA, but as victims of FMS. Many had also engaged with a range of self-help and self-improvement texts from those relating to diet to sexuality to health and illness. However, as Simonds suggests of readers of self-help literature, they did not read this material simply to be told what to think and how to feel but 'looked to self-help books primarily for validation of how they already felt, for inspiration, for comfort, for explanations of situations they could not understand' (Simonds 1992:7). For the majority of women whose stories feature in this book it was the CSA recovery literature that offered what they felt to be the best explanation for present dissatisfaction or unhappiness and the best route to a better, happier, more successful life.

Women's first engagement with therapeutic discourses was not necessarily through reading self-help literature aimed at victims of CSA. Pat for example, first read self-help material in an attempt to understand and improve her ME type symptoms, and did not believe she was a victim of sexual abuse until she recovered memories during a scientology session. Others, including Fiona and Beccy, immersed themselves in self-help culture ranging from that which identified physical problems to that identifying psychological ones before they focussed on literature aimed at victims of CSA:

> I used to go to the library and get all sorts of books on well being and how to, nutrition and how to get a healthier life style and I got into that. Through reading these books that helped with health I got into the other kind of books on self-esteem . . . I read books at the time like My Mother Myself by Nancy Friday and err, The Power of Beauty. This was the start after reading the nutrition books and health books I went on to these kinds of books And then that led me more to self-help books more targeted at self-esteem.
>
> (Beccy)

Beccy identified a clear development in her reading beginning with books on issues around the body, including those aimed at health and diet, and progressing to psychology and pop psychology books which were more likely to identify psychological difficulties together with causes and solutions which looked to a perceived damaged or problematic psychology. Fiona also drew heavily on self-help and self-improvement literature and, although not so clear about a progression did position herself as someone who turns readily to books:

> That's what I'm like; I'll go and look up books for things.
>
> (Fiona)

Whereas Beccy's reading started with books aimed at the body, Fiona's began with books which addressed the mind and included texts on assertiveness, relationships and sexuality. This reflected aspects of Fiona's life that she was unhappy or dissatisfied with but, as for others, this was more a sense of unease, than a clearly defined problem.

> Because I felt that something wasn't quite right... it was as if I was kind of trying to work out what was wrong with me cos I couldn't... I knew something wasn't right but I didn't know what it was or what to do about it.
>
> (Fiona)

Fiona was aware that she turned more readily to books than others and recognised that some might see her as different. It was therefore important to Fiona to construct herself as 'normal' and she did this by establishing a connection with the lives of other ordinary people who read similar material to her. Of her reading it was she says:

> General books that you would just buy in an ordinary bookstore about how to be a happy person or how to make your life more successful and that came in the book.
>
> (Fiona)

Women did not simply impose a new story, taken from the pages of the recovery literature, onto the present. If their new story were to be a success they would need to identify links between present unhappiness and the past and in doing so maintain some biographical certainty. For many women who entered adulthood with no memories of abuse, the harm story, with its guides for identifying symptoms, offered the first indication or confirmation that they might have been sexually abused as children. Not only did it provide a narrative framework that enabled them to re/construct their identities or sense of self and make sense of their lives. It also enabled them to rewrite their own personal biographies within a framework which accorded them at least some autobiographical certainty and connection with the past:

> There were lots of things that I suddenly thought about, that's why that's like that and it all slotted into place suddenly.
>
> (Rae)

It was also a story that could provide those with continuous memories with a connection between the present and the past:

> The clues were all there when you look back with hindsight. I was not quite the same as everyone else.
>
> (Angela)

Traumatic forgetting

All but five of the women entered adulthood with no memories of sexual abuse. The problem they faced was not making connections between present unhappiness and past abuse, but explaining a lack of memories. Traumatic forgetting, whereby traumatic memories are believed to be stored in the minds and bodies of victims, often as 'alternative memories', offered such an explanation, and featured in the majority of women's accounts. For some the idea of traumatic forgetting came first, whereas others used it to support a story they were already beginning to formulate. Beccy identified symptoms of abuse but had lacked the knowledge of traumatic forgetting, that, for her, was vital to constructing an abuse narrative. It wasn't until she learnt of traumatic forgetting that Beccy was able to rewrite her biography and connect the problems she identified in her adult life with a history of sexual abuse:

> I didn't have that piece of information that told me I could forget. I didn't know that you could forget something like that...So many times I've thought, yeh I mean the explanation it would, obviously it would make complete sense if I'd been raped or abused but I haven't. Because I didn't know that I could forget. So the main thing for me was to learn that I could forget. And then it made sense then it was like yeh, of course.
>
> (Beccy)

Traumatic forgetting offered women an explanation for how, as victims, they forgot their abuse, but it also offered those who entered adulthood with no memories a way to connect 'symptoms' with perceived abuse. Those who rewrote their histories within a framework of sexual abuse had accepted to some extent the idea of recovered memories and traumatic forgetting. However, even when the idea of repressed memories was introduced to explain forgotten traumas, the idea that past experiences could have an effect on adulthood was not entirely new to them. They may not have thought of repressed memories within the context of their own life stories but the idea of traumatic forgetting or repressed memories was not alien to them. Through a variety of cultural texts the women had already been introduced to the idea that negative childhood experiences might influence the thoughts, feelings and behaviours of adults. Many also believed, on entering adulthood, that something was wrong or not quite right in their lives. By the time they engaged with self-help and CSA recovery literature they were concerned with a variety of issues. They may not have connected these with traumatic childhood experiences, but the idea that they carried with them some inaccessible piece of evidence which might explain their feelings, was something many women brought with them to their engagement with therapeutic and recovery discourses.

Even some of those who ultimately rejected some aspects of their recovered memories did not necessarily reject the knowledge claims on which they were based. Hazel, Rae and Pat had all recovered memories of being abused by their fathers during hypnosis or scientology sessions and although they rejected the idea that their fathers had abused them they did not completely reject the knowledge claims on which these memories wee based and believed instead that they may have been abused by someone else. All three had initially engaged with these therapies to loose weight or, in Pat's case to alleviate ME type symptoms, and the idea that they had these problems because they were unhappy with their lives, possibly caused by some early childhood event was one that made sense to them. It was an idea that was reinforced rather than introduced to them by a therapist:

> She believed she had to uncover something yes, because she felt I didn't feel good about myself and so she had to find out why I didn't feel good about myself.
>
> (Rae)

> He said to me because I wasn't losing weight there was a reason why I wasn't losing weight and it all went back he said to my childhood. He said we'll regress and we'll go back and see what the reasons were.
>
> (Hazel)

When Hazel's hypnotist and Rae's scientologist drew on this understanding and suggested they needed to uncover the causes of their unhappiness, they were tapping into ideas that resonated to some extent with the women's pre-existing belief systems.

Making sense of unhappiness, identifying symptoms

A central message of the recovery literature is the need for healing, in which the reader must recognise they have been damaged (Tavris 1992). Central to the CSA recovery literature are the twin identities of victim and survivor. The aim of this literature is to help guide victims on the journey of healing and recovery but to claim the identity of survivor the formerly abused women must recognise that she was a victim and the effects this had on her life. This allows for the identification of symptoms, seen as evidence, in the lives of women who enter adulthood with no apparent knowledge of having been sexually abused as children. The foundations for this model of survivor are underpinned by the trauma model of child sexual abuse, which is 'the basic framework in the treatment literature for ordering and explaining the long-term psychological harm correlated with childhood sexual abuse' (Davis 2005:145). Whether or not they have memories of sexual abuse, victims are told they must identify themselves and recognise the damage before they can begin their journey to recovery, and much of the literature is aimed at helping the reader to do just that. However, when women read this literature and are presented with lists of possible symptoms, they are receiving ideas that are not entirely new to them. Whether through the novels of Margaret Atwood, episodes of 'The Bill', docudramas of women living with multiple personalities, or films about adult women wreaking havoc on the lives of themselves and those around them, readers of CSA recovery literature are likely to have been introduced to the idea that traumatic experiences can be stored as 'alternative memories' in the minds and bodies of, often unsuspecting, victims.

The majority of the self-help literature carries a relentlessly negative portrayal of child sexual abuse and its victims and encourages women to identify symptoms in their adult lives which can then be attributed to past childhood trauma. In much of the literature this takes the form of exercises in which women are presented with a series of questions and checklists to help them identify the effects of sexual abuse. One of the most popular self-help texts for victims of CSA, *The Courage to Heal* (Bass and Davis 1988, 2002) lists over 70 symptoms of childhood sexual abuse. These 'symptoms' cover a range of feelings and emotions, ambitions and expectations, abilities, and life experiences and include such examples as an ability to feel good, being able to protect yourself, being able to accomplish things you set out to, and even being a victim of rape or domestic abuse in adulthood. Whilst Bass and Davis recognise that there might be other explanations for these 'symptoms' they work on a theory of percentages in which ticking one or two may indicate bad luck but ticking a significant number indicates psychological damage.

The majority of the women who participated in this study based their life stories on 'alternative memories' which, for the most part, involved a redefinition of memory to include these perceived symptoms.

Identifying some of these symptoms was for many their first introduction to the idea that they had been sexually abused. As Beccy stated after reading a self-help manual:

> When I read I still didn't have any memories then, but I went yes. I mean if that's what happened that would explain it so much. That would really completely make sense but I still didn't have any memories then.
>
> (Beccy)

These symptoms were for some their only evidence to indicate they were sexually abused as children. All 16 women were able to identify 'symptoms' in their adult lives which could be interpreted as evidence of sexual abuse. These included general unhappiness or dissatisfaction with their lives, problematic relationships with sex and being overweight, or failing to lose weight. For a number of women it was a desire to address such 'problems' that first led them to engage with therapeutic discourses, not necessarily in the first instance those aimed at adult victims of CSA. The majority had no memories of sexual abuse and therefore the identification of 'symptoms' or 'alternative memories' was their first and often only significant 'memory'. Whilst this was enough for some to 'know' they were victims, others needed more concrete knowledge in order to be certain. For the majority of women the process of constructing their stories was more dynamic than simply identifying symptoms, even when this included an element of 'knowledge' or 'memories' bursting through.

The view of sexual abuse, memories and knowledge promoted within much of the recovery literature offered women a way to gain the more concrete knowledge they needed to be certain they had been sexually abused in childhood, together with an explanation for why they previously lacked such knowledge. This knowledge could be stored as 'alternative memories' in the minds and bodies of victims, held by an inner child who split at the time of the abuse or stored in the unconscious mind of the adult victim. It might surface spontaneously in the form of alternative memories bursting through, or women could access it by contacting that part of their 'inner child' thought to hold the alternative memories. The women did not feel constrained to remain loyal to particular texts or explanations, but drew on a range of ideas at different times. Those who developed a relationship with an 'inner child' did not necessarily rely on a static relationship with 'her' but developed different or evolving relationships with her as their own needs and understandings changed. Through their inner child they could try and access different or additional knowledge but she could also perform different functions and/or serve different purposes.

Whether or not it takes the form of ticking checklists, the process of identifying symptoms and making connections between adult and childhood experiences is fundamental to engaging with the recovery literature. This was particularly significant for those with no other memories and for whom 'symptoms' represented their only way to know, with confidence, that they were sexually abused. In identifying symptoms women were encouraged to confer significance on earlier events which in turn make the 'plot' seem inexorable (Lawler 2002). Symptoms are not always identified using the checklists featured in texts such as *The Courage to Heal* (Bass and Davis 1988, 2002) but a consistent message within the recovery literature is that if women can find themselves in the pages of this literature then they too can benefit from the life changing, or in some cases life saving, suggestions it promotes. In an attempt to reinforce and legitimate their message, the writers of these texts often draw on biographical vignettes, which are said to originate from women's own experiences. Survivor stories are used to reinforce or amplify the checklists, which themselves harbour the generic plot of the sexual abuse narrative (Plummer 1995). Although much of this literature claims to appeal to all victims, whether they have continuous memories or have inferred a history of sexual abuse through the correlation of symptoms, it is primarily the testimonies of those who themselves rely on the 'alternative memories' found in the checklists of this literature which are used to reinforce the negative message and which impede a more positive understanding of the experiences and consequences of sexual abuse in childhood. However, the life stories told by those who do remember their abuse can provide a more positive reading:

> I think that in a positive way, it has made me mindful of others, and the effect my actions could have on others.
>
> – I consider myself to be a very strong, determined individual as a result, and a good mother (as I am aware that my actions now could be damaging to my child's future).
>
> I work in a voluntary capacity, listening to women, when they need someone with which to share their problems. Again, I think I am able to empathize because of my own past troubles.
>
> (Emma)

Emma was confident that her experiences had both positive and negative consequences on her life, but for others this was not so clear. The relentlessly negative construction of sexual abuse led some participants to reinterpret critically, qualities which they as well as others might, under different circumstances, have viewed positively:

> I had an over developed artistic sensibility, read too much, travelled but had no emotional inner security.
>
> (Jenny)

Jenny drew on this negative construction of sexual abuse to re-evaluate what others, and possibly also herself at one time, might see as artistic talent, a love of books and reading, a desire to see the world and meet new people. Rather than celebrating these qualities, as others might be able to, Jenny came to see them as both problematic but evidence of a deeper underlying trauma.

Finding themselves in the recovery literature did, for some, develop from their own reading, but others were introduced to this literature by a therapist. A number of women saw therapists who used recovery literature, including 'self-help' texts, to help clients identify symptoms or evidence of sexual abuse. For some this involved using the literature as a workbook, sometimes photocopying sections or exercises for clients to do as homework. Beccy negotiated her way through a range of self-help and self-improvement material before her therapist introduced her to the CSA recovery literature, and in particular a book aimed at those with no memories of sexual abuse. Beccy did feel her life had benefited from the advice she had found in general self-help texts but it was the pages of *Secret Survivors* (Blume 1990) that provided her with an explanation for and answer to the difficulties she experienced in her adult life:

> It's aimed at people who might suspect that they've been abused but who don't have any memories. There's a checklist at the beginning with all sorts of questions... When I read it I still didn't have any memories then but I went yes, I mean if that's what happened that would explain it so much. That would really completely make sense but I still didn't have any memories then.
>
> (Beccy)

Beccy identified difficulties with sex as 'the main problem' in her life but, in rewriting her life story within a narrative framework of sexual abuse, she went on to identify a catalogue of other problems and difficulties which she believed could also be explained with reference to sexual abuse:

> I used to be scared of the dark . . . if I go into a restaurant I always put myself with my back on the wall. (Laughs) I never used to trust anyone, very suspicious of anyone. I always think that men fancy me, I always think that they want to have sex with me . . . I erm, lack of confidence, feeling bad about myself a lot, feeling that I am not good enough, that I can't do anything. (Pause) . . . You know the main problem with intimacy and sex, that's the main problem. That's pretty much it. Oh and yeh, always wanting to be in control. I'm a complete control freak, always feeling that I had to be in control. On top of everything, not being very spontaneous . . . problems with having fun and just relaxing . . . not being able to play ever. Always, always having to do things that were productive. (Laughs) . . . But I think that's pretty much it. But having problems with people in general, being a bit of a social freak, not being able to chitchat, not being able to just do light talking.
>
> (Beccy)

Beccy's view of CSA and its effects enabled her to link a range of difficulties to a sexually abusive childhood of which she had no memory. Beccy is not alone in identifying such 'problems' in her life, and whilst other interpretations could be offered these are noticeably absent from the recovery literature, where the reader is encouraged to look inward and not outward to explain themselves and their lives. As Beccy drew heavily on the recovery literature it is perhaps not surprising that alternative interpretations were also absent from her own narrative. Beccy found herself in adulthood with no memories of sexual abuse but nonetheless unhappy with her life, or aspects of her life. When she identified herself as a victim of sexual abuse she had spent many years reading self-help and self-improvement literature and seen her most recent therapist for 18 months. She had also invested heavily in therapeutic solutions to her problems and identified herself as the key to her own personal happiness. Through her reading of other self-help and self-improvement literature Beccy had already accepted there might be something within her that might provide both explanation and solution to her difficulties. However, it was her therapist who first introduced the idea that the underlying cause was sexual abuse:

> With all the symptoms I had it was very obvious I think she probably knew straight away but she never mentioned it. Then after a year and a half she took me through the checklist without showing me what the book was and then she said ok, well you've answered positive to

> three quarters of them so maybe you want to read this and tell me what you think.
>
> (Beccy)

Beccy's therapist was informed by an understanding of CSA that enabled her to identify abuse even in the lives of women who might initially be resistant to such an explanation:

> She said it doesn't mean that you, that it was necessarily you, it could have been that you witnessed something or you know, it might not have been you. It could be anything. It could be that you've witnessed your parents doing something to someone else, or someone in the family or even it could have been someone not in the family, all sorts, it could be anything it doesn't necessarily mean that it's you.
>
> (Beccy)

Victims no longer have to directly experience something to claim the identity of victim but can claim this identity through witnessing such events. This resonates with the idea put forward by Hacking who identified the possibility that, at least for some, it is possible to construct a story of CSA that might be 'true' of the past even if it was not 'true' in the past (Hacking 1995). Beccy did not take up this option, but the idea that she might have witnessed something was offered to her by her therapist. This is, as Hacking suggests, an option that makes sexual abuse narratives increasingly available to women in the late twentieth century, but it was not a route followed by the women who participated in this study. Beccy, for example, ultimately rejected this more tenuous link to victimhood believing herself to be a direct rather than an indirect victim or witness. However, it may be that this understanding did initially help her to believe she was a victim of some form of abuse as it provided a theory which explained her difficulties without the need to identify herself as the (direct) victim or her father as the perpetrator. For some women coming to believe they are victims may be a gradual process during which they first accept as evidence, symptoms they identify in their adult lives. This allows them to perceive themselves as damaged before they need to identify either the specifics of any abuse or a perpetrator.

Identifying oneself as a victim of sexual abuse can lead to low self-esteem and a negative self-image in which the self is seen as damaged and in need of repair, it can also be used to construct an identity in which the self, past and present, is seen in a more positive light. A number of the women were able to draw on the idea that they had been sexually abused to create a more positive self-image and develop optimistic relationships with their selves:

> It was a revelation to me. It brought me total self-respect and self-acceptance for the first time in my life... It was absolutely marvellous. Although it was terribly hard to come to terms with, in some central way it made (sighs) you know, it stopped life weighing heavy on me. It did bring light into an area of darkness just to remember.
>
> (Anne)

It was not only those who relied on making connections between assumed past abuse and their adult selves to identify themselves as victims, who were able to use the identity of victim to construct a positive self-image. For those who remembered their abuse, making connections between childhood experiences and adult difficulties could also be an important step that helped them feel better about how they functioned in the adult world:

> To actually identify that a lot of the things that were happening I could attribute to the abuse... having trouble with bonding to children erm... down to low self-esteem, being able to know about it was a big step and being able to make the connection was a big step.
>
> (Angela)

Locating themselves in the symptom lists of the recovery literature proved helpful to women for a variety of reasons. For those who deviate from prescribed norms of femininity, or what they believe is expected of them, a sexual abuse story can help re-establish or maintain a positive self-image and provide an explanation for what might otherwise be seen as 'failings'. Angela, for example, had trouble bonding with her children, but was able to use a sexual abuse narrative to establish a more positive identity and overcome the failings she had felt as a mother. We could also argue that a sexual abuse narrative does not challenge the construction of women as failures but merely provides them with a new way to explain perceived failings.

Whether or not they ultimately rejected their memories of abuse, the majority of women had at some point found themselves in the pages of the recovery literature. However, some also recognised that it would be hard, particularly for women, not to find themselves in the pages of numerous self-help manuals:

> If you look at any checklist from any magazine on various things it covers such a range of symptoms which can cover most things can't they... I just think you can always find yourself in a checklist. It's a very rare person who can't find themselves in a checklist... Especially women, I think women have problems with self-esteem and various issues because they're brought up differently.
>
> (Pat)

There is a similarity between the symptoms of what at first appear to be very diverse conditions. What they share in common is a view of women as both the cause of and solution to their own unhappiness and dissatisfaction within an idealised world which fails to acknowledge the material conditions of their lives. The stories of recovery told within this literature and employed by women to make sense of their lives may not be complex ones, fitting as they do within other common story telling frameworks (Plummer 1995), and drawing on common sense understandings (Showalter 1997, Tavris 1992). However, the women's negotiation of them was not straightforward. The women engaged with therapeutic discourses because they identified aspects of their lives or themselves they were unhappy or dissatisfied with, or found difficult. Through their reading they were encouraged to find themselves in the pages of the literature and, having done so, to accept their symptoms as evidence of sexual abuse. It took time for some women, but making connections between symptoms and past abuse did provide them with explanations:

> But I didn't at first understand. I thought I was depressed and having horrible thoughts.
>
> (Fiona)

> Most useful thing was eventually remembering enough abuse to know what ailed me.
>
> (Frances)

> The issues that were coming up at the time were very much related to self-esteem and very much related to how I felt about myself which all came from the abuse.
>
> (Angela)

The majority of the women accepted that sexual abuse in childhood could result in the catalogue of symptoms outlined above. However, they did not necessarily believe that all victims would experience these symptoms or that these 'symptoms' could or should always be attributed to CSA. Nor did their understanding of the consequences of sexual abuse remain constant either when applied to their own life or to the lives of others. An interesting reading was offered by Angela who recognised the importance of context:

> I think that for most people the crisis doesn't come necessarily from being abused it's everything else that's going on in life.
>
> (Angela)

For those who were sexually abused in childhood it may be that this context contributed to how they experienced the effects of sexual abuse or even how the sexual abuse they experienced in childhood effects them throughout their lives. For those who enter adulthood without memories of abuse, it may be that the context informed how they used a sexual abuse narrative to make sense of their lives. Some women may believe the recovery literature offers them the best way to address problems in their adult lives, but whether they believe these problems to be the result of sexual abuse, or only the result of sexual abuse, may not in fact (always) be relevant.

Being normal, connecting with others

Making connections with the experiences of others was important to many of the women and the idea of normality was a recurring theme in their accounts. Whether through reading the recovery literature or survivor auto/biographies, or seeing a therapist or counsellor, women were presented with examples and illustrations of how others experienced and survived being sexually abused as children and of how they coped with and ultimately recovered or healed. Many participants had felt different or 'abnormal' and, although not something they specifically sought, feeling normal was a benefit that many identified, particularly after reading survivor testimonies. The view that victims reacted normally to an abnormal experience was one that women found particularly helpful and reassuring, although how they made use of this varied according to their individual circumstances. The literature offered them a way to recognise or acknowledge they were in some ways different from those who had not been sexually abused in childhood, without necessarily having to see those differences as problematic. This literature also enabled women to make connections between their own lives and the lives of other victims and many found this to be a powerful experience, providing both reassurance and help to move forward.

Where women did identify evidence of difference, in the literature this was often shown as examples of survival or coping skills. Therefore, even when they identified thoughts, feelings or behaviours that were problematic, they did not necessarily have to renounce these immediately. Instead they could use their histories to maintain attitudes and behaviours that might otherwise be difficult to justify, or that they did not want or were not ready to give up. The belief that they were 'normal' proved to be important to the majority of women and helped them construct a positive image for themselves and accept themselves for who and what they were:

> You had self-respect and you imagined a small child being raped and you loved yourself instead of hating yourself.
>
> (Anne)

Sarah also used the literature to re-evaluate how she felt about herself, and found the similarities between her own experiences and responses and those of others to be particularly useful:

> I read people's responses/experiences at the back of the book and thought actually I know each people's an individual and to some degree how they respond is an individual thing but it was quite similar to mine. So I thought actually there's nothing wrong with me, it's a normal response and there's nothing to be ashamed of, so that was fantastic.
>
> (Sarah)

Julie, who visited a Parks Inner Child Therapy (PICT) therapist also found relief when she discovered her responses to being abused were quite normal:

> What I got from it more than anything was that I'm quite normal because I felt abnormal. It seems abnormal that it had happened but it was quite a relief to me really.
>
> (Julie)

Whereas Julie benefited from being told how her experiences were similar to others, some women needed to read this for themselves. We do not all process information in the same way and some women needed time to think about the new information which the context as well as the process of reading gave them:

> When I read those books I thought, oh god I feel the same way you know, this book is exactly describing how I feel inside... these books just everything was like black and, you know everything was clear. So then... I knew exactly, that's exactly how I feel.
>
> (Tracey)

Recognising themselves in the literature and comparing their experiences with those of others was clearly important to many women, particularly as it helped them view themselves in a more positive light. However, comparisons with others could also be problematic and might lead to feelings of inadequacy and even failure, especially if they read about experiences they felt were worse than their own:

> Some I've read and I've thought yes I can see, I can read them and I can think yes I can see why I have so many difficulties but then there's always the part of me that's saying well yeh but theirs is much worse than what you went through.
>
> (Angela)

Where comparisons with others has a negative effect, leaving women feeling they should be doing or coping better, women may feel in need of an explanation for perceived failures. This may lead some to search for evidence of further or more extreme or repeated abuse and others deeper into the world of hidden memories and multiple personalities in their search for such evidence.

Identifying experiences in common with other victims was particularly important to women who believed they were victims of abuse but who were not 'the first author of the story' (de Rivera 1998a). These were women who had not constructed a sexual abuse narrative through piecing together clues and identifying symptoms in their adult lives but were instead presented with an idea or story which they then had to test out. For these women the knowledge that there were others with similar experiences of 'forgetting' and 'remembering' was particularly influential in their coming to believe they had been abused, even if they later came to reject such a history. It was also important for those women whose biographies were based on the belief that they had recovered false memories. Hazel was not the first author of her story which was based on recovered memories. She had sought the help of a hypnotist as she was having difficulty losing weight and it was specifically losing weight that she wanted to address. Hazel recognised that she was unhappy with her self and her body and also that she did not have a good sex life and thought losing weight would help her feel better. Although she accepted there might be an underlying cause for her failure to lose weight, Hazel had not considered it to be sexual abuse. After her hypnotist suggested that sexual abuse experienced in childhood was the underlying cause of her difficulties, including problems she had with her weight, Hazel turned to the CSA and recovered memory literature. Hazel believed in the power of hypnosis to recover buried memories, but she also needed an explanation of her difficulties that made sense to her. It was important for Hazel to find similarities between her own experiences and those of others:

> I started reading the books because I wanted to see if what was happening to me during hypnotherapy was happening to other people in the books... I needed confirmation.
>
> (Hazel)

Hazel trusted in the power of hypnosis but at the same time she needed to have her newfound knowledge and experiences validated externally. Hazel was not alone in using the literature to help her confirm that she had been sexually abused a child. Pat also found this literature provided a valuable measure against which could compare her experiences:

> I started reading self-hep books. You've got all the symptoms, you've got the tiredness, you've got the depression, you've got every symptom possible for survivors.
>
> (Pat)

Many women were able to use the symptoms identified in the literature to help confirm or identify that they had been sexually abused, but some also acknowledged an element of choice in identifying themselves as victims. These women recognised that the symptoms identified as evidence of CSA could also be used as evidence of other experiences or conditions, and therefore there was an element of choice in the stories they chose to tell. Not simply because they picked a story they liked, but because they came across more than one story in the self-help and self-improvement literature that could be used to make sense of their lives.

It is clear that the storylines featured in the CSA recovery literature can be used to create a positive self-image, increase self-esteem and help women to feel normal and happy about themselves. However, these storylines can also be used, by those at the centre of the story as well as by others, to very different effect. Emma had engaged in two periods of counselling aimed at victims of sexual abuse. During the first period Emma had used a framework of sexual abuse to make sense of her life and construct a sense of her self as positive and normal, and this was important for how she viewed the present and the future:

> I think the important difference between the two sessions was that the first time, I really did need to talk about what had happened, to make me understand that I was normal.
>
> (Emma)

In the second period of counselling, following a miscarriage, Emma felt it was her therapist who used a framework of CSA to make sense of Emma's experiences. In doing so she dismissed Emma's very real feelings relating a miscarriage and constructed her as permanently damaged as a result of the abuse she experienced as a child:

> The second lot of sessions years later seemed so negative because I felt, she was trying to tell me that I was abnormal and always would be because of my childhood.
>
> (Emma)

The counsellor drew on a contemporary CSA story, not to reassure Emma that she was 'normal' but rather to construct her as abnormal and position her within a therapeutic framework in which her reactions to events, rather than the events themselves, were seen as problematic. At the same time CSA was used by her counsellor to dismiss external factors and to construct the problem, and potentially any future problem, in terms of Emma's perceived damaged psychology. As a way of making sense of her life, it was a story that Emma rejected.

Revisiting childhood

Our contemporary storying of childhood sexual abuse has expanded over recent decades to include areas that in the past might not have been interpreted as either sexual or abusive. This has enabled women to return to their childhoods and reinterpret some experiences as sexually abusive. As Hacking suggests, this has contributed to a muddying of the waters of the recovered memory debate as it enables women to put forward an interpretation of events which may be 'true' of the past but was not necessarily 'true' in the past (Hacking 1995). This might contribute to the emergence of 'recovered' or 'alternative' memories, but is not on its own enough to account for all those who have constructed a sexual abuse narrative based on 'recovered memories'. For many, and certainly the majority of those in this study, it was the harm story which provided the narrative framework, and conceptual underpinnings, that enabled them to reconstruct themselves as damaged and in need of healing as a result of being sexually abused in childhood. The 'memero-politics' identified by Hacking (1995), whereby past events are reinterpreted from a (different) position of knowledge and understanding in the present, is likely to have contributed to an increased acceptance of the extent of child sexual abuse and as such may have contributed to the contemporary phenomena of recovered memories. A reinterpretation of the past from an elevated position in the present may also account for some women's sexual abuse narratives. However, it does not account for the sexual abuse narratives, based on recovered memories, of those who participated in this study, except that the increased acknowledgement of recovered memories has contributed to a climate where it is easier for women to identify themselves as victims.

The women in this study may have revisited their childhoods, and some did reinterpret feelings or actions as consequences of sexual abuse, but they did not recover memories of abuse through reinterpreting childhood events as sexually abusive. Rather they identified alternative or hidden memories stored in the unconscious mind and body as evidence of abuse. Whether through reading self-help manuals, pop psychology and psychology textbooks, magazines and newspapers, or through listening to the radio and watching films and television, they were introduced to 'alternative memories' of CSA in the form of potential symptoms on a daily basis. These symptoms might have taken the form of 'adult behaviour patterns', 'acquired survival skills', or 'compulsive self-abuse,' or they might have taken the form of 'dreams' or 'flashbacks', and body messages (such as aches and pains). In revisiting their childhoods some women were able to identify symptoms of sexual abuse in the lives of their child selves. Some were able to use this to support the alternative memories they identified in their adult lives, whilst others were able to use the identification of symptoms in childhood to identify themselves as victims of CSA.

The idea of a normal child against which the sexually abused child could be measured was one that was drawn on by a number of participants, either by identifying with the abused child or by seeing themselves as different from the non-abused child:

> The clues were all there when you look back in hindsight. I was not quite the same as everyone else.
>
> (Angela)

> I think I was always the very good child and I think that's the other, in self-help books, the typical picture of the abused child was that you were always trying to please and I was definitely one of these.
>
> (Pat)

Angela and Pat both entered adulthood with no memories of sexual abuse and it may be that for them it was particularly important to find some supporting evidence of abuse in the lives of their child selves. Whereas Angela identified symptoms in the life of her child self, Pat identified the characteristics of the abused child in her child self. In doing so they were able to construct their child selves as victims of sexual abuse but it is our culturally circulating stories of CSA and the sexually abused child that enabled them to do so. Had different narrative frameworks been available they may have interpreted their childhoods differently and in doing so produced different narratives, in which they were not positioned as victims or constructed as damaged.

Women with continuous memories of abuse were often well aware of the signs evident in their childhoods, although as children they had not necessarily understood their experiences as sexual or abusive. A return to childhood did help some to recognise that what was done to them was wrong. Jay, who entered adulthood with the memories of years of sexual abuse, had revisited the self of her childhood and, by comparing her past child self to children of a similar age, was able to view her experiences in a different light:

> I found looking and talking to children of that age, then I found it more and more difficult to say well 'it was me encouraging him', 'it was me being flirtatious' because I kept thinking well at that age I shouldn't have understood.
>
> (Jay)

Jay had continuous memories of her childhood but it was through comparing her child self to others of a similar age that she was able to reinterpret her experiences as abusive. For those with unbroken memories of abuse, revisiting childhood also contributed to a fuller, more nuanced account in which sexual abuse, whilst clearly in evidence, was not always a central or organising theme. As Tracey says of her childhood:

> My mum used to tell me I was fat and just like, with sexuality this really hurts. She's giving me an impression that she doesn't think that I'm, 'no one would want me' you know and that 'what am I talking about', 'you'll never get there'. So she obviously thinks I'm not a very beautiful person and you know outside I'm not a beautiful daughter.
>
> (Tracey)

Woven through the accounts of Julie, Tracey and Jay were elements of emotional and psychological abuse which at times they all identified as being at least as significant as sexual abuse in contributing to the difficulties they faced in adulthood. These other elements also formed the background against which they interpreted their experiences of sexual abuse. They drew on the CSA recovery literature because it offered a way to address these difficulties but this should not be taken as a straightforward acceptance that sexual abuse was the main cause of, or sometimes even a contributing factor in, those difficulties.

Different lives, different stories

All the women had, at least temporarily, invested in a history in which sexual abuse featured as an organising principle but this was not the only story that could be told of their lives. Nor was it the most comprehensive. Those who lacked memories based their stories on a correlation of symptoms but those who were able to draw on concrete childhood memories provided a more sophisticated understanding to show that the context was as important as the sexual abuse itself. The context in which most children experience sexual abuse is one in which secrecy is a central feature. Jay's account illustrates how this secrecy helped to lay the foundations for how, as a child victim, she could be perceived by others and, which she believed, contributed to her experiencing other forms of abuse, including additional sexual abuse:

> It wasn't until then that I twigged that everybody knew about it and I'd been keeping this secret and it wasn't any secret, because everybody knew and that's when I started becoming angry. Because trying to keep a secret it led to other abuse.
>
> (Jay)

Current orthodoxy on child abuse constructs sexual abuse as the most damaging but as Jay's account shows, it is not always sexual abuse, or the sexual element of an abusive childhood, that is experienced as most damaging or difficult to deal with by children themselves:

> I found I couldn't take the psychological abuse at all No. I could cope better with the physical and sexual abuse than I could the psychological. That's why I walked out of hers' and straight back into the abuse, knowing it would be the same, hoping it wouldn't be but knowing it would be.
>
> (Jay)

Jay found the psychological abuse so much harder to deal with that she 'chose' to return to where she would be sexually abused. Jay's was not a story that fitted easily within our contemporary telling of childhood sexual abuse, and she did not find herself in the pages of the CSA recovery literature. Within this literature Jay was confronted with an understanding which, as it constructed victims as *innocent because they were powerless*, contradicted her own experience, and denied her claim to the status of innocent victim because she had exercised some power and chosen to go back.

Tracey also had clear recollections of an abusive childhood and whilst she focussed on certain aspects of her past and drew on sexual abuse to make sense of adult difficulties, she could have written a different history, which did not feature sexual abuse as a causal narrative. She could even have written a history in which sexual abuse did not feature at all:

> I felt denied of my childhood and that I didn't really have a childhood. I felt like I was born to make people like my family, make them be proud of me and not to live for myself and not to have a life. Basically I was like a slave to my family and as long as I brought on a good name for them or I made them proud of me it's all that mattered.
>
> (Tracey)

She could equally have written her life story with a focus on abandonment:

> It was because, yeh it was because my mother abandoned me and my father abandoned me as well. He died when I was seven, my dad. But he was like my, he was the best parent for me but I didn't know him so well so you know, I was abandoned. I felt abandoned in a sense because afterwards my mum took over and my mum and I didn't get on and she beat me up and she didn't like my dad at all. She took all her anger out on me.
>
> (Tracey)

Tracey's account focused on physical and emotional trauma, and made little reference to sexual abuse but it was sexual abuse that she drew on to explain adult feelings and dissatisfaction, including difficulties around sex and relationships. Her life story not only needed to make sense of these difficulties, she also needed it to act as a guide for living and it may be that she felt a sexual abuse narrative offered her the best way to do that. Sexual abuse is thought to result in sexual difficulties in the lives of adult victims and many CSA recovery manuals have sections to help victims deal with this aspect of their lives, but the 'sex education' Tracey received from her mother provides Tracey with an alternative explanation:

> Cos my mum would say its really horrible, its hurtful and you bleed and its painful and oh, its like a knife. She was saying everything to put me off, y'know to put you off the subject.
>
> (Tracey)

An alternative story could also have been written by Angela who thought witnessing violence (both physical and verbal) between her parents, was more significant than the sexual abuse she experienced at the hands of her elder brother, both in childhood and later:

> The violence in the house... I suppose had the biggest effect on me in normal day-to-day life, in being able to make friends.
>
> (Angela)

We can see in these women's accounts that the stories they chose to tell involved a degree of choice, determined in part by the usefulness of those stories as guides to living. In one woman's account we can also see how versions of stories might outlive their usefulness. Although she constructed a life story that featured sexual and ritual abuse, Anne remembered a childhood which included a catalogue of difficult or traumatic experiences. Hers was:

> A multiple problem middle class family... one brother died as a child... my other brother killed himself... he'd attempted suicide often as a teenager... he'd spent a year in a mental hospital... so it was clear to me that this family was a complete mess.
>
> (Anne)

Anne could have drawn on these experiences to write a life story that (to an outsider) adequately made sense of difficulties she experienced in her adult life and whilst she still made reference to these events, Anne no longer positioned them as central or even particularly influential to her life story. Whilst we can only speculate as to why Anne chose to tell the particular story she did, we can say that the latest version of her story is one that is more reliant on our collective storying of childhood, and sexual and ritual abuse than it is on Anne's memories of her childhood.

Making sense and a better life

The success of the CSA recovery literature is measured, like other aspects of self-help and self-development literature, by 'the extent to which fear gives way to inner confidence and despair to hope' (Kitzinger 1993:231). Its success relates to women's perceptions of how their lives have improved. The emphasis is on the inner world of women's psychologies in which the measure of success is determined by how they perceive themselves within the world rather than how they perceive the world in which they live. Another important measure of success for women whose narratives were organised around CSA is the extent to which they believed those narratives to make sense of their lives. The majority of the women in this study clearly did believe that sexual abuse explained their lives, even if it had not yet helped them to make improvements, but there were some for whom this was not the case. For these women, it was necessary to find a new way to make sense of their lives and whilst FMS offered an explanation for the recovery of 'false' memories, it did not offer an explanation for what might have lead women to engage with those therapeutic discourses through which they recovered such memories. It is perhaps for this reason that those who rejected completely the memories they once believed in found it difficult to move forward with their lives.

5
Making Contact: Knowledge and the Inner Child

We knew something had happened. The children knew something had happened but not quite why or how it happened.

(Anne)

Introduction

The inner child may be conceptualised in a variety of ways but some form of inner child self occupies a central position in much of the CSA recovery literature. She is often seen as the holder of knowledge, the damaged part of the adult victim for whom time stopped still, and that part of the adult victim that needs to heal. She can also be understood as a child like part of the adult victim or survivor and it is therefore possible to engage with 'inner child work' without acknowledging an inner child. The majority of the women identified an inner child, or childlike part of their adult selves, as a valuable, although not always straightforward or unproblematic, concept. Most of those who acknowledged their own inner child believed they were introduced to the concept during the course of their healing and recovery, although even here the idea of an inner self, who could be childlike, was not totally alien to them. The inner child, in some form, is a pervasive presence in many aspects of contemporary culture. She can be found in the pages of popular literature, autobiographies and magazines, on both the small and large screen through her appearance in TV soaps, films, docudramas and documentaries. She has also played the occasional role in advertisements, encouraging viewers to look after, pamper, or indulge themselves and has featured in celebrity autobiographies such as those of Roseanne and Oprah Winfrey.

Women were introduced to the idea of an inner child who could influence their thoughts, feelings and behaviours, through being encouraged to identify evidence of her in their adult lives, before they were introduced directly to (the idea of) their own inner child. Identifying the idea of an inner child who could operate in, and exert influence over, the lives of adults also made it easier for women to identify their own inner child and although the majority did acknowledge an inner child she did not fulfil the same function nor did they all view her in the same way. How women conceptualised her, the role she played in their lives, and the degree to which they relied on her varied in part according to the level of knowledge they had about their abusive histories. For some she was simply a damaged part of themselves who needed healing but for others, as the holder of knowledge, she was central to the writing their life story. Women took an active role in identifying the influence their inner child, or children, had on their adult lives, but when it came to uncovering the hidden knowledge held by this child they did not always play, or believe themselves to play, such an active part.

Uncovering knowledge

The inner child may have a certain uniformity and take on a particular and well defined role within the recovery literature, but the inner child, or child self, of women's accounts was more fluid and their engagement with her more complex and pragmatic as she developed in response to different and sometimes fluctuating needs. Needs that were themselves determined in part by the memories they brought with them into adulthood. An important role women needed an inner child to perform was to provide evidence of their abusive childhoods. For some this might involve uncovering childhood memories, but recovering memories is rare (Bass and Davis 1988, 2002) and it is therefore more likely to involve recognising or identifying symptoms in their child and adult lives. This was particularly important for those who entered adulthood with no concrete memories, without which they would be unable to recognise themselves as victims but was also important in order to recognise they were damaged and begin the journey to healing and recovery. It was this that encouraged self-identified victims to look for evidence of sexual abuse in their adult lives and correlate present difficulties or unhappiness with past (childhood) traumas. For those who did not remember, on entering adulthood, that they had been sexually abused in childhood, the identification of symptoms may have helped them to construct a life story based on sexual abuse but it did not necessarily provide them with enough certainty. Where this was the case women needed other forms of knowledge to support their accounts. For many in this position, an inner child not only provided them with information or evidence she also offered an explanation for how they 'forgot' this information. However, it was not necessary for women to recognise or make contact with an inner child to gain access to additional knowledge which could also be seen to have been stored in the unconscious minds of victims. Often women recognised both sources of information and negotiated their own unique path between the two.

Many women took an active role in identifying symptoms of sexual abuse and used this information to make sense of their lives. Having something to attribute their unhappiness or dissatisfaction made it easier for them to identify these 'symptoms' as evidence of childhood traumas. Contrary to popular understandings, the majority of those who enter adulthood with no memories of childhood sexual abuse but believe themselves to be victims, are unlikely to recover memories (Bass and Davis 1988), and this was also the case for those who participated in this study. Those who did recover what they believed to be memories (which in many cases were later rejected as false) did not see themselves playing an active role in their recovery, largely because they believed these memories were already present, albeit sometimes deeply buried. However, although they believed they played a secondary, less active role women did not necessarily see themselves as entirely passive in the process. Often 'recovered memories' came to women in a form not readily understandable, such as dreams or hypnosis. Therefore, although the women did not believe they played an active part in uncovering memories, they recognised the measures they took to interpret or make sense of their newfound knowledge, which in some cases involved seeking the help of experts. This itself could be seen as creating knowledge, and although this understanding was resisted by the majority of participants it did offer some, those who wanted to reject their abuse narrative, a way to explain and/or reject 'memories' that could be redefined as wrongly interpreted.

Spontaneous knowledge

Whether held by an inner child or a damaged part of the adult women, the surfacing of knowledge of childhood trauma is believed to be spontaneous, and controlled only by an inner child or childlike part of the former victim. However, it is not only the knowledge on which a sexual abuse narrative is based, but the narrative itself, that is beyond the control of the adult victim, and her therapist if she has one. There is only one story that can be told, and it is a story dictated by the 'facts'. Survivors may be able to change how their stories continue, substituting different subplots and endings, but the story they tell of their abuse and its consequences is the only story that can be told. This enables women with no memories, whose stories are based on 'alternative memories' and a correlation of symptoms, to maintain confidence in the stories they tell, without which some may come to doubt their memories or wonder if they have 'made it up'. This is particularly important at times when women are faced with denial, such as when they might accuse their perceived abusers, or in a climate of general scepticism, such as that surrounding the 'recovered memory wars'. This understanding of traumatic knowledge is also an important defence against accusations of 'false memories', as no one can be responsible for the creation of memories which are just waiting to emerge. This knowledge is held or stored by an inner child, a child like part of the adult victim, or as a body or sense memory and can spontaneously surface without the influence or involvement of the victim herself. The surfacing of such memories is often said to be triggered by some event or experience in the adult victims life. Whilst these triggers could relate to negative experiences or feelings, such as being revictimised, they could also relate to positive experiences, such as having children, meeting a partner, or successful life experiences, or important times in a persons life story.

This view of spontaneous, traumatic knowledge, bursting to the surface, without them exercising any control or influence, was a view that resonated with many of the women. Whether or not they developed a relationship with an inner child, many felt they had acquired knowledge over which they had no control. It was knowledge which, they believed, had always been present, albeit unrecognised or buried, and took a number of forms. Often surfacing through dreams and flashbacks it could also surface in the form of feelings and emotions and whilst some women recognised an inner child at work others believed this knowledge came from a damaged part of their adult selves. Not all the women believed this knowledge spontaneously and inevitably broke through and some believed that accessing knowledge needed, at least some of the time, to be worked at. This reflected advice they found elsewhere in the recovery literature which encouraged them to work on themselves in order to be ready to receive knowledge of sexual abuse.

The CSA recovery literature provided a number of explanations for how knowledge could be buried and how it might be accessed. It might be held by an inner child who split at the time of the abuse, stored in the unconscious mind of the adult victim, or stored as alternative memories in the minds and bodies of the child victim. It might surface spontaneously or victims might need to contact that part of their child or adult selves who held it and women did not feel constrained to remain loyal to only one explanation. They also developed fluid relationships with the inner child, and there were times when they felt compelled to develop a more intense relationship with an inner child if, for example, they had not been able to access knowledge they believed would adequately explain their lives, either to others or to themselves. Spontaneous knowledge provided women with additional knowledge or supporting evidence, but when it broke through into their consciousness it could also be experienced as overwhelming. Fiona had times when she felt besieged by knowledge held by her inner child:

> It was as if I wasn't able to keep the lid on it anymore and the memories just popped out, just came out. But I didn't at first understand. I thought it was because I was depressed and having horrible thoughts...I wasn't able to control them anymore and out they came.
>
> (Fiona)

This was different to Beccy's experience of accessing knowledge, which she experienced as hard work and something she had to work at, if it was not to remain unavailable to her. Neither Beccy nor Fiona entered adulthood with memories of abuse but both believed they were the victims of sexual abuse through identifying symptoms in their adult lives and believed they could discover more solid evidence of their abuse, in the form of buried memories. Although they conceptualised her differently, an inner child played a central role in both their attempts to access this hidden knowledge. Whereas Fiona often felt overwhelmed by her inner child there were times when Beccy felt she had to actively seek out her child self:

> Try and connect with myself as a child because, to help me get the memories back.
>
> (Beccy)

Elsewhere Beccy refers to the surfacing of a different form of knowledge over which she also felt she had no control:

> I get emotional flashbacks, I'm not reacting to what's happening.
>
> (Beccy)

Knowledge which surfaced in the form of emotions and feelings was important to a number of women. Not only did this knowledge provide supporting evidence for their stories but women also believed it could provide them with a direct connection to their abuse, and to the abused child they once were. Women did not just remember sexual abuse, but some also believed they were reexperiencing the abuse or at least the feelings they experienced at the time:

> If I get really upset, that seems to be the age that emotions regress back to. And where I can't talk about what's going on, I'm not able to verbally express or tell anyone or ask for help and I feel really upset because I can't do that at that age. All I can do is express how I feel and you know, in emotions, in crying or shouting or rage, whatever physical way I can I'm expressing these strong feelings. I'm too young to be able to talk about them and that wee person wants listening to.
>
> (Fiona)

> We'd get more upset and you know, she [the therapist] would follow my upset.
>
> (Anne)

This connection to their abused child self was particularly important to women who had no other memories through which they could connect their adult and child selves, as it enabled them to maintain or establish some biographical continuity. Knowledge, or an inner child who held this knowledge, could be accessed through a number of routes. Anne, for example, would sometimes put her self in a trance:

> Because that's what you have to do to let the little ones talk.
>
> (Anne)

Anne was clear that it was 'the little ones' who knew and were therefore in a position to talk about the abuse. This knowledge might not provide detailed information about what happened or who was involved but, as it was seen as an inner child reexperiencing the abuse, many women felt it provided enough information for them to 'know' they had been sexually abused. As the source was understood to be their child self, women saw this knowledge as an accurate reflection of feelings and emotions relating to sexual abuse. It was, they believed, a form of knowledge which did not lie.

In addition to hypnosis and trance like states, women employed a range of methods to contact their inner child and gain knowledge of their abuse. Angela used a number of techniques to access information held by her inner child including the writing exercises suggested in the literature, which encourage readers to write letters to and from their inner child. Letters to their inner child should offer love, support and the knowledge that she was not responsible for the abuse. In writing letters from their inner child, women are encouraged to let her speak to them, and let their adult selves know how she felt. Angela was one of the few women to follow this advice and felt a powerful connection with her child's emotions:

> It's much more intense than just writing to your inner child if you like, because it's feeling what she's feeling.
>
> (Angela)

The view that the adult self can return to the time of the abuse and feel, for themselves, what the child once felt, was a common theme in many of the women's accounts, as was the idea of the past encroaching into the present:

> What we are doing is feeling the pain that we couldn't feel as a child.
>
> (Jenny)

> The past was a daily reality to me, I was living in the past I couldn't escape it, it was with me all the time. Memories erm... feelings, the past was haunting me I wasn't able to get on with my present.
>
> (Fiona)

It was important for women whose biographies were based on alternative memories to identify a source of information beyond their adult selves as this also distanced them from the construction, or at least the details, of their narratives. If knowledge was attributed to an inner child, then so too must the writing of the story, as it was she who provided the details and cast of characters. As Fiona says of the memories that informed her own story:

> They were just squished down, now they're out in the open and here's a chance to sort them out.
>
> (Fiona)

Fiona did not choose to look for buried knowledge of abuse but seized on an opportunity presented to her, by implication by someone other than her adult self who had access to this knowledge. Whilst she believed her child self responsible for the emergence of this knowledge, it is the adult

Fiona who used it to make sense of her life and construct a narrative in which this knowledge occupies a central and causal position. Sarah also seized an opportunity presented to her adult self, 'when the memories came through', and chose to see a psychiatrist in the process of constructing her life story. Like Fiona, the adult Sarah does not claim these memories as hers, and thereby succeeds in distancing herself from the process by which they surfaced.

Not all the women made contact or developed a relationship with an inner child but of those who did, the majority did so with only one child. However, Anne recognised hundreds of inner children, of whom she had so far made contact with over twenty. For the majority of women, uncovering knowledge was more important than contacting an inner child, although many did develop supportive relationships with this child. However this was not so for Anne, for whom making contact appeared more important than uncovering knowledge. For women who had no memories but who relied on an inner child to provide knowledge, this usually involved the child self transferring knowledge and in doing so letting go of their knowledge, which in turn freed the adult to let go of their child self. In Anne's account the memories stayed with, and belonged to, her inner children who seemed more 'real' to Anne than the inner children of the other women. Anne's inner children did share their knowledge but they did not relinquish it, and in turn Anne did not own this knowledge, nor did she relinquish her relationship with her children. Ann's adult self, although given access to knowledge, remained distanced from the memories Anne attributed to her children:

> We knew something had happened. The children knew something had happened but not quite why or how it happened.
>
> (Anne)

Anne shared her life with her inner children in a way that the other women, perhaps more concerned with integrating and moving on, did not. Each of Anne's inner children had their own memories and often the memory and the child surfaced together, in what Anne described as a traumatic experience:

> Your mind gets so used to the horrors that, I mean you are shattered... because there's another child each time that surfaces and each memory is different.
>
> (Anne)

Often the children surfaced when Anne was not awake:

> The children come with the dreams into the memories.
>
> (Anne)

Although Anne's adult self remained somewhat distanced from the knowledge held by her children, like Fiona, she did take some responsibility for making sense of it.

Anne was not alone in understanding her emotions and feelings to be an inner child reliving experiences of abuse. It was a view that helped to make the experience and the knowledge very real to women, and was particularly important for those for whom this was their only source of knowledge. However, women did not need to develop a relationship with an inner child in order to access this knowledge which could be attributed to their unconscious or a damaged part of their adult selves. Even those who recognised an inner child as an important source of information did not rely solely on her for information. Fiona, for example, in addition to knowledge held by her child self was able to access other memories:

> Not visual memories, more memories of touch and smell and sound because this happened at night. Either it was dark or I was closing my eyes but I don't remember really seeing a lot of things going on.
>
> (Fiona)

She was able to do this because, informed by the CSA recovery literature:

> I remember my other senses have got memories.
>
> (Fiona)

Beccy also drew on the idea of alternative memories held by the senses, in her case to explain a lack of memories relating to what she called the main problem:

> Sometimes I do get memories coming back and sometimes I don't. But sometimes I just get feelings I don't get any images.
>
> (Beccy)

Of the women who entered adulthood with no knowledge Sarah was the only one who did not rely on alternative memories. Sarah had recovered 'recall memories', validated by others, and did not rely on either form of memory to 'know' she had been abused, and this contributed to her confidence in her sexual abuse narrative and her identity as a survivor. Sarah implied a level of spontaneity when she talked of her memories coming through, and believed additional memories would surface if and when they needed to. She also believed knowledge might be brought to the surface by her unconscious, and therefore not under the control of her adult self. Although happy to let this knowledge surface spontaneously, there were also times when Sarah was less patient and considered a more proactive approach:

> Because if my conscious or whatever needs to bring it out, it will bring it out. I don't know if I go to hypnosis it might bring it up then.
>
> (Sarah)

Sarah believed she could actively seek out knowledge, but believed it was knowledge that already existed. Whilst she acknowledged that she could play an active role in bringing it to the surface, did not see herself as responsible for it, or for the story that she came to tell.

The inner child of women's accounts

The inner child is often seen as a distinct personality who not only holds knowledge of past abuse but also controls the thoughts and actions of adult victims. However, not all women accorded their own inner child such a degree of autonomy. Not all the participants recognised an inner child but of those who did, all developed their own unique relationships with her, and granting, or acknowledging, varying degrees of autonomy, power and knowledge. Some like Sarah and Anne, recognised an inner child or children as very separate from their adult selves, with access to knowledge unavailable to their adult selves, but for others she was more fluid and the degree to which they saw her as separate varied over time. A number of women believed that the presence of their inner child or children was in itself telling them something. For Anne the mere presence of the children that told her she had been abused, and the more children she came to recognise the more (severe) the abuse she believed she had suffered. Whereas Angela found that her inner child often came when she was finding life difficult, and this she believed was:

> Normally a clue to me that there's something deeper going on that I need to deal with.
>
> (Angela)

All the women had engaged with the self-help and CSA recovery literature to some degree and it was against this background that they constructed their histories and, in some cases, developed a relationship with an inner child. Some went on to identify a clear influence between their reading of the CSA recovery literature and the inner child they developed a relationship with. Fiona dedicated a lot of time and energy to her inner child, and believed she became more separate after reading *Rescuing the Inner Child* (Parks 1990). Not sure if it was 'positive' or not, Fiona said that since reading the book:

> Part of me is a very separate part of me now whereas I'd never before had that idea in my head. That part was more integrated into all of me but since I've been into that idea of starting to think about it more there seems to be more of a distance between me and myself when I was wee.
>
> (Fiona)

Beccy also acknowledged a childlike part of herself but was much clearer about this child self, and did not see her as a separate personality:

> Yes I see it as part of my mind rather than something separate.
>
> (Beccy)

Echoing the idea of time having stopped still, Beccy believed her child self had:

> The memories that me as a child who was abused... Yeh. Obviously it's myself telling myself but it's that part of my mind that's been shut out.
>
> (Beccy)

It was an idea she returned to later when she talked of using photographs to access knowledge held by her child self. Although not a separate personality, Beccy did credit her child self with a degree of control over her adult self and the process of healing and recovery. Beccy felt she had a long way to go in terms of healing and attributed this in part to her failure to uncover, what she believed were buried memories of severe sexual abuse, held by her inner child. She had considered a variety of techniques, including hypnotherapy and regression therapy, to help uncover this knowledge. She also attributed her failure to engage with these techniques to the child part of her mind:

> I haven't done much of it because I'm quite resistant to it. I want to but my mind's resistant to it so its not quite worked so far.
>
> (Beccy)

Although the majority of women entered adulthood with no knowledge of sexual abuse not all recognised or developed a relationship with an inner child. The idea that memories could be stored in their unconscious minds and/or bodies provided some with an alternative explanation for how they could forget traumatic experiences as well as how they could recover forgotten memories. Even those who believed their inner child held memories did not rule out the possibility that additional memories might be stored in their unconscious minds and bodies. This enabled women to employ a range of techniques aimed at both contacting an inner child and accessing knowledge held by her, and accessing and interpreting alternative memories. At times women thought their knowledge surfaced spontaneously or was triggered by events or experiences and at other times they sought out additional knowledge. What was important was their belief that this knowledge was waiting to be uncovered. Whilst some of this knowledge was clear, sometimes they felt it was in need of interpretation. Although there were occasions when they believed they might have some control over accessing or preparing themselves to receive or interpret this knowledge, the women all firmly believed they had no control over the content.

Interpreting knowledge: Help from the experts

Whether based on continuous, recovered or false memories those women who continued to believe in their sexual abuse narrative in some form, believed they played an active role in constructing their biographies. The majority of the women believed they were victims of sexual abuse through uncovering hidden knowledge and alternative memories. However, not all their knowledge was easily understood, or in some cases even clearly related to sexual abuse, and for some this meant seeking out experts to help with interpretation. Although Fiona was certain the knowledge she uncovered related to a history of abuse she felt she needed the help of others to understand what it was telling her:

> When I realised what it was about, what the memories were about then I sought out a counselling service specifically . . . they could help

> me understand what I was feeling and what was happening and what was the best way forward.
>
> (Fiona)

Fiona shared with many women the belief that her inner child was responsible for bringing memories to the surface but her adult self was responsible for making sense of it, but this was very different to Anne. Anne believed hundreds of inner children held knowledge of sexual and ritual abuse she experienced as a child, and had so far contacted over twenty, from whom she learnt of her abuse. Much of this knowledge came to Anne, the 'front personality', in the form of dreams. It was her inner children, not her adult self, who were in control of the process and who took responsibility for choosing when it was safe for her to know more:

> The people inside you know they are only letting out as much as I can take.
>
> (Anne)

Anne was certain that in her dreams her alters were telling her about the abuse but this information often needed additional work, either because it was in a form not easily understood, but more often because it was incomplete:

> I go with my dreams and often it's just a fragment when I wake up. It's just a sentence and the whole thing comes out of that. In the therapy session we just work on the fragment.
>
> (Anne)

Anne was acutely aware of the recovered memory controversy and the possibility that some might challenge her memories and dispute her narrative. She was therefore keen to distance her adult self from the emergence of memories and the production of knowledge, and therefore from accusations of false memories. Whilst she was clear that her knowledge of an abusive childhood came from her 'alters', a lot of work was involved in turning the 'fragments' she received from her inner children into a narrative. Anne may have begun with fragments, which often came to her in dreams but, together with a therapist, she has used these to construct, or piece together, a complicated and involved narrative, populated with a host of characters, many hundreds of whom she had yet to meet. It was also through her dreams that Anne first learned she shared her inner world with hundreds of alters:

> I had a dream that chanted my name, and then a dream about a long list of children.
>
> (Anne)

Again, she felt she needed the help of a therapist to interpret these dreams:

> She thought I might have more people than one inside and I thought oh no . . . then one notices a long list of names and pictures of these teenagers and all called the Children's Brigade.
>
> (Anne)

Anne was certain that the knowledge she obtained from her inner children related to ritual and sexual abuse, but there were times when she wanted more. The recovery literature includes exercises aimed at helping adult survivors recover buried memories and heal from their abuse. Some of these are aimed at the inner child and others directed towards the adult self and Anne was able to draw on these to develop 'whole packages' for her children:

> Often I write two lots of things and then a number of poems, and then a chant to the goddess from them so they get a whole package.
>
> (Anne)

There are times when the adult Anne appears to be writing, but elsewhere it is clear that she believes the children are responsible for the words on the page:

> I write the poem from inside, from them.
>
> (Anne)

Communicating with an inner child is one of the techniques suggested in many recovery manuals for accessing knowledge and healing the hurt or damaged part of the adult victim. This often takes the form of letters which can be written between the inner child and the adult self, and between the inner child and their abuser or a guardian. The majority of the women were aware of these techniques and although not many made use of them, the idea of communicating with a child self did reinforce the view of an inner child who held knowledge, and feelings, that they could gain access to.

All the women had read at least some self-help and recovery literature aimed at adult victims of sexual abuse. Some had also read more widely on the subject of sexual abuse, healing and recovery and this had clearly informed their understanding of their own situations and the stories they came to tell. Anne in particular had read widely on sexual and ritual abuse, recovered memories and multiple personalities. This had informed her understanding of how an abused child could 'split', how memories be hidden, how she could make contact with an inner child or children, and in doing so access their memories of abuse. Anne used this understanding to find further evidence of abuse and identify additional personalities, who could add to her knowledge. Anne found many of the techniques in the self-help and recovery literature but had also drawn on auto/biographies. She had, for example, learnt of the potential for her inner child to communicate to her adult self in the form of writing through Sylvia Fraser's autobiography *My Father's House* (1987). It is here that Fraser tells of the role her inner child played in the writing of her novels, how her inner child 'learnt to type' and how she 'presses the keys, throwing up masses of memories – stream of consciousness stuff' (Fraser 1987:149). With this knowledge Anne was able to explain some of her own writing and in the process identify her inner children at work:

> As a writer I'd always found it rather suspicious that I'd totally work with six characters and I'd manage complicated plots and things, like you know, and I could write fast and it was very complicated and all that.
>
> (Anne)

Like Fraser's inner child, Anne believed her inner children took over the adult Anne and were responsible for writing complicated stories. This idea of an inner child taking over was also used by Angela. Here she uses the idea to explain a letter she wrote to her parents although, unlike Anne, Angela did not believe it was her inner child who wrote the letter:

> My inner child was the one that forced me to write it.
>
> (Angela)

Angela did not rely on her child self to know that she was sexually abused but in identifying her as the force behind the letter she did identify this child self as the one who possessed knowledge of the abuse.

Actively seeking knowledge

In addition to knowledge which took the form of symptoms, the majority of women with no memories relied on hidden knowledge, which was seen to surface spontaneously and inevitably. There were also times, even for those whose knowledge surfaced spontaneously when they felt the need to actively seek out additional knowledge, or supporting evidence. For some women spontaneous knowledge did not fully explain or make sense of their situation whilst for others a lack of perceived improvements in their lives lead them to seek out additional causes for their failure to find happiness or satisfaction. In addition to interpreting spontaneous memories, the literature included ideas and techniques that could be used to access hidden or buried knowledge. Many of these techniques involved contact with an inner child, including writing letters and drawing pictures, but others such as guided flashbacks and interpreting dreams could be used by those who did not recognise a child self. Anne was particularly open to ideas aimed at contacting an inner child and employed a range of techniques including writing letters and cards to her inner children. She also recorded the content of dreams, in which she believed her inner children communicated with her, and attempted a number of guided flashbacks, although ultimately she found these too traumatic:

> I did a sort of guided flashback if you like, sort of jiggling about in a chair and things, as if I was being raped and then it was clear that I was being raped by different people if you see what I mean . . . and I did about two of those and then I couldn't cope I began to fall apart. (Anne)

Anne's experience was very real to her and whilst she was clear that in her flashbacks her inner children were reexperiencing the abuse, it is a technique that can be employed by those with no relationship with an inner child. For many women, the need to access additional knowledge related to the degree of certainty they had in their narratives and their identities as victims, as well as the extent to which they felt their lives had improved. The confidence they had in their memories or their need to search deeper for additional memories did not remain static but was itself mediated by a number of other factors, not all of which related to the strength of their memories

At one point Fiona claimed:

> There's enough in my memory that I know what happened, I know who did it.
>
> (Fiona)

However, there were also times when she considered returning, to:

> Get in touch with my wee self at two-and-a-half/three.
>
> (Fiona)

Fiona was certain she had been sexually abused but also felt her knowledge was only partial and limited. She believed the difficulty she had in accessing adequate knowledge indicated a greater degree of trauma and therefore also a greater depth to her memories, and had contemplated other forms of therapy:

> They might know ways of getting at things, you know, subconscious things that consciously I wasn't really getting access to.
>
> (Fiona)

Fiona was considering trying to access knowledge she did not have, but it was her understanding of the effects of sexual abuse that allowed her to identify the existence of such hidden knowledge by the feelings she had in the present. At the same time, her investment in a sexual abuse narrative, recovered memories and healing could also be seen to encourage her to look deeper for hidden knowledge because she was still unhappy with her life. The idea that particularly traumatic experiences might be more deeply buried and therefore harder to uncover was shared by Beccy. Although Beccy believed the information provided by her inner child was an accurate reflection of past events and therefore not open to interpretation, she also believed there was a correlation between the proximity of knowledge to the 'main problem' and the difficulty this knowledge had in reaching the surface:

> Mostly I never get nothing, when it's a bigger thing that's touching on the main sexual problem erm, I err...I get feelings but I don't get any memories. So all the feelings come but I can't remember anything.
>
> (Beccy)

Beccy had spent over 10 years healing and looking for memories. Although certain she had been sexually abused, Beccy had recovered no concrete memories despite numerous attempts to access knowledge held by her child self. At times she relied on patience, hoping that memories would surface when she was ready. She also attempted to access this knowledge with the use of photographs of her self as a child, particularly where she looked very unhappy, and would presumably be more closely connected to traumatic experiences, which she would look at before she went to bed and:

> Ask that little girl that I was what happened, just to help remind me, you know ask her.
>
> (Beccy)

However, even patience was not a passive exercise for Beccy. She did not simply wait for the memories to come but actively worked on herself, through healing and making her self stronger, to prepare her self and make it ready to receive this more difficult, and presumably more traumatic knowledge. All the time unsure what she needed to heal from, only that it was traumatic.

Not the first author

Whatever route they came by their memories of sexual abuse, the majority of women believed either their child or adult self was responsible for those memories and therefore for the stories they came to tell. However, five women did ultimately reject at least some aspect of their sexual abuse narrative and claimed to be the victims of false memory syndrome and these women believed they were not 'the first author' (de Rivera, 1998b). Whilst this should not necessarily be taken to indicate their stories were less reliable or accurate, it may be an indicator that they were less confident, or had less investment, in their stories than those who were the first author.

The majority of the women were able to identify symptoms in their adult lives, but for those who were not the first author, the idea that they had a history of childhood sexual abuse was one that was first introduced to them by a therapist. Although they may have been able to identify symptoms they did not gain access to 'other' memories or knowledge of abuse without assistance from a therapist. Ultimately all five women came to reject as false, at least some aspects, of the memories they recovered during therapy, although the degree to which they rejected their narratives and their explanations varied. Only Daisy and

Nicole eventually rejected as entirely false the memories they had once believed, or at least invested, in. Hazel, Rae and Pat rejected only some aspects of their memories, and maintained some belief in their abuse narratives. For them the difficulty was not in believing they were victims of sexual abuse but believing their fathers had abused them, and this was the aspect of their memories which they ultimately rejected. All three had all engaged with some form of therapeutic practice to address specific concerns in their adult lives, and their memories of sexual abuse first surfaced during such sessions: during hypnosis in the case of Hazel and Pat and during a scientology session in the case of Rae. Hazel and Rae both wished to lose weight and Pat wanted to address ME type symptoms. They also identified additional difficulties, mainly around sex, that could be attributed to sexual abuse. The idea that their symptoms resulted from being unhappy made sense to them, and when a therapist suggested they needed to discover the hidden cause of their unhappiness he tapped into ideas that resonated with the women's existing belief systems. As this included the idea of knowledge stored in the unconscious mind it could accommodate the idea of knowledge held by an inner child or traumatised part of the adult self:

> I've always been like that and I used to wonder what I was pushing to the back.
>
> (Rae)

The majority of Hazel's knowledge was gained through dreams and regression, and relied on a hypnotist to interpret. With the help of her hypnotist, Hazel used regression to go back to the time of her perceived abuse as a way of accessing knowledge of past traumas. She also revisited or replayed her dreams during her sessions where they were interpreted by her hypnotist and provided additional support for her narrative.

> And he would analyse them. It could be like I said about a house and a red box and I would be the house and dad would be the red box and it had been squashed . . . Things like that.
>
> (Hazel)

Hazel could identify supporting evidence in her adult life, but the idea she had been abused in childhood came from her sessions with a hypnotherapist, with each visit adding to her story:

> Every time I was at hypnotherapy I'd come out with another memory of abuse, every time.
>
> (Hazel)

Whatever stories the women told of their lives, they did so in an attempt to make meaning and whilst some women ultimately rejected their stories, or aspects of their stories, they were stories that had at some point made sense to them. Hazel initially believed the interpretations provided by her hypnotherapist and recognised they had made some sense to her. When she came to question her biography, she also recognised that there was no one truth in the analysis of dreams but rather it was possible to read dreams in different ways:

> Sometimes a dream makes sense. Yeh sometimes they do don't they, they do make sense sometimes. But those dreams I don't know he just made things out of them.
>
> (Hazel)

Hazel eventually questioned the interpretation of her dreams but, like Pat and Rae, did not reject the idea that hypnosis could uncover knowledge of traumatic events stored in her unconscious. All three believed in, and had engaged with, this idea before and during the therapy in which they had uncovered evidence of abuse. Pat and Rae also believed in past lives, and were open to the possibility that had been sexually abused in a previous life, rather than this one. It was perhaps this that made it difficult to reject totally, the idea that they had been sexually abused:

> I've always believed that anything that comes out in hypnosis is the truth, and I couldn't get away from that, I kept saying well it must be true because it's hypnosis it must be true.
>
> (Rae)

It was this belief that prevented Rae from returning to the hypnotist:

> I was terrified of knowing, I didn't want to know anymore... I was terrified what I was going to dig up. I wanted to know if you know what I mean but I didn't want to know.
>
> (Rae)

Hazel also had faith in hypnosis and the knowledge recovered during her sessions:

> I believed everything, I believed everything.
>
> (Hazel)

A belief in knowledge stored in the unconscious mind had contributed to their acceptance, albeit short lived, that they were victims of sexual abuse perpetrated by their fathers. When they came to doubt their memories it was this same belief that enabled Hazel, Rae and Pat to construct an alternative story, in which they rejected the specifics of their memories and the characters involved, but not the underlying plot. For Pat and Rae it was a belief in past lives that enabled them to maintain a belief in hypnosis or the unconscious and retrieval of buried memories of sexual abuse. It was, importantly, a belief that also provided a way to remove their fathers from the story, and they did recognise an element of choice in the stories they told:

> I had to say well look if I haven't been abused in this life I must have been abused in a previous life. That has to be the answer. Whether or not it is I'll never know but I had to believe that that was the answer because I had to cling on to something.
>
> (Rae)

> So I thought well this could have been in a past life or it could have been something I'd seen on television or something initially.
>
> (Pat)

Although identifying herself as a victim of FMS Pat, like Hazel and Rae, was keen to distance herself from the bfms stance that malicious or misguided therapists implant false memories into the minds of weak and vulnerable victims. Rather than blaming others for the information in her head she believed it came from within:

> He doesn't lead you at all there's just no ... Oh yeh it's very intense. Yeh I mean it's coming from you.
>
> (Pat)

Although Hazel did not share a belief in past lives, she too was able to accept an explanation which did not challenge her view that she had been abused, but only challenged the role her father was said to have played in that abuse. As she suggests:

> I just think its real, that I really do think its real. I've said to K... I'm sure something happened but not with my dad. Absolutely positive something happened.
>
> (Hazel)

All three acknowledged that their own wishes and motivations played a role in the explanations they eventually put forward. In ruling out any possible role her father may have played in sexually abusing her, Rae acknowledged that her reasoning was based to some extent on the outcome she wanted:

> But I couldn't rule out the possibility that I'd been abused, I could only rule out dad's part of it. But whether I have ruled that out in my head because I loved him so much and protected his image I don't know, I honestly don't know and I'll never know will I.
>
> (Rae)

Hazel, Rae and Pat shared a view of how knowledge could be stored in the unconscious mind that enabled them first to explain how they had been sexually abused and later to explain how they had come to uncover 'false' memories of abuse. However, it was a view that did not challenge the idea of buried knowledge and therefore, although they were able to construct a new narrative based on false memories, they could not do so with certainty:

> When I think about my dad and I look at his photo in the dining room, yeh I always wonder; did you or didn't you?
>
> (Hazel)

> I will never know whether I've been abused or not. I've still got that bit in my head... No I'm still not sure.
>
> (Rae)

> You know there are always questions still unanswered that will never be answered and that's the frustrating thing.
>
> (Pat)

Hazel, Rae and Pat had all rewritten a biography that, whilst it made sense to them, was based on some uncertainty. Daisy and Nicole had also rejected their memories but the responsibility they took for, and the investment they made in, their stories of both CSA and FMS was very different. In rejecting their memories, they also rejected the knowledge claims on which they were based. Although they had both once believed themselves to be victims of sexual abuse they rejected both their memories and the idea that traumatic knowledge could be stored in the unconscious mind of victims. The majority of the women were moving beyond the identity of victim but Daisy and Nicole seemed firmly attached to this identity, at the same time as they distanced themselves from a history of sexual abuse. Their rejection of hidden knowledge had informed their narratives, and whilst these no longer featured CSA they did feature FMS, in which one victim identity was replaced with that of another. It did not seem to be a positive identity, one that helped them look optimistically to the future, but instead focussed on the past, albeit the immediate past of therapy. Maybe at its heart it too contained an element of doubt. All those who rejected at least some aspect of memories introduced to them by others had found a way to make sense of their lives. However, it was one shrouded in doubt and uncertainty, and it may be that they are all to some extent condemned to 'a state of autobiographical limbo' (Tietjens Meyers 1997) in which they can never be certain. Neither Daisy or Nicole had such doubts but it is hard to imagine that even for them there would not have been at least some seed sown during the course of their therapy even if, like the other three, it only referred to the identity of the possible abuser. They had after all once believed, or at least invested in, these stories.

Memories, knowledge and the child within

'Memories' in some form were central to women's sexual abuse narratives. However, for the majority of women the memories they recovered were not concrete or recall memories but 'alternative memories' – a correlation of symptoms with assumed past abuse. Whilst these memories could be held by a damaged inner child, women did not need to accept the concept of an inner child or develop a relationship with their own inner child to access such memories as they could also be stored in the damaged, and therefore child-like part, of the abused women's psychologies. These memories, which surfaced in the form of symptoms, were seen as the influence of the damaged inner child or child-like part of the abused adult, exerting an unhealthy influence over their adult lives.

Much of the information accessed by the women was felt by them to come from their inner child but they also accessed information, often in the form of dreams and flashbacks, which they felt might have come from either their damaged child or adult selves. There were also times when they were unclear where their memories originated and other times when they drew on different understandings to explain the origins of their knowledge. Whilst the source of their memories was significant to others, it did not seem to be of relevance or importance for the women themselves. What was important to them was that their memories made sense and they had enough confidence in them to construct a life story that made sense of their lives and could act as successful guides for the future.

6
Life with the Inner Child

She's brilliant yeh yeh. Full of fun and laughter, fantastic.

(Sarah)

Introduction

The child, or child-like, self who features in discourses of childhood sexual abuse recovery occupies a central position in relation to both knowledge and healing. The inner children who populated the accounts of the women who participated in this study are more complex and women's relationships with them more fluid than she appears in much of the literature. Although she occupies a central position in the literature, as the holder of knowledge and as the damaged self in need of healing, the inner child of women's accounts was much more than this. How they understood her and the relationships they developed with her were informed as much by what they wanted in the present as they were by their need to explain the past or plan for the future. Clearly an explanation for storing and retrieving traumatic memories was significant to those who lacked memories but believed they were sexually abused but even for those without memories providing knowledge was not always the central role played by an inner child or child self. At a time when women are under pressure to conform to particular norms of healthy adult womanhood the inner child offered a way to 'deviate' temporarily from these norms without having to identify deviant behaviours or feelings as problematic, as long as they were able or willing to attribute such behaviours to an inner child. Whilst an inner child provided many women with access to knowledge of past abuse, she also offered a way to express feelings and emotions and enabled them to satisfy a desire to play and engage in what might otherwise have been perceived as childish activities.

The adult woman and the inner child

Not all the women accepted the concept of an inner child or developed a relationship with an inner child. Among those who did, their relationships and the role the child self played in their lives varied according their individual needs, wishes and circumstances. For some an inner child was a vehicle through which they could express feelings and emotions, but for others she was much more real than an idea. Whilst some were able to express feelings and emotions through a child self, others believed such expressions came direct from their inner child, who was seen to exert varying degrees of control. Fiona and Beccy felt it was often not their adult selves who were in control of or reacting to a situation, but believed it was their inner child who was reacting. However, they did not share the same understanding of who or what this child was:

> I was quite often being very upset if we had a conflict . . . I started to think well how am I feeling when this is happening, what's going on in my head because I'm not here and I'm not now. I'm not feeling like I'm in my own house and that I'm 37 years old, what am I feeling like and I felt like I was a young child and I was lost.
>
> (Fiona)

> This part of my mind that's causing the emotional flashbacks is still emotionally a child. It hasn't worked it through and developed so in a way it's getting in touch with that part of my mind that's still reacting to what happened. So yes I see it as part of my mind rather than something separate.
>
> (Beccy)

Whereas Fiona believed her inner child took over, Beccy did not see her child self as separate and did not create the same distance between her adult self and the feelings and emotions she experienced. Beccy believed it was a damaged and childlike part of her adult self, who held knowledge of her abuse, who took over at times of distress or difficulty and reacted and influenced the thoughts and behaviours of the adult Beccy. Both women drew on the harm story, survivor discourse and the inner child but applied them in ways that best suited themselves and their situations. However, although Beccy made it clear that she did not see the inner child as separate, she did confer a level of autonomy and control on the child part of herself that, at times, was not dissimilar to the level of control Fiona believed to be exercised by her inner child.

Women who entered adulthood with continuous memories of abuse did not need to contact an inner child to access knowledge of their abuse, although she could provide additional information. She is however, conceptualised in the literature as damaged and in need of healing and portrayed as a continual presence exerting an unhealthy influence over the lives of victims. She is therefore as important to healing as she is to the retrieval of buried knowledge, and victims are encouraged to contact her whether they need to access knowledge or as part of their healing. A number of women read Parks' *Rescuing the Inner Child* and two, including Julie, also engaged with Parks Inner Child Therapy (PICT) which uses guided flashbacks as a way to contact the inner child and recover knowledge of past abuse. Julie did not need PICT to access knowledge, but she did make use of guided flashbacks. She believed her inner child was holding her back and used guided flashbacks to communicate with this child self:

> I got her to calmly talk to me and what have you, and in the end I'd go back and meet her again and this particular time I sort of explained to her that she wasn't very well and that she really did need to go and be sort of healed really. I didn't really want to send her off to a psychiatrist or anything so her guardian angel came and took her away and she went off with them. In a way, it's not like I've abandoned her completely, its like one day she'll come back but she'll be healed.
>
> (Julie)

Whereas some women were introduced to their inner child through therapy or recovery, others were already aware of different aspects of their personalities, even if they did not conceptualise this as the inner child of CSA recovery, and sought out particular therapies to help them make contact with these inner selves. The concept of an inner child resonated for Julie, who had long been aware of different facets of her self in different situations:

> I always knew I'd got this, well split personality, this childish side, not childish but no I was very aware of my inner child . . . I felt I'm an adult with my children and there are times when with my mother I felt like a child and that was a side of me that I didn't like . . . I was

> very aware that there was somebody else... So there were these three personalities already there before.
>
> (Julie)

The inner child was an important companion for many women, but like other companions the relationships they developed and how they viewed her were fluid. For some she was an aspect of their personalities, for others a separate personality, but what was important was that she helped them deal with or articulate a range of thoughts and feelings. Through her women were able to identify and tap into different aspects of their own personalities. For Julie it was a part of her she did not like, but many women felt that in communicating with and comforting their inner child they discovered more positive aspects of themselves. The notion of a hurt, damaged child, although used in the literature to encourage women to return to a time when they were weak and vulnerable, was also recognised by women to offer the possibility of a fresh start, an opportunity to put right problems created in childhood, and for some the chance to identify an innocence they had not recognised. Growing up again and (re)parenting their inner child was a recurring theme in a number of women's testimonies:

> The whole idea of dysfunctional patterns and re-parenting our inner child was one that I found very useful. It was necessary in order for me to get in touch with my vulnerability and my feelings again after building a powerful wall around them.
>
> (Jenny)

Although contacting an inner child directed women to identify a weak and vulnerable part of themselves, when combined with the idea of reparenting her, it also helped some women to identify a stronger and wiser part of their adult selves:

> It was very useful and I actually found myself being wiser than I realised I was. It was as if I was being able to tap into some wisdom that I had that I didn't even realise was in there when I was trying to parent my child.
>
> (Fiona)

Not all the women acknowledged an inner child and of those who did, not all developed a positive or even meaningful relationship with her. In the case of Hazel, it was her therapist who developed a relationship with Hazel's child self. The child who held knowledge of Hazel's abuse did not burst spontaneously into Hazel's life or consciousness, neither was she brought into the world by Hazel, but surfaced only during hypnosis. The entirety of Hazel's therapeutic encounters was conducted, not between her adult self and the hypnotist, but between the hypnotist and her ten-year-old child self. The adult Hazel was not involved in these sessions and felt little control over or ownership of the process:

> I'm a 10 year old; I'm talking as a 10 year old. Yeh the words one uses as a 10 year old... Yes as a child for about two years.
>
> (Hazel)

Hazel had visited the same hypnotist for two years and in that time, with the exception of practical arrangements such as making the next appointment, he had only engaged with Hazel's hypnotised 10-year-old child self. The adult Hazel had been given information generated during these sessions but was not able to engage with the sessions or discuss the memories or knowledge, or even talk about how she felt about the experiences of sexual abuse, recovering memories and hypnosis. One of the few occasions when the adult Hazel was able to talk, as an adult, of her experiences, was when she was interviewed during the course of this research. Hazel ultimately rejected her memories and believed her hypnotist had misinterpreted the knowledge stored in her unconscious or held by an inner child. Hazel did not develop a relationship with an inner child, and therefore did not engage in those activities, suggested in the literature, aimed at making contact with this child, either to heal or access additional information. She had read self-help manuals to help her understand how she might have forgotten and then recovered memories of sexual abuse but this was a solitary exercise, in which she did not talk to others. Although, after she rejected her memories, she met with other retractors, this was more by way of listening to their stories than it was telling her own.

Although she did not develop a strong relationship with an inner child, or child self and did not ultimately reject the idea of an inner child, Hazel did reject her hypnotist's interpretation of knowledge this child was said to hold. A more critical view was held by Jay who believed the inner child was created in therapy, a product of inner child work, who could develop a life of her own.

> I found the inner child strange. I couldn't really cope with that one. I tried but I couldn't get my head round it.
>
> (Jay)

However, even Jay found a way of using the inner child in a way that helped her own understanding and recovery:

> It was looking at other children who were the same sort of age as when I was abused because I did blame myself. I found looking and talking to children of that age then I found it more and more difficult to say well it was me encouraging him, it was me being a flirt because I kept thinking well at that age I shouldn't have understood. I shouldn't have been able to flirt, not sexually... so I suppose you could use inner child as err, looking at it a bit differently but I looked at it that way.
>
> (Jay)

Jay rejected the inner child but was able to compare her child self with the innocence and vulnerability she saw in other children of a similar age to her abused child self and it was this that helped her to see that she was not to blame.

Acting your age

A central theme of the contemporary sexual abuse story is that it is an overwhelming experience that leaves a devastating mark on its victims. This is combined with the view, widespread within self-help culture, that adult women are not only powerful but have the right to lead happy, fulfilled and successful lives. Where women fail to claim this right the causes and solutions are said to lay within their individual damaged psychologies. Where this understanding is combined with the concept of the inner child, the nature and process of healing takes on a particular meaning which has consequences beyond that of individual women. The inner child becomes central, not only to the retrieval of knowledge, but also to the process of healing, as it is she who has been damaged and therefore it is she who is in need of healing. The inner child or child self can also be used as a measure against which women's healing can be judged, as women 'grow up' and move from 'childhood' to adulthood where they are healed and can claim their rights as fully functioning healthy adults. Along the way, as 'children' they are encouraged to engage in those activities and behaviours appropriate to those who have not yet reached adulthood.

The path to healing is mapped out in two ways. It is an ongoing journey of discovery and personal development. Alternatively women can contact their inner child and learn to parent her, and through this reparenting can help her to 'grow-up' and develop without the damaging effects of abuse into the strong powerful woman she should or would have been. Whichever route women choose they are offered the promise of becoming, or finding, a strong powerful woman, able to claim her rights to happiness, fulfilment and success. However, they must (first) accept they have been damaged and their damaged psychologies or damaged inner child needs looking after to enable them to heal. At a practical level, whether they acknowledge an inner child or child-like inner self, women must accept they are weak, vulnerable, and therefore childlike, and they can therefore pass easily from acknowledging an inner child to acknowledging a child-like inner self. The CSA recovery literature has helped to construct formerly abused women, thought to be in need of healing, as weak and vulnerable, and childlike and in doing so has helped to extend the construction to include others who display similar 'symptoms'. In this way all those who are unhappy or dissatisfied can be constructed as weak, vulnerable, in need of healing, and childlike.

Whilst the recovery literature does encourage women to engage in 'childish', or children's, activities and at times to 'become a child' we should not assume women follow this advice as if following a set of commands. The inner child was not only more or less real, and more or less separate to different women, but she represented different opportunities and fulfilled different functions for different women. For some she offered a way to engage in activities they found difficult but saw as beneficial or enjoyable to their child and adult selves. For others she offered the possibility of a fresh start and the opportunity to put right problems they thought were created in childhood. The hurt inner child who needed to be healed, occupied a central position in much of the literature, but she was not always a central character in women's lives. Even women who recognised an aspect of their inner child who needed to be healed did not restrict their relationship with her to healing, but engaged her in a variety of activities. The majority of women identified an inner child in their lives but their perceptions of her, how real she was, the contact they had with her, who controlled that contact, and their relationships with her varied considerably. A number of women found she provided an important outlet or mechanism through which they could participate more fully in life. She helped some engage in artistic or playful activities, and activities that helped them release tension or let off steam, or simply enjoy life more. Both Beccy and Fiona, for example, participated in playful activities with their child selves but Fiona also took part in more creative activities with the help of her child self. Beccy did not recognise her inner child as separate, but did find in her a way to work on aspects of her (adult) life and personality she felt needed to be improved. This child self provided a way for the adult Beccy to learn to enjoy life more. This was something Beccy found difficult and therefore even learning to enjoy life was experienced by Beccy as part of healing and that needed to be worked at:

> It's something I have to work through as well. Because I need to be able to play, I want to be able to play. I want to be able to erm ... to go into an imaginary world and really feel things when I want to.
>
> (Beccy)

Beccy used her inner child to represent a part of her adult self but for other women the inner child, or children, was more real or separate. However, women's perception of their inner child was not always straightforward, and might relate to how they saw contact with her as a way to help their adult selves. As the following exchange shows, although Fiona identified her child self as separate, she also used her as a way to engage in activities which she felt would benefit her adult self:

> Looking after the inner child I think is more basic it's cuddling up with my teddy. I keep a teddy by my bed and if my inner child is feeling tearful and afraid I'll go to bed and cuddle my teddy and have a wee cry and that's how I take care of my inner child. [J: But the teddy's not your inner child?] No no. No my inner child is in me, not a separate part of me it's always me, actually me. My inner child's cuddling the teddy. It's me as an adult telling myself to get into bed and cuddle the teddy and keep myself warm and have a wee rest and it's my inner child that's doing that, that's lying in the bed cuddling the teddy. When my inner child has been comforted, had a little cry, cuddled the teddy and I'm calm and it's my adult self that gets out of bed and carries on with the day. I'll look after my inner child as well with music. I actually like to dance about. If I've got the place to myself (laughs) not if my partner ... I'll put on music that I like and I'll have a wee dance about the place and just feel happy. Sometimes just to relax and feel happy and I do that when I'm on my own but not when I'm with anybody else. That part of me feels safest when it's just me and her. If I want to dance I would go with my friends out dancing or out with my partner out dancing but I would do that in the company of other people but erm, for that part of myself to be able to express her happiness and joy she would want to do that

> with just me there, not anybody else. Colouring in, I went through a period, not recently, but when I used to have a colouring in book and crayons and just lie on the floor and colour in. I'd feel quite calm and happy doing that.
>
> (Fiona)

The relationship Fiona developed with her inner child was not only informed by her reading of the literature but also by discourses of femininity and what she accepted as appropriate thoughts and behaviours for adult women. Fiona acknowledged some activities engaged in by her child self were beneficial but without her they would have challenged Fiona's perception of herself as a mature, healthy adult woman. Her inner child allowed her to engage beneficial, pleasurable or fun (childish) activities without threatening this identity. Many of the women contacted a child self but Fiona and Anne both developed particularly important and intense relationships with their inner child. Both women clearly drew on the advice found in the recovery literature, but they had also used their own judgement in choosing which activities or behaviours to entertain and which would be unhelpful. Together with counselling and reading recovery literature and survivor auto/biographies, Fiona participated in self-help and support groups, and Internet sites. Whilst she found most of these helpful she did find one, which encouraged a particular embodiment of the inner child, to be particularly disturbing. Fiona was happy to entertain her inner child and allow this child self to participate in a variety of activities including Internet chat rooms, but felt those chat rooms aimed at her 'inner baby' were a step too far:

> I didn't find useful the idea of actually talking in a babyish voice or trying to regress myself physically but maybe I got that idea on the Internet. I didn't think that was very useful.
>
> (Fiona)

For observers who fail to recognise the potential of some recovery discourses to infantilise women, it is perhaps worth visiting a chat room where victims' 'inner babies', are encouraged to 'talk' in a language of goos and gahs. However, rather than simply being rendered infantile through the activities she engaged with as her inner child, Fiona was able to maintain a positive self-image through this child self. She found she could engage in 'childlike' behaviour but at the same time distance her adult self from this behaviour. However, Fiona's relationship with this child self relied on accepting that only particular thoughts, feelings and behaviours are appropriate in healthy adult women, an idea vigorously rejected by Jay. Jay believed the concept of an inner child encouraged women to believe that, as healthy adult women, they should deny themselves certain feelings, experiences and behaviours. Therefore if or when women want to participate in such experiences and behaviours they are discouraged or directed to do so, not as healthy adult women, but only through their child selves. Jay felt the idea of an inner child not only threatened her sense of identity but denied the very real feelings her adult self had in the present:

> I know sometimes you feel like a child and feel vulnerable and scared and everything else but are we not allowed to feel that as adults... Yeh I feel vulnerable now. That's what I have to deal with. I'm living now not then.
>
> (Jay)

Jay felt it was unhelpful and even unhealthy for women to separate themselves from their thoughts and feelings, whether or not this separation occurred through an inner child, and believed it would be healthier for women to recognise and take responsibility for the way they felt and behaved. Jay had experienced years of abuse but she had also spent many years learning from her experiences. Although she still experienced difficulties relating to those experiences, Jay was secure enough in her sense of self and what it meant for her to be a healthy adult woman, to be able to challenge the popular construction of adult womanhood, which enabled her to also reject the concept of an inner child, but this was not so easy for others. Jay also had unbroken memories of her abuse and therefore, unlike other participants including Fiona and Anne, did not rely on an inner child to provide knowledge or autobiographical certainty. Jay was, therefore, better placed to recognise potential problems with the concept of an inner child and likely dangers that might emerge in women's relationship with her.

Multiple children

Fiona and Anne both accepted only certain thoughts and behaviours to be appropriate for women, but used the inner child, or at least the concept of an inner child, to mediate the effects this had on their own adult lives. In different ways their inner child provided temporary release, and relief, from the straightjacket of contemporary womanhood. However, whereas Fiona made contact with one inner child, Anne had contacted many. Through, dreams, flashbacks and inner child work Anne had identified hundreds of alters who she believed were created as a result of some form of abuse in her childhood, of whom she had so far contacted over 20. The majority of Anne's alters were people, of whom one was a boy and the rest were girls. Anne and her alters lived 'as a group' and her relationships with them more intense than the relationships the other women developed with an inner child. Unlike the other women Anne often used the pronoun 'we' when talking. At times Anne's group of alters took on the characteristics of a family, with Anne at the head, and at other times it was more like a group of friends. Whether a family or a group of friends, each member had different characteristics, although they were somewhat one-dimensional. Through her inner children Anne engaged in similar activities to other participants but she did so to different effect and for different reasons. Anne's inner children were very real to her; she gave them names and developed individual and unique relationships with each of them. She also recognised and, through the things she bought them and the activities she facilitated, encouraged in them strict gender attributes. Anne's alters enabled her to engage in certain activities but perhaps more importantly they enabled her to negotiate a path for herself that involved traversing between different gender roles, ways of being and identities. Anne's alters were a mixture of animals and children of which all but one were girls, and whilst the girls helped maintain a position of vulnerability and helplessness, the one boy provided Anne with an occasional escape from this role. The girls:

> Like colouring in books, they love glittery stuff, all the girly stuff.
>
> (Anne)

Anne saw them as sweet, charming, innocent children who needed protecting and looking after:

> They're lovely.
>
> (Anne)

And

> I've got a lot of very sweet little children, you know, who are delightful and great fun, sort of ingenious and I've tried to train them not to take sweets from strangers or go off with them.
>
> (Anne)

Anne invested a lot of time and emotion in her inner children, and they repaid her in their own ways. She wrote poems to them, and bought presents and cards, an idea suggested in much of the literature. She even celebrated their 'birthdays', keeping as special the day each one surfaced, and thereby keeping each child special. Many of these cards and gifts were kept and were on display around her house. Although great fun at times, Anne's children could also be very demanding:

> I found the children kept wanting bracelets you know. They thought bracelets were great. And Minuet who picked up the worst of the abuse, I got her a beautiful . . . you know I went into the shop, I knew I wanted silver because I realised there were predators in my system who were anti me and I felt it was like possession, you know I needed exorcism. You know I thought you stopped vampires with garlic and silver so I went off to try and get something silver.
>
> (Anne)

Anne was very generous to her children in a way that she was perhaps unable to be generous to herself. Whilst she may not have been able pamper or treat herself, buy presents or indulge her own needs and desires Anne had found a way to do this through her inner children. However, it was not only the giving of presents that was directed towards her inner children but, in times of distress and upset, reassurance and comfort was also directed towards her inner children. One way Anne provided this, particularly to the smaller children, was to play them a tape recorded by her therapist:

> Many of the children inside listen to that tape now, when they're panicking.
>
> (Anne)

> Cos a little baby hears voices you see, don't they.
>
> (Anne)

Through her children, Anne was able to buy nice things, to read books and listen to tapes. She was able to take time out for herself and to go for walks across the park. She was able to talk about her feelings and even to seek out a therapist. It may be Anne felt unable to undertake these activities for her adult self but she was able to do them through and for her inner children. The CSA recovery literature claims to be empowering, but it did not help Anne's adult self undertake these activities, and may even have prevented her from doing them 'as an adult'.

The messages contained in this literature may also have prolonged the life of her inner children, without whom her adult life might have been constrained by a need or desire to conform to the stereotypes of conventional womanhood.

Dag, the only boy among Anne's alters enabled her to move beyond the straightjacket of femininity and find in herself not only a personal strength, a masculine toughness as she saw it, but also an ability to stand up for herself and her 'family' and to protect them from the outside world. Dag did not simply conform to a generalised young male stereotype. Rather he conformed to a particular stereotype of troubled or troublesome male youth. Even his first appearance was in what could be perceived as a particularly male environment. He first surfaced by a football ground and when he wrote it was always using graffiti:

> You know stroppy kids kind of thing, you know, graffiti artist, tough graffiti artist.
>
> (Anne)

Anne did not buy Dag sweets or girly presents such as colouring books or bracelets. Instead she bought him that characteristically male accessory – a football. Dag might have been damaged and he might be troubled but he was also tough and, by implication, able to look after himself. He could also, by implication, look after and protect her adult self and the rest of her inner children. Dag was a young man 'with attitude' who had something to say and he used a language and method that was very different to the timid and gentle one of his fellow inner children, and even from the adult Anne. Of all her alters Dag was the one Anne seemed to have the most affection and the most admiration for. He was perhaps the one she wanted to be. He was the one:

> Who had to be incredibly courageous you know, all the time. The daring one.
>
> (Anne)

But he also bore a resemblance to her father:

> His eyes are just like my dad's.
>
> (Anne)

Whereas Anne occupied the role of the female head of her family, or mother, Dag could be seen to take on the role of a father figure and it was through him that Anne was able to bridge a gap between the father she blamed for her present difficulties and one she felt guilt over. Anne had a somewhat ambiguous relationship with her father and it may be that Dag was, or represented, the father she always wanted: a head who was strong, courageous and able to look after and protect the family. She may not have found this in her own father but she was able to create it, or recognise it, to some extent in Dag and her 'new' family. It was her father who Anne believed was one of the central figures in the circle who ritually abused her. However, he was also someone about whom in his later life she felt some guilt. Unlike her friends who looked after elderly parents, Anne had moved away and left her father to look after himself. Whilst she expressed guilt over her failure to look after her father, she was able to draw on her history of abuse to justify her behaviour and relieve at least some of that guilt.

Although she can be used to construct victims as childlike the concept of an inner child was significant to many women's sense of themselves as mature, healthy adult women. This was because their inner child helped them maintain an identity of healthy womanhood as it distanced their adult selves from those aspects of themselves that deviated from this role. They did not deny the childish side of themselves, they simply allocated it to a childish inner self. However, it was an identity that not all women embraced and their child self could also help to avoid such an identity. Anne did not appear to be happy to construct the identity of mature womanhood for herself, and indeed this might have been an identity she wanted to avoid. Even as a teenager she had not been sure she wanted it at all:

> Because in my teenage years I had no intention of growing into a woman at all, it just sort of happened.
>
> (Anne)

Anne's inner children may well serve a different function. The girls who populate Anne's world displayed the feminine characteristics with which she was uncomfortable but they remained largely very young girls who:

> Like colouring in books, they love glittery stuff, all the girly stuff.
>
> (Anne)

They were not young girls growing up into young women and as such might have helped Anne to avoid such an identity for her adult self.

The only inner child who carried any real suggestion of maturity and growing up was Dag, the only male among Anne's alters. His presence, linked as it was with power and authority, might indicate a recognition on Anne's part of the vulnerability and inferiority inherent in the position occupied by women, even at the beginning of the twenty-first century. Whatever gender they embodied all of Anne's alters insulated and protected her from the outside world. Even as very small children they could sometimes:

> Feel to me like protectors, parents or something.
>
> (Anne)

In much the same way as very small children are sometimes reported to have telephoned emergency services when a parent is in trouble, Anne believed it was one of her inner children who telephoned her therapist, when she was having a particularly difficult time:

> One of my inner children called up B, my therapist. It had to be that person because, you know, it wasn't me on the phone. It was somebody else.
>
> (Anne)

Becoming whole?

Much of the literature identifies an inner child or child self as central to both uncovering knowledge and healing. It is through recognising and healing their damaged child self and thereby leaving the identity of victim behind that formerly abused women can go on to embrace the identity of survivor. There is usually only one inner child, and becoming whole and integrating the child and adult selves is an underlying theme running through much of this literature. However, whilst there is usually only one inner child in the CSA recovery literature, the inner child is not usually limited to one and the aim is not always integration in that literature aimed at or written by victims of ritual abuse. Becoming whole through healing and integrating their inner child was also a theme running through many women's accounts, not all of the women saw integration and the letting go of their alters or child selves, as a desirable goal. An inner child had enabled many to experience a variety of activities and feelings and therefore, if they were to let go of their inner child, the one who facilitated these experiences, they either needed to relinquish them or find alternative ways of engaging. Whilst for some this might involve allowing their adult selves to engage in 'childlike' activities, others were less likely to allow their adult selves to be 'childish'. Therefore, although integration was a goal to aim for, a number of women found the idea of becoming whole ran counter to their experiences of healing and recovery. This was particularly so for those who engaged with inner child work or relied in some way on their inner child. We can see that some women, such as Anne, welcomed the separation between their adult and child selves, others found it disturbing. Fiona, for example, did not feel more whole but increasingly separate from her child self and while this could be seen as part of the process of healing, it was something Fiona was concerned about, suggesting that a sense of wholeness was something she thought she should aim for. Becoming whole and finding her 'true self' were seen by Sarah as fundamental to healing and it was through healing and connecting with her child self that she believed:

> I became my self and became whole.
>
> (Sarah)

A number of women had a clear image of their inner child as the young child they had once been, an image sometimes supported by photographs. Julie had pictured her inner child in this way and had chosen to send her away to be healed. However, she was also very clear that her inner child was a (damaged) part of her adult self. It was, she believed:

> The side to me that was inhibiting me.
>
> (Julie)

Sending part of herself away enabled Julie to move forward in her life and become stronger and able to welcome back her inner child, who as a part of her would also be stronger. It could also be seen to reflect a lack of confidence, as there were aspects of herself that Julie did not feel able to work on. Women developed their own understanding of their child self, and Julies' was different to others who chose to keep this child self with them as they believed they needed to help her heal. Unlike other women, Julie did not feel strong enough to help her inner child. However, Julie did have other real children to look after at the time of her healing, and this might have influenced her ability to deal with a childlike or needy aspect of her self. It may also be that some women, unlike Julie, needed their inner child to help them uncover knowledge or evidence of their abuse, and possibly also of the damage done to them. It would be hard to send their child self away under such circumstances. Integrating their damaged child self was for many an important part of healing but they did not all take this to mean that, on healing, they had to give up their child. The continued presence of this child should not necessarily be taken as evidence of the ongoing effects of sexual abuse or be used to distinguish between those who were abused and those who were not:

> She's never going to go away, as in there are times you know, as a human being, we feel a bit like a child.
>
> (Julie)

The issue of integration also featured in much of the literature on multiple personalities but within this area there are those who argue that integration should not necessarily be the only or overriding aim (Whitman and Shore 1994). This was an idea picked up by Anne who had intense, at times overwhelming, relationships with the children who shared her world. Whilst she believed these inner children needed to heal, she was less clear about the need, or desirability, for integration:

> Whether they'll merge or what happens I just don't know . . . but to my mind the thing to do is to just love them all and when they surface you need to tell them that they're not going to get hurt any more.
>
> (Anne)

Whilst she was aware that much of the literature encourages survivors to integrate their personalities, Anne had recently read a book that challenged the orthodoxy of this:

> It's helped all of us, you know, begin to realise, you know, not to try and sort ourselves out like all these easy books tell you to but to just kind of go along with it and take whatever happens week by week because it's, you know maybe you'll end up getting to know all the children like before, you know or maybe they start integrating a bit along the way.
>
> (Anne)

The inner children with whom Anne shared her world were very real to her. So real had they become that Anne did not always see it was her role, as the adult or front person, to make decisions for the rest of 'the group':

> I realise that there are people in there who know much more than I do about what happened and who are much wiser than me in what needs to be done. I mean there are so many different people but Anne, the front personality, is beginning to realise that she is only part of the big system.
>
> (Anne)

For many of the women who acknowledged an inner child, integration and becoming whole were important steps on the road to recovery and health. However, for Anne integration did not appear to be a goal:

> You get used to existing as part of a group. Even the front personality gets used to existing as part of a group.
>
> (Anne)

Anne's whole life centred around this group which had come to represent both her family and friendship networks and without which her life would have been very lonely.

Who is the inner child?

The inner child of women's account was a 'child-like self' who fulfilled different needs and functions, for different participants at different times. For some she was simply an aspect of their adult selves, for others the part of them that had been abused in childhood that remained damaged and waiting to be healed. Whereas some women needed her to provide evidence of their sexual abuse, others entered adulthood already in possession of such knowledge and did not have the same need. She got in the way for some women, but for others she provided a way to engage in activities and behaviours that might, without her, be seen as in appropriate. For some she was a reminder of who they were and for others a companion or friend on the journey to healing and recovery. Not all thought her a useful or beneficial companion but of those who developed a relationship with her, all felt they developed the relationship that suited their needs and circumstances best.

What was clear from women's accounts was that the inner child who populated their stories need not be the weak, vulnerable child evident in much of the CSA recovery literature. Neither need she always be a reminder of a past filled with unhappy or traumatic times. Instead she could be a representative, or possibly a reminder, of happier times: of a child and a childhood not always filled with hurt and vulnerability. In Sarah's case, literally a snapshot of a happier self:

> I have an inner child oh yes. Stay there I'll show you my photo of my inner child [leaves and returns with a photo of herself as a child] This is a photo I love, this is my inner child she's beautiful, just her face and the laughter it's brilliant. She's probably about four. She's brilliant yeh yeh. Full of fun and laughter, fantastic.
>
> (Sarah)

Sarah had found a place for her inner child where could recognise *'the fun and laughter'*, not just the trauma and abuse she experienced as a child. However, a number of women also recognised another, more problematic side, to the inner child and inner child work.

7
Problems with the Children

I mean, who is going to be the inner child?

(Anne)

If you have five, or six, or eight of them it's going to get rather crowded

(Jay)

Introduction

The inner child maybe central to much of the CSA recovery and recovered memory literature but where she comes from and how she enters the world is left relatively untouched within much of this literature, although her aetiology does come under harsher scrutiny within the literature on 'multiple personalities'. Whilst her origins may not be central to debates on a solitary inner child, the way she enters the world as one of a number of alter personalities, is central to debates that focus on multiple personality syndrome (MPS – a term commonly used by the women who participated in this study) or Dissociative identity disorder (DID) as it is now known in the professional literature. This is in part due to the focus of two separate but related arguments: whereas the recovered memory wars focus on the truth or falsity of sexual abuse claims, the focus within the arguments around MPS/DID is on the emergence of alters. Therefore, although an inner child, itself a form of multiple personality albeit usually limited to only one alter, plays a central role in recovered memory discourses and the CSA recovery literature, attention is focussed on the knowledge which she is said to hold. In the MPS/DID debates the focus is not on the knowledge claims but on the alters themselves. However, although unproblematic within much of the literature, the origins of even a singular inner child, and the role she might play in their lives, whether related to accessing knowledge, to healing and recovery, or to other more day-to-day activities, was not unproblematic to the majority of women in this study.

One of the few areas of agreement within the recovered memory debates is that hypnosis is significant in the surfacing or creation of multiple personalities. According to the false memory syndrome foundation (FMSF), MPD is an 'iatrogenic behaviour syndrome, promoted by suggestion and maintained by clinical attention, social consequences, and group loyalties' (McHugh 1993:5). Although there is recognition of the vast body of literature, including self-help material, currently in circulation, it is assumed that this suggestion is made by a (hypno)therapist. As with recovered memories, those (largely women) at the centre of these debates are seen as passive recipients or hosts for these numerous personalities. However, the identification, creation or surfacing of alter personalities does not always take place within a guiding framework of hypnosis and women themselves play an active role in the process. The emergence of more than one inner child is likely to be influenced by the value women place on their relationship with an original inner child and the investment they made in her as a source of knowledge and a companion on the road to well being. However, we should not look for a straightforward relationship between an un/successful relationship with an inner child and the emergence or not of multiple inner children or personalities. To understand this relationship we must look at the lives, in all their complexities, of those who developed a relationship with one or more inner children.

Four women identified problems with some aspect of the inner child or inner child work, albeit for very different reasons. Beccy and Fiona both developed a relationship with an inner child which they recognised could be problematic. Anne, who identified hundreds of inner children, had so far developed a relationship with over 20 and was concerned that much of the literature denied the existence of multiple alters and directed women to recognise only one. Jay was concerned with the very idea of an inner child, who she believed was created during the course of inner child work and could take on a life of her own. Jay was also concerned that the inner child could be used to indulge inappropriate feelings and behaviours, and deny adult women the opportunity to express themselves. These women cannot be taken as representative or used to explain how all multiple personalities come into being. However, their accounts and their concerns do shed some light on the subject and offer alternative routes for the emergence or creation of multiple personalities, including an alternative to hypnosis which allows a role for the women themselves, Their accounts also demonstrate the need for caution when it comes to promoting inner child work.

A problem of separation

The inner child was conceptualised as hurt and in need of healing and therefore contacting her was seen as necessary, or at least beneficial, but a number of women expressed concern over how she could be perceived, or might develop or even separate over the course of therapy or the journey to recovery. Beccy and Fiona both developed a relationship with an inner child or child self but conceptualised her in different ways. Beccy understood her child self as a part of her adult self damaged in childhood and, although not concerned about the relationship she developed with her own child self, was aware of potential dangers and expressed concern about the relationships others might develop:

> They're all you so is it good to be so separate? Like this one had that personality and this one had that personality and this one had that one. I'm thinking what, they're all you. So I think there can be damage somewhere there of not integrating everything and not working through some things because you think, oh well that's not me that's that inner child there, or that inner child there. When really, it's all you.
>
> (Beccy)

Beccy was one of the few women to engage directly with the recovered memory wars and this clearly influenced her engagement with this research. Careful to avoid criticism of her own therapist she was keen to distance her from practices that could be criticised by others. As a result, although she expressed concern around the inner child, Beccy made it clear that she was not rejecting something from her own therapy but something she came across in the literature. Beccy believed that seeing their inner child as separate from their adult selves could direct women away from working through problems, seen to belong to a separate child self, and thereby prevent them from healing. This separate inner child could also be used as an excuse, or even an indulgence, by some women, and this was a view shared by Jay. Where problems or behaviours are attributed to a child and not an adult self, the adult woman can avoid responsibility for actions attributed to the child self. A further concern for Jay was that women might not respond to events but see those events as happening to a separate inner child and this might direct them away from the self work they need to undertake:

> So I feel in a lot of ways the inner child, as well as being dangerous and everything else, it takes you totally away from what you really should be concentrating on.
>
> (Jay)

The inner child was not a new concept to many of the women occupying, as she does, a central place in many contemporary cultural texts, and a number had already made contact with an inner child in some form before they before they came across her in the context their recovery. Fiona's introduction to her child self resonated with a pre-existing feeling that she shared her life with someone, and the literature offered her a way to contact and interact with what she later identified as her inner child. Fiona was not entirely comfortable with the relationship she developed with this child self, who she saw as increasingly separate. Although Fiona had once had a positive relationship with her inner child, who had proved a helpful and cheerful companion, she had become increasingly separate and developed a will of her own, capable of exerting an unhealthy influence over the adult Fiona who was:

> A bit afraid of her at the moment because she is the one who has caused me all this upset.
>
> (Fiona)

Beccy did not see her child self as separate, and therefore continued to believe she was under the control of the adult Beccy, unlike Fiona who had surrendered a degree of autonomy to her child self. Fiona's relationship with her inner child was important not only as a means to recover memories but also, as we saw in the previous chapter, as a way to engage in activities that she might otherwise find difficult. Although she recognised that her inner child had become more separate since she first entered therapy, as she believed her to be real, she did not believe that a separate inner child was created in therapy. Therapy, and healing, had merely enabled this inner child to flourish. However, this was not a view shared by everyone.

Creation

Beccy and Jay both expressed concerns abut the inner child and the dangers of different aspects of the self splitting off to create new personalities and, whilst Beccy was unclear how this might happen, Jay believed the creation of one or more inner personalities was the result of inner child work; a therapeutic technique in which women are encouraged to contact and communicate with an inner child self or selves. Within the context of recovery from childhood sexual abuse, this often involves writing letters to and from the inner child and enabling the child to draw pictures, seen as the child communicating information. It was the child who was damaged by, and held knowledge of, their abuse and women were encouraged to attribute thoughts, feelings and behaviours believed to result from the abuse to their child self. However, as Jay recognised, in doing so women could create a personality, or personalities, who they might see as separate and with whom they might develop a relationship:

> So I did write some stuff and I found I'd given a name and then I thought hold on I'm making this into a real person, somebody who's not me. But by making her a real person am I not encouraging it and I became quite scared then.
>
> (Jay)

Jay entered adulthood with unbroken memories of multiple forms of abuse, involving different abusers, spanning most of her childhood. Consequently, she did not rely on an inner child for knowledge and did not have the same incentives as some to identify or make contact with an inner child. However, Jay came to reject inner child work and the idea of an inner child for a number of reasons. Abused over many years Jay was faced with the problem of how old this child might be. She could either choose an age at which to contact her self as a child, possibly related to how hurt this child was thereby focusing exclusively on the damage or hurt experienced by this child self, or she would have to contact this self not once but many times, at different ages. An additional concern, also recognised by Jay, was that inner child work encouraged women to identify different feelings and attribute them to different personalities. In order to distinguish between these different personalities they can be given names, but the process of naming can itself establish these personalities as 'real':

> I said no because if you're trying to acknowledge somebody at a certain age then you're looking at that person as an individual and to me that usually means looking at it and giving it personality or a name and something like that. Now if you have five or six or eight of them it's going to get rather crowded. That's when I realised, when I'd given them names and things like that and I thought... it was getting me crazy it was like a multiple personality and I thought no, I'm stopping this now.
>
> (Jay)

Jay rejected the idea that childhood experiences of sexual abuse led a damaged child to split and believed instead that the inner child, or children, were created in therapy through inner child work. This not only encouraged women to focus exclusively on the damage or hurt experienced by their child selves but more worryingly, could lead them to identify multiple inner children. Whether according to age or discrete personality traits, Jay recognised that inner child work could itself create multiple personalities and, whilst Beccy was the only other women to express similar unease, we can see echoes of these concerns in the personalities who populated the inner world of Anne. Although it was a concern that Jay felt was not appreciated by her own counsellors she believed if she continued with inner child work it would lead her into an even more difficult situation than the one that led her to seek therapeutic help:

> Yes it was multiple. And I was thinking I don't want to end up getting sectioned for having multiple personalities.
>
> (Jay)

The possible age of her inner child or children, a concern not raised by others, and the possibility of developing multiple personalities, were not the only reasons Jay rejected inner child work. Jay had tried inner child work but eventually rejected it as unhelpful, counterproductive and at times dangerous. Returning to the inner self of her childhood, particularly her teenage years, was especially disturbing to Jay:

> As a teenager I could be rebellious, I could be angry and I could be quite destructive especially to myself. Did I want to bring a child out like that?
>
> (Jay)

It was when she returned to this difficult period in her life that Jay found the process particularly harmful:

> I'd never cut myself but I did when I was doing the inner child work and that's when I stopped the inner child therapy and I stopped cutting myself.
>
> (Jay)

Jay was clear that it was her adult self who now experienced the effects of having been abused as a child and, as it was this adult self who lived in the present, it was she who had to deal with those effects. Jay felt safest, and most in control, when her adult self rejected the inner child. Jay learnt in her childhood that life as child was unsafe and it was a lesson she learnt again as a result of inner child work. She experienced first-hand of some of the dangers of inner child work but her concerns were not limited to her own situation. Like Beccy, she felt that attributing thoughts and behaviours to an inner child, or children, could be indulgent and might direct women away from addressing issues faced by them, as adults, or deny them access to certain feelings and emotions that as adults they were led to believe were inappropriate. Inner child work, she argued, served to deny adult women the expression of feelings and the articulation of thoughts which were seen within the therapeutic community as inappropriate whilst encouraging women to indulge in childish and/or irresponsible behaviour. Once they had identified and made contact with an inner child women were encouraged to re-parent her, but as Jay recognised, it was a style of parenting that could be viewed as irresponsible:

> Saying they've got a right to be angry and everything else but I think well no if you're trying to parent a child you have to be a responsible parent . . . I do feel it's giving yourself permission, not to be indulgent, but to be very destructive. And I don't think that's going to help anybody so I stopped doing that as soon as I twigged what seemed to be happening.
>
> (Jay)

Although she rejected much of the 'childish' behaviour encouraged through inner child work, Jay did not reject all behaviour defined as 'childlike'. Instead she questioned those behaviours prescribed for adult women and those behaviours which are prohibited, within which women can only engage in certain behaviours by accepting they are performed by a child self:

> I felt as though it was an excuse to let things run riot in a way, which I don't suppose is always a bad thing but do we need an excuse, it could be we want to do it.
>
> (Jay)

> Why say the inner child's angry. Why not just say you are angry and I felt as though maybe the inner child was becoming an excuse.
>
> (Jay)

Some women were content to engage in 'childlike' activities, such as dancing, playing with teddies, or taking themselves to bed when upset, through their inner child. However, Jay believed they should be able to engage in these activities if they chose, not as children but as adults. She recognised that ideas surrounding the inner child prohibited certain behaviours in adult women whilst they encouraged others, neither of which are beneficial or healthy. An additional concern, again recognised by Jay, related to how women who developed a relationship with an inner child might be treated by others. The literature not only encouraged women to contact an inner child, but to indulge her and enable her to engage in 'age appropriate' games and other activities, including holding birthday parties for her and asking their partners to read her bedtime stories. A prospect not relished by Jay:

> Because you're asking your husband to effectively treat you as you were treated as a child . . . so for both sides I think it's very dangerous.
>
> (Jay)

A number of women clearly benefited from engaging in some of the activities that the CSA recovery literature encouraged them to attribute to their child selves. Whilst I am not suggesting we deny women the opportunity to engage in all these activities I do believe that we should question why a grown woman would want or need to take on the persona of a child in order to engage in particular activities or recognise particular thoughts, feelings and emotions. Equally I believe we should question why a grown man would want their partner to do so.

Anne's children: 'Living as a group'

The problems identified by Jay, relating to inner child work and multiplicity can be recognised in Anne's account of identifying herself as a victim of ritual abuse living with multiple personalities. However, Anne had a very different understanding of the inner child and did not see the emergence of her personalities as problematic. Rather than being created through inner child work, Anne believed that:

> During a severe physical trauma there's a point where the mind and body split.
>
> (Anne)

Inner child work was problematic for Anne, not because she did not identify with the idea or recognise her own inner child, but rather because she recognised (too) many:

> Because if a lot of us have got inner children, I mean who is going to be the inner child?
>
> (Anne)

Anne believed she experienced continuous abuse throughout her childhood, but whereas Jay saw a problem with creating personalities out of the experiences she had at different ages, Anne embraced these potential inner children. However, unlike Jay who was secure in the plots and characters of her life story, Anne relied on these inner children to construct her biography, and without them her story would have been limited to the remembered traumas of her childhood, which largely centred on her reactions to others. Anne's concern was not that inner child work might create multiple personalities for those who engaged in this work, but that most therapists would fail to recognise more than one inner child. A major problem identified by Anne lay with therapists and writers of self-help manuals who failed to recognise that those with particularly traumatic experiences may have split many times during abusive childhoods, creating many alters, and making contact might itself be traumatic:

> What I would really like to caution about this inner child stuff is that for multiples it is terrifying to have people want to do inner child work on them... They [therapists] should never ever assume that anybody has just got one inner child. Because if you are severely disturbed you will have more inner children and I think it is appalling that therapists aren't taught this and go about trying to castigate you.
>
> (Anne)

Believing inner personalities are created at the time of trauma, Anne felt inner child work should allow for the possibility of many children and should be designed to help all of them rather than focus on just one. Identifying and contacting more than one inner child might be traumatic, but as Anne said of her own experience:

> It's been marvellous to surface the inner children.
>
> (Anne)

Anne began her healing journey over 20 years ago, although the story she told of her life had been drafted and edited many times during this period. Once believing she was a victim of sexual abuse, Anne went on to reject this storyline and, in the course of rewriting her biography, identified herself as a victim of ritual abuse. She was not the only woman for whom sexual abuse may once have provided an explanation for unhappiness but which, over time, was no longer felt to be adequate. However, unlike those who rejected as false memories of sexual abuse and identified themselves as victims of FMS, Anne had invested heavily not only in a therapeutic solution but also in the idea that her problems stemmed from childhood trauma, and more specifically from ritual and sexual abuse. Anne was also, again unlike those who claimed to be victims of false memories, the first author of her story. Whilst we cannot speculate on whether or not Anne was the victim of sexual or ritual abuse we can see in her narratives a 'progression' from childhood trauma through incest to prolonged ritual abuse in which she appears no nearer her goal of a happy and fulfilled life. Having invested heavily in therapeutic discourses Anne needed an explanation for why the difficulties that led her to seek therapy continued and this she also found in the therapeutic literature. It was only a small step for Anne from believing her difficulties stemmed from childhood trauma to looking deeper to uncover knowledge of even greater and prolonged trauma, stored in her unconscious or held by an inner child or children.

As Bauman suggests, in constructing our life stories we are confined to the options on offer (Bauman 2001), and in Anne's account we can see a number of options that were considered before being rejected in favour of new, darker, more disturbing plot lines and narrative frameworks. Whilst some might argue that this process is taking Anne closer to the 'truth' of her troubled life we might also argue that her investment in therapeutic discourses is itself the driving force and even the narrative framework within which she constructs her life/story. If the latter is the case it may prove difficult for Anne, should she want to, to even begin to construct a life story in which, leaving her therapeutic lifestyle behind, she is no longer fully immersed in world of healing and recovery, populated as it is by hundreds of alternative personalities.

Anne's life story is one filled with pain, tragedy and loss. In her own words she had 'always needed therapy', had 'always needed something' and spent many years trying to decide if it was her 'mother or father that was causing the problems'. In earlier versions of her narratives Anne identified herself simply as coming from a middle-class family with numerous problems. It was a family in which one brother died as a child, another brother made a number of suicide attempts as a teenager, spent time in a psychiatric hospital and did eventually kill himself, and her mother, who also suffered from depression, spent time in a psychiatric hospital. Anne had enough knowledge of her childhood to write her biography within a narrative framework that did not involve sexual abuse, for which she had no memories. Indeed early on in her life Anne had constructed such a story based on concrete memories of childhood and it was only later that she came to believe, first that she had been the victim of incest, and later, that she had been ritually abused as a child and with multiple personalities she existed as 'part of a group'. Anne had no memories of sexual or ritual abuse, beyond the 'alternative memories' or symptoms identified in the literature, but she did have access to a traumatic history. This was a history which, seen to provide an adequate explanation for unhappiness or dissatisfaction in their adult lives, might be used by others to construct a very different narrative to the one constructed by Anne. However, Anne did not feel that the continuous memories she had of her childhood and adolescence adequately explained the difficulties and unhappiness she experienced as an adult, or at least her 'failure' to heal from them.

Anne recognised her unbroken childhood memories indicated a painful and traumatic time, but was also influenced by our contemporary view of child sexual abuse which constructs it as more traumatic and damaging than other childhood abuse or trauma. Anne had identified a narrative framework within which she was able to rewrite her life story based not simply on childhood trauma, or sexual abuse but on what she came to identify as childhood experiences more traumatic and damaging. These newly discovered experiences provided Anne with a framework which she believed was adequate to make sense of her life without the need for the sexual abuse subplots of her earlier narratives. Anne's biography is now based on many years of living as a ritual abuse victim, and itself includes a progression from a simple story of childhood loss, through a story of incest, to another more complex and traumatic story, a story with more severe consequences and a more damaged cast of characters. It also, like all stories we tell of ourselves, offers us a way of being in the world and in the case of Anne, whose life is contained by her stories, it also offers companions to be in the world with. Whilst this life story provides Anne with many things including companionship, it is also possible that it may make it difficult or even prevent her from moving beyond her family of alters, should she want to.

During the course of her healing and her involvement with therapeutic discourses Anne identified a growing number of alters, the first of whom she initially connected to sexual abuse. She was initially unable to do inner child work and believed this was because she had more than one inner child, itself an indication that she suffered more serious abuse over a prolonged period. This, she believed, resulted in very scared and damaged children and so rather than attempting to make contact with them as her adult self, she left it to the inner children to make contact first. Anne's narrative was not simply informed by having more than one inner child but the inner personalities who shared her world were, she believed, very different from those created as a result of 'mere incest'. Unlike many multiples, Anne's system did not include adults, which she linked to the severity of her traumas and the ages at which they occurred. This absence was also, Anne believed, related to the particularly traumatic abuse she experienced and the lessons her children learnt as a result of that trauma:

> I was expected to have adults in my system but I didn't trust the adults you see.
>
> (Anne)

The only adult in Anne's system was Anne, the front personality. She was the one who had 'been out in the world' and was the one who was involved in the research for this book. Anne's inner children were the 'totally traumatised children' found in the ritual abuse literature. Her understanding explains not only why she has the personalities she has but also why she did not benefit from the 'sweet pretty little books' aimed at the multiples of the sexual abuse movement. Her inner world was not populated by the:

> Happy little children and happy little adults who get to know each other and some of them go off to work and some of them do this and that.
>
> (Anne)

A constant theme within the sexual and ritual abuse literature is that of splitting and often within the ritual abuse literature the more extreme or traumatic the experience(s) the more split personalities a survivor is likely to have. The explanations and advice provided by therapists, self-help books and auto/biographies, clearly played an important role for Anne not only in explaining and making sense of her life but also in validating her experiences. Whilst it could be argued that Anne structured her life around therapeutic discourses, she was not tied to any single one. There are 'no rules' she said, 'everybody does things different'. Where the literature no longer provided an adequate explanation or way of living, or possibly when her relationships with an inner child or children developed beyond the literature, she was prepared to move beyond her existing narrative. This sometimes involved contacting new alters but latterly had also involved contacting the inner children of her inner children, and reflected an increase in the level of trauma she believed she experienced. It was not only an increase in the number of potential personalities that resulted from ritual abuse but, as Anne learnt through her reading, these personalities develop very differently:

> You've got an entirely different pattern of multiple personalities... You've got all the totally traumatised children... And then you've got the predators who are on the side of... you know. I'm now beginning to understand all this. And then you've got the children who surfaced during the abuse yes, the abused children, the predators and protectors. I've got animal protectors. This I think is beginning to be you know, maybe people who've suffered more serious ritual abuse, that you are a very small child so you've got animals, it's lovely.
>
> (Anne)

In a further development traumatic experiences such as ritual abuse, may not simply result in additional alters but the alters themselves may develop personalities of their own. Anne's life revolved around her inner children. Her days would be spent with the children and her evenings would often be spent, possibly when they had gone to bed, talking about them to those adults willing or able to listen, usually on the other end of one of a number of helplines. At the time of our interview Anne had become aware of the possibility that there was more to her inner children than she first realised. Rejecting books she was once 'wild about', Anne's reading had become more focussed on ritual abuse and it was here, specifically in reading *Ritual Abuse* (Smith 1993), that she first realised an extra dimension to her children:

> It's helped at least one person surface and it's helped all of us, you know, begin to realise, you know, not to try and sort ourselves out like all these easy books tell you to but to just kind of go along with it and take whatever happens week by week... But I found the simple advice of other multiple personality books simply didn't tell you the horrors and the difficult structures that these tortured children had to invent.
>
> (Anne)

The structure of multiple personalities is said to be such that in extreme cases of abuse the personalities may depart, leaving one particular alter to take the abuse. It is under these circumstances that an alter may herself develop inner personalities, an explanation Anne applied to her own life:

> They were talking about children who took the abuse would also fragment into sub-personalities and I now realise because three of them who took the worst abuse have surfaced and they have sub-personalities I think now. I may be wrong but I think they're sub-personalities of Minuet, the dear little girl who took most of the abuse.
>
> (Anne)

Anne found, within the field of multiplicity, an explanation not only for the difficulties she experienced in her adult life but also for why those difficulties continued. She also found an explanation, and possibly a justification, for why she had not integrated her inner children, even after years of therapy:

> I couldn't do the exercises. I mean, the ritual abuse thing was just so different so I mean sometimes you know I would get upset.
>
> (Anne)

> Well no because I'm a ritual abuse survivor, the book is geared to people with a different experience.
>
> (Anne)

It was not a failure to work on herself that meant Anne continued to experience problems. It was because she was a victim of ritual abuse.

However, there were times when even this was not enough and she needed to claim to be suffering from ever more extreme forms of abuse:

> I could never get help by the books. I think what happened to me was too severe.
>
> (Anne)

> I was right, you know off the... out of the books as it were. I always was the most severe case in anything I read.
>
> (Anne)

Ritual abuse not only explained why Anne, and other victims of such abuse, continued to have difficulties it also significantly changed the relationship they might have with evidence and their inner children. Having relocated to the world of multiple personalities Anne was no longer under pressure to provide evidence of abuse, as multiplicity was evidence enough. Nor did she feel under pressure to integrate. As a guide to living, the life story Anne constructed, informed by ritual abuse literature, did not require her to write her inner children out of her narrative. Instead it was narrative framework that encouraged the storyteller to include these new family members as integral characters in their ongoing biography. This was an aspect of the ritual abuse literature that Anne enthusiastically embraced. Anne did not need, or perhaps increasingly could not, to go beyond the 'packages' she prepared for her alters. However, as her life was increasingly centred on her inner children, Anne had become increasingly isolated. Again she did not look outside the therapeutic world of multiple personalities to address this problem. Identifying herself as a victim of the most severe trauma provided Anne with more than just an explanation for her continuing difficulties. The 'survivors' world', she said:

> Has given me a home, a base and area of dialogue... suddenly I'm in an area of growth and discussion and beingness. And that also has been fantastic. That's since I've discovered the sort of survivor's movement as it were. You know there are people to whom you can talk about this.
>
> (Anne)

Finding the survivors movement did not offer Anne a way to overcome her isolation, instead it provided her with a way to mediate that isolation. Beyond her inner world of troubled children, the people Anne talked to are those within the survivors' movement, who understand

and are willing to talk to someone who identifies themselves as a victim of ritual abuse and who shares their life with hundreds of personalities. Although she has spoken with a few ritual abuse survivors with multiple personalities, the majority of those to whom Anne talked in this survivors' movement were those at the other end of a helpline. Going through her list of helpline numbers Anne was able to tell me those that she found helpful and those she did not. She talked to women at the end of helplines all over the country and spoke of them as if talking of good friends or family members. The women she found particularly helpful were those with a particular understanding of and empathy with the inner children of the ritual abuse world:

> It was fantastic to find they take you on board as a person. They would know me and I would call up and I would talk to someone I knew.
>
> (Anne)

> I got to know all the [service] people which was lovely. Then [city] started getting new people at [service] and I got to know them. I got to know... at [city] a tiny bit. The [city] people were great. They were never there but they would always call back.
>
> (Anne)

She also subscribed to a number of newsletters, for sexual and ritual abuse survivors. On reading these she commented:

> You're almost in touch with the people out there aren't you?
>
> (Anne)

Anne might have been *'almost in touch'* with some of these people but the only people she was really in touch with were those who inhabited her own inner world. She brought them to life through communicating with them, writing them poems and drawing them pictures, sending them cards and buying them presents. She helped maintain this reality by displaying these gifts, although it was primarily only Anne who saw them. Whilst this was a life Anne seemed happy and content with most of the time, there were indications, such as when she was almost in touch with those beyond this inner world, that it was not enough. The survivors' movement might have contributed to Anne feeling special and given her a sense of belonging, where she might otherwise have been even more isolated, but this survivors' world was itself a very restricted one. Anne may have been looking to expand her world, but so entrenched had she become in the world of multiplicity that it was difficult for her to look elsewhere and it is perhaps no surprise that her life expanded through an increasing family of inner children.

Anne's story reads not so much like a 'detective novel' in which she uncovers perpetrators, but more like a coming of age or family saga in which she goes through life developing new relationships, but only with children and the occasional animal. Anne was one of the few participants whose narrative relied on inner children and/or 'alternative memories' who made reference to the recovered memory debate. Throughout her account Anne made it clear that she believed her alters had always been present, albeit unrecognised, and was careful to distance herself, and her therapists, from their creation. Like Beccy, she engaged to some extent with the recovered memory wars, and this informed the explanation she gave for the emergence or surfacing of her alters. Throughout her account Anne referred to the ideas of others, therapists, writers and survivors, as a way to reinforce and validate her own account and to some extent to distance herself from its construction. Whereas Beccy had claimed validity for her story by distancing it from the accounts of others, Anne claimed validity for her story by demonstrating its similarity to the stories of others found in the literature. Anne reinforced her claims through her descriptions of reading although it was not always, or at least not only, her adult self, who read this material:

> It's been stuff that nobody else has told me. You know, it's just my inner children who've had those experiences. And then in this book they talk about the experiences and the inner children just, you know, it's so fantastic to them that it's written down.
>
> (Anne)

Anne's inner children sometimes read this material and it was through them and the connections they made that Anne was able to piece together a story that explained her life. In many respects it was their story, not hers. However, they were not restricted to reading the literature, but did also communicate directly with her (their) therapists:

> Once or twice [a counsellor] at [a service] talked directly to the children who were feeling very panicky and that helped but that's quite strange.
>
> (Anne)

Much of the CSA recovery literature encourages victims of sexual abuse to contact their inner child and encourage her to write letters and draw pictures both to communicate knowledge and as part of the healing process. This was something that Anne also came across within the ritual abuse recovery movement:

> Sometimes there's different people inside me talking you see... B [a counsellor] at Christmas said she wanted me to write every week...She said she wanted me to write every week and moreover she wanted the person who talked in the therapy to write. That was when we realised she didn't want Anne the front person to write and it turns out, I thought it was a young child but it was clearly much more, you know a major part of the system.
>
> (Anne)

So far Anne's children had only talked directly to her therapists when the adult Anne, was absent. However, Anne was optimistic about the possibility of her front personality being present with her children and for them to be able to engage in conversation together:

> It's complicated this, it's about co-consciousness. Have you come across the term? It's new to me. But I've never had co-consciousness, I think most people have it from the age of three onwards or so, something like that I don't know. You know when there's someone there that can say wait a minute this is going to be tough but we'll be ok...But anyway I'm beginning to get it a bit which is fantastic, it's a great thing isn't it. It's marvellous. It means you don't have to get so upset you know.
>
> (Anne)

Again, Anne identifies her experiences as different to other victims, and evidence of more extreme or traumatic ritual abuse, which provides an explanation for why she has come to this later or more slowly than others. It also reinforces her claim that she is not responsible for the unfolding of her life story. Rather than developing co-consciousness because she read about it in a book, Anne believes she has only recently recognised the possibility of co-consciousness, and later than other victims of ritual abuse, because her life experiences were so much worse than others. If her experiences were less severe, she believes, she may have developed the ability to communicate directly between her inner children much earlier, and before she was introduced to it through her reading.

Anne worked for many years at developing a relationship with some of her alters. She was only beginning to look at the possibility of developing relationships between herself and individual alters and between all those with whom she shared her world. She was also aware of how much of her life was taken up with the children:

> So much to do in life... you need an extra day to do anything.
> (Anne)

The harm story of the child sexual abuse recovery literature enables women to construct a life story located within, and arguably constrained by, a particular narrative, which in turn helps them negotiate their adult lives. The discourses around ritual abuse and multiple personalities help women construct different life stories, again located within and constrained by particular narrative frameworks, in addition to providing them with a different set of tools with which to negotiate their lives. The emergence of multiple personalities and their acceptance, albeit within limited arenas, has also helped to create a space and time in which those stories can be both told and heard, if not by everyone, then at least by some. The sexual and ritual abuse literature not only provided an explanation which Anne could draw on to explain her own life but in doing so it introduced the possibility that she shared her world with a number of alternative personalities. Although she did not simply follow a script set out in the literature her experiences did to some extent echo the developments documented in the literature, which she attempted to explain by identifying her own experiences as more severe, traumatic and damaging.

Sharing her world with a population of inner children and animals had become so much a part of Anne's life that it was more 'real' to her than the one outside, populated by 'unitary people'. Constructing a ritual abuse narrative helped Anne to make sense of and explain her life. It also provided her with the tools and maps to negotiate a path for herself, with which she felt comfortable and at times 'special'. Unlike those for whom the inner child was a means to gain access to knowledge of abuse, Anne's inner children did not (need to) provide evidence. Their presence was evidence enough and the emphasis was on making contact and developing relationships. Anne's life involved little contact with the outside world but was centred around her inner children. She had for the last 20 years:

> Been virtually invalided out of the work world because I'd get ill all the time and things.
>
> (Anne)

Unable to work and with limited outside contact, Anne's friends and companions were the personalities, animals and children from her inner world and those from outside who were able to enter this inner world and who she felt able to let in. Each child received a package, including poetry, presents, sweets and cards, and Anne's life revolved around producing these packages. It may be that when she had completed a package for one child she moved onto another. There were after all hundreds still waiting. However, there were also suggestions that she was beginning to want more from these relationships. Women engaged with the recovery literature for a variety of reasons which for many involved developing a relationship with an inner child. Many were searching for knowledge, others looking to make sense of their lives, and others looking for a brighter happier future or a combination of reasons. It may be that some were also looking for companionship. What they all wanted, albeit in different ways and measured against different criteria was a 'better' life. Anne's life did not seem to live up to the promises of empowerment and success but she did seem most of the time to be satisfied with it: it may be that for her MPS offered a new way to be an unhappy person (Hacking 1995).

The inner children of women's accounts

The concept of the inner child illustrates once again that women's engagement with ideas promoted within the sexual abuse recovery literature, and encapsulated in the harm story and the healing discourse, were not always embraced with open arms or accepted in their entirety by those who engaged with these discourses. It also illustrates the extent to which these ideas have permeated some of the everyday cultural texts that many of us are familiar with, and therefore the extent to which they were already familiar to those who engaged with the literature aimed at adult victims of childhood sexual abuse. Not all the women identified an inner child or developed a relationship with her and of those who did, not all saw her as separate. However, many did accord her considerable influence over the lives of their adult selves. The inner child was evidently a valuable companion who helped some women understand, make sense of and move on with their lives. For others, she was someone with whom they shared the present. However, she was not an unproblematic concept even for those who shared their lives with her. Women had an ambiguous, at times problematic and at times helpful relationship with their own inner child.

8
The Contradictory Self

> *Personhood... is not a matter of simply choosing a role that one somehow becomes aware of.*
>
> (Grodin and Lindlof 1996:5)

> *I am pleased and happy to be the person I'm becoming.*
>
> (Sarah)

Introduction

Within sociological writing on the self, Craib (1998) argues, we are given 'a choice of being either a "plurality" or "assembly" of parts or a "more or less unitary" self' (Craib 1998:5). Missing he argues is what 'goes on "inside" the bearer of identity or identities, and the process of internal negotiation which this involves' (Craib 1998:4). The late twentieth and early twenty-first centuries have seen a turn to the self and a 'frantic search for identity' (Bauman 2001:152) but the identities we construct do not indicate a stable, core self, unchanging through each individual's progress through life (Hall 1996). The self of late modernity is a process, continually under (re)construction rather than something we have. It can be seen as a project to be worked on (Giddens 1991), and improved, to be continually reconstructed in light of new experiences, challenges and understandings. Yet, paradoxically, at the same time as we are being urged to work on this self, we are urged to embark on a journey of discovery, to uncover our true, or core self. This is the contradictory self of the self-help and the CSA recovery literature (Woodiwiss 2005). In this chapter I look at these contradictory formulations and explore women experiences of finding, constructing and putting back together their own selves, both core and makeable, static and becoming.

The self of the recovery literature

The self of the twenty-first century is located within a therapeutic culture (Furedi 2004) and bombarded with advice on how to be a better, happier, authentic self together with warnings of what might happen if this advice is not followed (Woodiwiss 2005, 2006). For Giddens, therapy and the reflexive self are intricately linked. Therapy, he suggests, is a secular version of the confessional, 'not simply a means of coping with novel anxieties, but an expression of the reflexivity of the self' (Giddens 1991:34). This reflexive self is, like the self of pop psychology and recovery, a powerful self which is thought to have real power over itself and its future happiness and well-being. A central theme of much self-help literature is the idea that the reader is in some way damaged (Simonds 1996), and therefore needs to recover and this involves personal not political change (Plummer 1995, Showalter 1997, Simonds 1992, Woodiwiss 2007a). Although some self-help literature includes an element of recovery that would benefit the external world, in the majority of the CSA recovery literature the focus, at least until the victim is healed, is the inner world of the individual. The selling point is the promise of a new and better self but it is a self which requires not only potentially years of time but often considerable financial and emotional investment.

However, there is a central contradiction in the formulation of the self, promoted by the writers of self-help texts (Simonds 1996), also evident in the CSA recovery literature (Woodiwiss 2007a) and whilst this might appear problematic, such a formulation proved useful to many women as it enabled them to negotiate their own path to construct the selves they were happy or at least content with. Encouraged to find their true, powerful, inner selves, which may be buried under layers of trauma and abuse but which remain untouched by that abuse, women were also told that, through hard work and dedication, they could become the selves they want, or even should, have been. This inner or core self, whilst essentialist in conception, is portrayed in the self-help literature to be 'realized through a construction process based on instruction by therapeutic experts, hard work and interactive expression' (Simonds 1996:16). A key subplot in the CSA recovery literature is the harm story, which constructs victims as so (inevitably) damaged that the effects of their abuse can be identified across all areas of their adult lives. Such a relentlessly negative construction requires a therapeutic response and this is provided by a 'healing discourse' (Davies 1995) which offers victims a way to leave their symptoms behind by drawing on the contradictory formulation of the self. Whilst it is not always clear what is meant by the self, Whitfield, author of a number of books, provides some clarity when he compares recovery to removing the layers of an onion:

> Each layer is a manifestation and consequence of the false self and our attachment to it. And each layer surrounds, constricts and imprisons our true self... Underneath all these layers, at the core of our being, lies the goal of recovery and our true identity: our True Self.
>
> (Whitfield 1995:259)

In some texts readers are told they cannot escape from or leave the past behind:

> There is no such thing as absolute healing. You never erase your history.
>
> (Bass and Davis 1988:167)

Elsewhere, they are offered more choice. Like many writers in this field, Herman helps victims to identify the effects of CSA on the self but goes on to suggest how they might move forward:

> Her task now is to become the person she wants to be. In the process she draws on those aspects of herself that she most values from the time before the trauma, from the experience of the trauma itself, and from the period of recovery. Integrating all of these elements, she creates a new self, both ideally and in actuality.
>
> (Herman 1992:196)

There is an imperative within the recovery literature that suggests a failure to embark on a project of the self, with its central element of healing, will lead to a catalogue of ills, from unhappiness and dissatisfaction to victimisation, and self-sabotage. This literature promotes itself as a means of 'self creation', 'damage control' and 'revival' whilst at the same time promises to reveal the 'true' self (Simonds 1996).

Negotiating the contradictory self

We may understand or conceptualise it differently, but a sense of self, of who we are, is important to how we are and what we do in the world. In engaging with the CSA recovery and self-help literature the women were presented with a formulation of the self as both static and evolving, both unitary and fragmented. Their engagement was itself illustrative of an uncertainty or dissatisfaction with who they were and how they saw themselves. In addressing these questions they had to negotiate the contradictory self of the recovery and therapeutic literature. Within this literature they were presented with the concept of a core self, a self which could be returned to undamaged by their abuse, and a self as a project, which could be worked on and developed to create a stronger more powerful self able to negotiate a successful path through life. They were also presented with a damaged self in need of healing. This was the self that needs to be worked on, as a project of correction and putting right, of who not to be, as much as a project of improvement, self-development and who to be. The selves who populated their lives and featured in their biographies were many and varied. The women brought their own understandings to the process of recovery and, drawing on formulations of the self promoted within therapeutic discourses, they used and created different selves. The majority articulated a sense of self or 'I ness' (Scott 2001), even though there had been times for many when they had lost sight of this self. However, what or who this self was, varied not only between different women's accounts but also within their individual accounts. A significant number of the women had negotiated their way through a range of therapeutic and self-help texts either before or during their reading of the literature aimed at adult victims of childhood sexual abuse and it is therefore not surprising to see evidence of more than one influence in the conceptualisations of the self who populated their life stories.

The core self

Women engaged with therapeutic literature for a variety of reasons, in response to different questions and different challenges. The different formulations of the self they came across within this literature, and elsewhere, did not provide answers but did offer women ways to workout their own answers, and the majority did not feel constrained by any one understanding of the self. In constructing their sexual abuse narrative they were forced to engage with, but not necessarily to adopt, the idea of a core self. This was a self that could be returned to and, through removing the effects of abuse, could be freed to become the person she would have been. Not all the women accepted a core self untouched by the abuse and, of those who did, not all embraced this self uncritically or straightforwardly. Of those who recognised a core self only some believed this core to be untouched by their abuse. Fiona was among those who recognised a core self, but she rejected the idea that this self was untouched by the abuse:

> My core self was abused... There's not a core me that I can remember before being abused... I haven't any memories before that... when I talk about me – that's somebody who was abused. It's part of who I am, I can't separate myself from it... I don't know who I was, who I would have been.
>
> (Fiona)

The significant factor for Fiona was the young age at which she was abused and it is because of this that she thinks the abuse is 'always going to be part of who I am' (Fiona). Whilst Fiona recognised a core self she did also acknowledge that this core self was not static. However, Fiona was not always so certain of her core self. It was important to Fiona that she knew who she was, where she was going and what life was about but there had been a time in her life when she was uncertain. Not only had Fiona lost sight of who she was and 'fallen apart' but there was a suggestion in her account that who she really was, her core self, did not exist before this:

> I feel that I've got a core inner self that wasn't there before that happened... if that hadn't happened I might not have got that real sense of who I am.
>
> (Fiona)

The idea of life events contributing to the formation or creation of the self informed the narratives of a number of women including Angela:

> I don't believe personally that you could deal with the abuse and then become a different person because you are the person you are because of the abuse... the abuse is a part of who I am the same as everything else that's happened in my life is a part of who I am, some good bits some bad bits.
>
> (Angela)

Whilst Jay did believe she might have become the same person had she not been sexually abused, this was not because she believed the abuse did not touch her core self or the self she was becoming:

> Would I still be the person I am now if the sex abuse hadn't happened and in a lot of respects yes, because of all the other things that went on.
>
> (Jay)

Rather, Jay believed the other abuse she experienced was likely to have contributed to the creation of a similar self.

A number of women including Beccy, Sarah and Jenny, talked of a 'true self' but, like the core self, this was not always a self who could be returned to untouched by the abuse. Women's understandings of this true self were largely informed by the CSA recovery literature but they did also draw on other influences. Sarah had engaged with a variety of therapeutic practices over many years and the formulation of the self she drew on was informed by a range of therapeutic discourses that extended beyond the CSA recovery literature:

> There was a tape we worked on called the meaning of the stone child erm and erm, which is stories of I'm not sure if they're red Indian but these stories like Jungian and one of those is erm like a, you have a flame or a light inside you and that never goes out but through stages of life which is the inner self it gets small but it's still there and with mine it's just grown.
>
> (Sarah)

It was a self which Sarah believed had:

> Always been there but it just needed to come out and grow basically and it has
>
> (Sarah)

Although a number of women identified a 'true self', the degree of autonomy and control they felt she exercised, particularly in terms of emerging or coming out into the world, varied, as they felt more or less in control of this aspect themselves. Whereas Sarah believed her true self had 'come through' without her working at it, Jenny actively sought out her inner self. This idea of seeking, finding or uncovering the self featured in a number of women's narratives. They did not all conceptualise this self in the same way:

> I have a true self that is me... My true self is my soul/spirit – is all I maybe am and then I am in this body which is me as well, and then there's my mind and what's in my mind has been programmed by what happened to me as a child... and my mind most of the time actually is the thing that controls my body and there's this thing that controls my true self.
>
> (Beccy)

Beccy believed her true self, or soul, was a constant presence in her life: sometimes the 'I' that was doing, but it was also a self that could be controlled and 'shut out'.

A number of women, including Jenny and Sarah, contrasted their true self to a 'false self'. This false self was formed in childhood and, like the inner child, exerted an unhealthy influence on their adult lives. It was conceived by some as a facade or cover hiding their real selves. Sarah, for example, conceptualised her false self as a masquerade hiding a true self trapped, she believed, as a result of her abuse. She had, she believed:

> Been living in a sort of fictional, masked world for so many years... Yeh and it's [my true self] come through.
>
> (Sarah)

Whilst Sarah held a negative perception of her false self, this was not so for Jenny and Tracey who identified some protective value to a false self: Tracey drew on the idea of a mask as a form of protection in adulthood. It was something that not only concealed a more authentic Tracey but could be used by the adult Tracey to keep others at bay and portray a different or even false self to the outside world. However, it was for Jenny a self rooted in childhood:

> In order to survive in our dysfunctional families we form a 'false self' which serves our growth until there comes a time when this self becomes restrictive and we begin a journey to a 'self' that is more reflective of our 'true self' or soul.
>
> (Jenny)

Like other childhood coping skills, Jenny also believed the false self could outlive its usefulness.

Fragmented self

A consistent sense of self was important to all the women, but they were not all able to maintain a continuous connection with, or a sense of, self and the idea of a lost, fragmented or shattered self was one that featured in several of their stories. A number of women also felt it important to maintain some continuity between the self they identified before they were sexually abused and their self after the abuse and/or their recovered memories of it. They had all been encouraged to recognise the damage caused by CSA and it may be that, in maintaining some continuity between their before and after selves, they could also resist the view that the abuse had destroyed them completely, without which they may have found it difficult to contemplate recovery or attempt to heal their selves. Identifying a part of themselves that survived the abuse may also have been important in the construction or telling of a life story which maintained at least some continuity with, an often unremembered, past. A lack of continuity can be seen in the accounts of those who ultimately came to reject their stories of sexual abuse.

Healing and recovery was, for most of the women, intricately bound up with their sense of self and who they were. It was through their process of recovery that they were able to work out who and what they wanted to be, and reconstruct a self, or selves, of their choosing. A number of women talked about this process beginning with an experience such as 'falling apart':

> I felt quite anxious and unstable and fragmented and I didn't have a sense of who I was, where I was going, what it was all about... well I had a sort of crisis like a breakdown and I really didn't know who I was. Everything fell apart.
>
> (Fiona)

Although the experience of losing their sense of self was in many respects a frightening experience, like Fiona, a number of women also talked about it leading to their being able to work out who and what they wanted to be. A 'breakdown' enabled them to remove or delete aspects of themselves they were unhappy with and in doing so identify, or construct, a self comprised of characteristics that they were happy with. It could be a painful period but, as in Fiona's case, it was also one in which she began to identify a core self:

> And almost decide who I was going to be then. This bit I would remember, this bit feels right, this bit's me that bit's not me.
>
> (Fiona)

Like the majority of women, Fiona drew on contradictory notions of the self found in the recovery literature but her sense of self was also linked to the confidence she had in her self and her place in the world:

> Ever since then I've had a kind of idea that I can cope with what comes along in life because I know who I am now and I know myself.
>
> (Fiona)

It was possibly a lack of confidence in their place in the world, perceived as a lack of self, that first directed some of women towards therapy. It was certainly important to Fiona's regained sense of self that she 'knew' herself and where she was going. Fiona referred to her self as a 'core' but it was also a self in process, one she was responsible for creating. There was also an ever-present self, similar to the self who featured in Beccy's narrative, and this was the self that was unable to hold everything together but who remembered which bits were Fiona and which bits were not. This idea of being able to create a new self, without rejecting entirely the old self, is an important feature of self-help literature, particularly that aimed at victims of sexual abuse. It is an understanding that enables this literature to encourage its readers to recognise they have been damaged whilst also being able to promise empowerment and a better life.

The idea of a lost or fragmented self was, for the majority of women, a temporary state of being. It was, they believed, a consequence or symptom of their abuse and could be addressed through healing and recovery, in a process that would not only enable them to piece their selves back together but also choose who and what those selves would be. Whilst some women, talking about a time before they began to recover or heal, had made reference to a shattered or fragmented self, this was not necessarily a lost self but it was for some a self who felt lost:

> I think I was pretty much out of touch with feelings and had no real sense of self or emotional maturity.
>
> (Jenny)

Many of the women had experienced themselves as fragmented, disintegrating or lacking a sense of self and they often equated this with a lack of confidence with themselves. Whereas Jenny experienced this as losing touch with her feelings, others experienced it as an emptiness:

> I was left with a big empty void and then starting to rebuild it bit by bit.
>
> (Angela)

Women drew on a range of ideas and concepts associated with the self, including those they found in CSA recovery literature, but they did not necessarily employ them in the same way or attach the same meanings to them. In much of the CSA recovery literature the idea of fragmentation was linked to the inner child, and therefore healing was connected with integrating the adult and child self. However, not all the women made such a connection, and for many, healing and becoming whole was linked with finding their true self, or rebuilding a shattered self, rather than with integrating an inner child or children. However, with the exception of Anne, for those who had made contact with an damaged, hurt, inner child, the ultimate aim was to heal this child self and as a result the child and adult self would integrate and become whole.

The 'front person' as self

Nowhere was the idea of a fragmented self more evident than in Anne's account of living with her inner children or alters, who she says:

> Don't operate in the outer world.
>
> (Anne)

There was often a sense of despair or panic evident in women's stories when they talked of falling apart and separation from their adult self, but this was not so in Anne's world. Here the focus was on embracing multiple identities rather than focussing on separation and falling apart and there was therefore no drive towards integration and putting the self back together. However, Anne did acknowledge that others might view her inner children differently:

> My goal isn't specifically to integrate but it seems to be thought that it can help them [inner children].
>
> (Anne)

In contrast to the stories of other women, Anne's story contained a sense of contentment, achievement, expectation and very often pleasure:

> It's been marvellous to surface the inner children.
>
> (Anne)

These children, or other selves, allowed Anne numerous possibilities for being (herself), but there were also times when she made reference to a lack of, or at least an incomplete, self. This lack was something she had felt particularly acutely before she began to recover and make contact with her inner children:

> I mean, there wasn't much of a person because I've needed therapy... I was a very wounded person struggling along trying to look like everybody else.
>
> (Anne)

As the only woman who existed as 'part of a group' and identified multiple inner children or, one might argue, aspects of her self, Anne's experiences and understanding of self were in some respects very different from those of other women. Anne talked about these different personalities, about their experiences, what they did and said, what they enjoyed, and how they differed from each other, but throughout the interview and her life story, there was also a constant presence in the form of her 'front person' or her adult self. This front person shared a name with her adult self, but, unlike the names of her inner children (or selves), it was a name she frequently changed. Ostensibly to conceal her identity and whereabouts from her abusers, this might also have been related to how she felt about her self, and might even have been an attempt to leave that self behind. This was a self of whom she says there wasn't 'much of a person' there she says, and even what there was 'trying to look like everybody else'. Whatever the case Anne always took her inner children with her, distanced from her adult self, but never quite separate and never left behind. It may be that these different personalities also gave substance to Anne's (sense of) self. Anne's acceptance of herself as important was fragile, but the arrival of new inner children, not only gave her self new dimensions, they may also have helped to support a fragile belief in herself.

The self becoming and the self that should have been

Within traditional responses to sexual violence, recovery is measured according to a 'return to normal functioning' (Kelly 1988), and therefore to a pre-existing self and this is also evident in the CSA recovery literature. When applied to adult victims of CSA, particularly when the abuse occurred at a very young age, it is not possible to locate a time (or a self) prior to the abuse and therefore, instead of returning to what was, victims are encouraged to return to a 'true self'. By removing the effects of abuse victims can return to a self that would or should have been, to live the life they should have lived. Victims are advised:

> The little part of you that is already whole can lead the rest of you through the healing process.
>
> (Bass and Davis 1988:156)

> That person you want to become is already with you.
>
> (Bass and Davis 1988:156)

Within the same texts readers are told:

> It may take some time before you begin to get the first inklings of who you are becoming.
>
> (Bass and Davis 1988:166)

They are encouraged to 'release their inner strength' which is equated with the self, freedom and self-determination:

> The self that's been hiding all these years, the unique and loving person you were meant to be. Together, we'll help free that person so that your life can finally be your own.
>
> (Forward 1989:12)

The self of the recovery literature is a contradictory one but it was this contradiction that enabled women to create a self, or selves, that suited their need and wishes. It enabled them to identify damage but also offered a way to erase that damage and decide who they wanted to be. Whilst for some this involved returning to what would have been, for others it involved deciding what they wanted to be. The idea of 'being' and 'becoming' was embraced by a number of women and helped them connect past (childhood) selves with present and future selves, at the same time as it offered a way to leave behind a damaged self and create a self no longer scarred by abuse. For many it was a connection to their child self that was important. They may have wanted to leave their abuse behind they did not necessarily want to leave behind their abused (child) self. In fact much of the CSA recovery literature healing relies on not leaving this child self behind.

Many women acknowledged a core self, possibly untouched by abuse, but also embraced the idea of a makeable self which for some was also understood to be the self that would have been. This makeable self enabled women to take control and create a self (or selves) they wanted and was particularly important for those who felt they had had little prior control over their lives. Although this makeable self was very important to women the idea of the self that would or should have been was also important. It was a belief in this self that provided women with a justification or rationale for healing, which may have been particularly important for those for whom the healing process was a lengthy one. Healing could be seen, not as an indulgence, but a process of reinstating their true selves and returning life to normal, or how it should have been. For some women, such as Fiona, the self was linked with inner confidence. Although Fiona recognised a core self, which she believed was damaged by her abuse, rebuilding 'self confidence' so as to be able to recognise, who she was and who and what she wanted to be, was an integral part of finding this inner self:

> It's hard if you separate it out because obviously you don't know what kind of person you would have been if this thing hadn't happened to you. You might be quite the same as you are (laughs) you know, you don't know. Cos those things happened so young that they're part of you, your personality as you are growing up and you can't separate them out.
>
> (Fiona)

The confidence she gained in 'knowing' her self was also translated by Fiona into a confidence and an optimism in her self and her future:

> I felt like I could cope with whatever life could throw. I would be able to deal with it because I'd found an inner confidence. I knew who I was and I knew I had the ability to cope with things and that was all good.
>
> (Fiona)

Julie believed she had a core self untouched by her abuse, both physical and sexual, but also believed she had a say in the person she was to be. For Julie the self was tied up with the life to be lived and it was a life she claimed as her own, to be lived by her in the way she chose:

> How I personally feel is that there is something in me that's definitely untouched. There is no doubt about that I would say definitely.

> I mean it could be argued but that's how it feels to me...This is the person I am and this is the person I always wanted to be.
>
> (Julie)

Linked to the idea that victims should start again to become the person they should have been was the concept of an inner child in need of re-parenting. However, only Jenny referred directly to contacting her inner child in order to start again as a significant feature of her healing and felt she:

> Had to become a child again to really grow up again healthily.
>
> (Jenny)

In starting again and reparenting herself Jenny felt she could let go of the trauma she experienced as a child and could grow up (again):

> Building a relationship with myself, slowly, slowly releasing pain and trauma, being re-parented in a healthy way.
>
> (Jenny)

Women engaged with the recovery literature because they were unhappy with the life they were living. The idea of a life meant to be lived suggested they might be living the wrong life but could live a different one which, as it would untroubled by the effects of CSA, offered the promise of happier, more successful times. This was linked to the idea of the self becoming, but a self who should have been living this life. The self who should have been and the life that should have been featured in a number of women's stories. Although they did not conceptualise their recovery as a return to the inner child, a number of women did refer to a process of 'becoming' in which they believed, on recovery, the self they were 'becoming' was the self they (and their inner child) would or should have been. Sarah conceptualised this as her inner self who needed to 'come out and grow'. Whereas Julie, believing her abuse interfered with the person she could have been, used healing to help her get back to that person. As this suggests, this was a person that Julie always believed existed, albeit not in evidence in her adult life before she embarked on her road to healing, rather than someone completely new.

> What I do with my life now is the person that deep down I always felt I could be. It drives me...I feel the core of me is the person that put

that stuff to one side and continuing to be that person that I want to be. But I think that's always been inside me.

(Julie)

Julie embraced the idea of a core self, but was at the same time clear that who she was or would become was down to her. It was important to Julie to recognise the positive role she played in her own healing and recovery, and the making of her self, which in turn had helped distance her from a life in which she (like her brother) might have become an abuser. Healing enabled women to make choices they might not have been able to make before, but healing was itself also a choice. Having made this choice women felt able to take control of their lives:

> Now I've got this knowledge of myself and my childhood I then wasn't prepared to be the person that I was.
>
> (Julie)

And

> This was all untangling stuff so that I could move forward in my life. I am the person that I really want to be. That's what came out of the first lot of counselling.
>
> (Julie)

Like the majority of women, Julie believed her childhood experiences, including sexual abuse, contributed to the self she had become. However, her understanding also allowed for that self to be remade and the effects of sexual abuse removed, if she had the strength and confidence to remake herself as the person she wanted to be.

> Well I always thought that the person I am today is a result, I think, of my childhood and the person that I've always wanted to be or the person I am today and the person I'm going to be in the future is the person that I would have been had I not had the, you know, if I wasn't so inhibited by my childhood I suppose. So I suppose I would like to say that I find that the abuse has inhibited me and the person that I'm going to be is the person I would have been had I not had those experiences. I would have grown confident.
>
> (Julie)

Confidence was also important to women's sense of self and how they saw their place in the world. Like Fiona, moving forward and becoming the person she wanted to be was, for Julie, linked to (self) confidence. Confidence was something she believed had been taken from her but her therapy, she believed:

> Healed me enough to be confident enough to go forward. To be the person that I wanted to be. Yeh definitely yeh. Yeh I don't think I could even elaborate on it really.
>
> (Julie)

Reaching adulthood was for Julie the significant factor in being able to leave behind (negative) ideas and beliefs learnt in childhood and choosing who to become:

> I believe every child starts off with the right intentions and then you just become moulded into something. As you get older you can choose to stay that way or you can move on. That's how I see it. I think at 3ish you are learning things from other people. You are copying, mimicking and your words are very much other people's words. Then when you get to a certain age you are the product of how you're brought up. I think you can choose to be whoever you want to be. You get to an age where I think I chose to be who I want to be today.
>
> (Julie)

Julie was able to remake herself as the person she wanted to be, but at the same time this person was the person she thought she would have been if she had not been inhibited by her abuse. It was important to Julie, and others, that they were able to remove the negative effects of sexual abuse but it was also important to acknowledge the positive role they themselves played and the contradictory self allowed for this. Angela took this a stage further as she recognised not only the negative effects of being abused but also the positive effects of overcoming that abuse. All her experiences, including her responses to them, contributed to the person she was becoming:

> You never stop learning. Whether that be about the actual abuse itself or whether that be about the effects of how I view myself or the effects on my relationships that I have with the children or how I deal with them growing up…Cos I do think if I hadn't been abused

> then I wouldn't have been forced to have to be strong and so I would probably never have found out how strong I could be or what I could do.
>
> (Angela)

Some women believed healing would enable them to become who they would have been if they had not been abused, as it would remove the effects of abuse to free them to become this self. Others recognised in the self they were becoming, a process which included their abuse, their recovery and their experiences in-between. This was an understanding that could also be shared by those who recognised in themselves a core self. Believing the self to be, at least in part, influenced by traumatic or abusive experiences did not necessarily lead to a negative construction of the self as damaged, although this was reliant on their ability to heal. Sarah's assessment of who she was reflected the views of most of the women when she said:

> I think, I am glad and happy about the person that I've become... I am pleased and happy to be the person I'm becoming.
>
> (Sarah)

Most women were happy about who they were and who they could be, but many also felt that there were times when:

> All these things get in the way of what I really am and what I could be.
>
> (Beccy)

An alternative view was offered by Jenny who went through life with:

> A general feeling that somehow all was not well, that I perhaps wasn't living the life I could or was meant to.
>
> (Jenny)

But suggested:

> Perhaps... this is the path I was meant to have trodden and would have done so sooner or later.
>
> (Jenny)

Jenny believed in 'meaningful suffering' and therefore the life she was meant to live and the life she was living may have been one and the same. While Jenny recognised a core self she also believed:

> My experiences have influenced the person I am and altered the flow of my life – (the life that my ego desired for myself). But as I believe in the idea of meaningful suffering then I can no longer untangle how I think my life ought to have been from how it is i.e. this is my soul's path.
>
> (Jenny)

Jenny believed her life was mapped out, although this did not mean she did not need to work on her self, at the same time as she identified an ego which might have chosen a different path.

The self and false memories

Rose has suggested that through their 'passage through therapy' women become 'attached to the versions of themselves they have been led to produce' (Rose 1989:251). However, the majority of women did not feel they had been 'led to produce' versions of themselves although they were attached to their new versions of themselves, but this attachment was less clear for those who rejected at least some aspects of the memories on which these versions of themselves were based. The experience of recovery, healing and finding (out) who they were had a positive outcome for the majority of women, but those who believed their stories were based on false memories were often left with misgivings and languished in a state of autobiographical uncertainty. The process through which women identified once believed in memories as false not only challenged their confidence in their memories, and not only those relating to sexual abuse, but as their memories were linked to their perception of themselves, this process also challenged their sense of self. Rejecting their memories created a fissure in women's biographical narratives that threatened to fracture their sense of identity and it is therefore not surprising that their stories were littered with expressions of doubt and uncertainty. Women articulated varying degrees of uncertainty but for some it translated into an inability to even recognise who they were and whether they had changed:

> Whether it's altered me as a person or not I don't really know because I don't know . . . I honestly don't know because I've got nobody to tell me if I'm any different now.
>
> (Rae)

Rae was reliant on a (significant) other to tell her who she was and her account suggests she did not have a strong sense of self or a strong connection to a past, whether in childhood or more recent. Similar uncertainty featured in Hazel's account, where she linked a lack of confidence in her memories to a lack of confidence in herself:

> I lost a lot of confidence; I lost an awful lot of confidence in myself. I don't trust my memories anymore. I do not trust my memories. I can't remember, I can't remember names anymore, people's names. I can't remember places, I can't remember.
>
> (Hazel)

Hazel's uncertainty not only led her to question her memories, it also led her to question more everyday knowledge, including the names of people and places. Although both women had an explanation for their false memories that enabled them to maintain some biographical continuity, the recognition that they had once believed in memories that proved to be false did lead them to question their biographies and threatened their confidence.

Women's confidence in their memories, and therefore their narratives, was significant to having a secure sense of self. It was a belief in their memories that connected women to the past, and it was a connection to the past that enabled them to construct an identity through which they could maintain continuity throughout their lives. This continuity or constant presence was also significant to women's self-confidence and sense of well-being. Maintaining this connection to the past may also have been important to women's ability or willingness to draw on the different formulations of the self presented in the recovery literature. It may be that their biographical certainty, their confidence in a connection between their selves in the present and their sexually abused selves from childhood, enabled them to dip in and out of the contradictory formulations which many found so helpful. Those who rejected their memories, not only lost this connection to the past, and therefore the selves they were, but this in itself may also have made it difficult to draw on the contradictory self that others found so useful.

The question of truth or falsity was important to women but, as Rae's account shows, a sense of self was at least as important. It was their sense of self, as someone who could successfully go out into the world, that most of the women were ultimately attempting to find or construct. Rae rejected her memories of CSA and, believing she was the victim of FMS, sought the help of a therapist but her therapy did not attempt to establish the truth or falsity of her memories but focussed on Rae's sense of self:

> No I remember her saying that erm, what we need to restore in you is your original image of yourself and that's what she worked on.
>
> (Rae)

Rae remained uncertain about whether she had been sexually abused or not but she had gained some limited confidence in her self. She did not return to a core self untouched by abuse, but was able to return to a self who had not been abused by her father, even if it was a self who might have been abused by someone else. This was important to Rae, possibly because it helped her maintain some confidence in her biographical narrative and those who were influential in the making of that narrative. Perhaps reflecting her continued uncertainty, this 'reconstructed self' had an unreal quality to it. It was a self Rae did not fully believe in and which she needed someone else's help to construct.

The majority of women recognised only one life but a number of women believed in a self who existed in previous lives and would continue to exist in future lives. This helped them explain how abuse could be forgotten and later remembered and enabled some to explain how they had uncovered 'false' knowledge of sexual abuse in childhood: they were abused in a previous life and the perpetrator was not who they originally accused. The sexually abused self was different at the same time as it was the same. Whereas Pat and Rae believed they were victims of sexual abuse in a previous life, Sarah thought she might have been an abuser in a previous life. She also thought that the abuse she experienced in this life might help her in the next:

> In another life I might have a better childhood because my karma is going to be built up.
>
> (Sarah)

A self to live with

A sense of self as something to be improved, developed and healed played a central role in women's engagement with the sexual abuse recovery literature and their construction of a sexual abuse narrative. They were able to draw on the different formulations of the self promoted within this literature in response to different questions and challenges and did not adopt uncritically the conceptions of the self they found. In taking a pragmatic approach women did not find the ambiguities and contradictions inherent in these different selves problematic but instead found them useful. Engaging with these different formulations women navigated their own path to a self that was both makeable and innate, both a process and a thing. It was something/one they believed had been abused, and something/one that could leave that abuse behind.

Women were not constrained by either a static self or a self in the making but were able to draw on both to construct a self that they were happy with and which helped them give meaning to their lives. However, there was another self populating their biographies. This was a self who, as a constant presence, connected them with their pasts and to their futures. For some it was their only connection to an abusive past. This was the self who chose to learn from their experiences, a self who put them back together, who rebuilt them bit-by-bit, who chose who they were going to be and who was glad and happy about the person they were becoming. Some gave names to the occupier of their 'inner space' (Craib 1998), such as the soul (Sarah, Jenny), the spirit (Beccy) and the front person (Anne), whilst others spoke of a true self (Beccy, Sarah). It was a self who helped them negotiate the contradictory selves of the recovery and therapeutic literature but it was also much more than that.

9
Healing and Growing Up

Everybody has got work to do their whole life.

(Fiona)

I think there is always something that we can always work on for ourselves.

(Tracey)

Introduction

The self of the twenty-first century is located within a culture in which the claim to victim status provides one of the most legitimate routes to recognition (Furedi 2004). This therapeutically informed self is bombarded with advice on how to be a better, truer, happier, authentic self, but there is another, more sinister side which carries warnings, or even threats, for those who do not follow the advice. Failure to heal may condemn victims to a life of misery, devoid of happiness or success, in which they are likely to be victimised again in adulthood (largely women) or victimise others (largely men). Therapy may appear to be empowering and liberating but it has helped to institutionalise a regime of self-limitation (Furedi 2004). The powerful, self-determining self, the self of the human potential movement (see Maslow 1970, Rogers 1970) and the reflexive self of Giddens (1991) is undermined at the same time as we are encouraged to connect with it. No longer limited to seeking help to cope with difficult and traumatic experiences we are increasingly encouraged to seek help to cope with everyday ups and downs. Suggesting we need therapy to cope with or survive ordinary or mundane experiences such as parenting, divorce, work or redundancy, and even sporting events such as the world cup, undermines the apparently liberating and empowering message of therapeutic discourses. We may use this culture and appropriate different aspects of it but we cannot entirely escape being limited by it (Furedi 2004). The women whose stories have featured in this book have used, appropriated, and at times been limited by a CSA recovery literature informed by a therapeutic culture that encouraged them to construct themselves as damaged and in need of healing. However, as this chapter will show, most of these women have also attempted to move beyond these limitations and, in writing a new chapter for themselves, redefined their own healing and recovery.

Healing the self, recognising the threat

The watchword of self-therapy, and the recovery literature, is 'recover or repeat' (Giddens 1991:79). It is not just that we might wish to embark on our own project of the self but there is an imperative within this literature that suggests a failure to do so will lead to a catalogue of ills, from unhappiness and dissatisfaction to victimisation, self-sabotage and, for some, ultimately suicide. This literature promotes itself as a means of 'self creation', 'damage control' and 'revival' but with an ever present threat of what will happen in the event of failure, and it does so whilst promising to reveal the 'true' self (Simonds 1996). Sexual abuse in childhood we are told 'derails normal personality development' which may cause behaviours that further damage the victim (Levenkron 2008:15) Whilst the harm story encourages victims to construct themselves as damaged and vulnerable to further abuse, the healing discourse offers a way to remove this damage and create a self that is both powerful and healthy. It is only through healing can they address their vulnerability, a state itself equated with childhood and a lack of maturity. Encouraged to contact their inner child or child self, victims must learn to 'reparent' her, in order to 'grow up' and become the woman they would have been (Ainscough and Toon 1993, 2000, Bass and Davis 1988, 2002, Dinsmore 1991, Parks 1990). Sexual abuse is thought to be so devastating that it cannot be healed and therefore empowerment and future happiness is achieved not from overcoming sexual abuse but from removing or undoing its effects. The view that time stopped, leaving the abused child stuck at the time of the abuse, allows for this as the adult victim can return to the time of the abuse and, with the help of trusted friends and therapists, 'grow up' to be the powerful woman she should have been.

The literature aimed at adult victims of sexual abuse in childhood promotes a 'flawed model' (Kelly 1996) of a cycle of abuse and carries an implicit threat for those who do not choose the path to healing and recovery. For these women, continuing to be 'damaged goods' is seen as likely (Bass and Davis 1988, 2002, Dinsmore 1991, Herman 1981, Parks 1990), or even inevitably (Forward 1989), to lead to an ongoing life of misery and suffering. A significant subplot links the sexually abused child with future abuse, and identifies formerly abused men as potential abusers (Lew 1988, 2004) and formerly abused women as potential victims (Bass and Davis 1988, 2002, Dinsmore 1991, Herman 1992, Levenkron 2008, Parks 1990). Feminist analyses of violence against women (e.g. Armstrong 1978, 1994, Kelly 1988, Kirkwood 1993, Russell 1982) is disregarded in favour of a new form of victim blaming in which the victim is held responsible for abuse enacted upon her (Kelly 1996), as victims are often said to choose abusive partners (Bass and Davis 1988, 2002, Herman 1992, Parks 1990, Dinsmore 1991, Levenkron 2008). In the 1980s theories of 'learned helplessness' and the 'masochistic woman' (Walker 1979, 1984), which constructed victims as responsible because of their faulty psychologies, were rejected. However, the CSA recovery literature also constructs women as responsible due to a combination of their perceived damaged psychologies and their failure to heal.

Breaking the cycle

The idea that, as damaged goods, they must heal in order to avoid repeating past traumas and victimisation, was familiar to women but not all accepted the link between past and future abuse. However, as part of the process of making sense of their own lives and the lives of others, some did believe that, without healing, they might go on to abuse others or at least enable others to be abused. In some cases they did this with reference to cycles of abuse they identified in their own family histories:

> I don't know how she was raised, she never talks about her childhood so I can imagine it's probably something similar to what I went through.
>
> (Tracey)

A number of women, including Beccy and Tracey, not only accepted that their own lives showed evidence of damage, but also believed they might be responsible for future abuse. The healing discourse offered them a way to break this cycle:

> I still remember when my mum first beat me and when I first got molested and now I feel like ok I was molested that was then... I'm gonna treat my kids with respect and I'm never going to do what happened to me. I'm really glad that I'm doing this because when I have kids I don't want to pass anything like this on. I must break the cycle and that's what my mum should have done ages ago.
>
> (Tracey)

Whether they had continuous or recovered memories, women were able to revisit their childhoods and find 'evidence' that not only supported their narratives but reinforced the message contained in the cycle of violence subplot. Beccy had no memories of sexual abuse experienced at the hands of her father but found in her shared family history what she believed were the foundations for her abuse:

> In my family there is a whole history of alcoholism and emotional abuse. At least I know there was emotional abuse in the form of neglect mostly but also some emotional abuse. And er probably a history of sexual abuse but I can't verify it or anything but I have strong suspicions. And none of these people worked it through.
>
> (Beccy)

Rather than believing people are born as abusers, Beccy accepted that those who go on to abuse others have learnt to do so through their own experiences of abuse. Whilst she did not believe they would inevitably go on to abuse others, she did believe that to avoid this outcome they needed to heal and undo the damage done to them. It was this failure, or refusal, to work through the effects of their abuse that Beccy believed caused members of her own family to go to abuse others:

> I believe 100 per cent of people who sexually abuse children have been abused in some way. They might not have been sexually abused but they've definitely been abused emotionally or physically or in some way. I believe that 100 per cent yeh.
>
> (Beccy)

Beccy accepted a negative construction of victims but like Tracey was able to resist this construction for herself by embarking on a healing journey and thereby taking a different path to the one laid out for her by an abusive history:

> I'm aware so there's no damage. I'm the end of the line. The abuse stops with me, that's it... I think if you deal with it you'll be fine. If you don't then very possibly you will abuse your children, at least emotionally I think.
>
> (Beccy)

Beccy had no concrete memories of sexual abuse and was unable to identify an abuser but was able to use the harm story to apportion at least some blame with her mother. She used this story to distance herself from the possibility of repeating her mother's sins:

> None of these people did anything about it. My mother doesn't want to do anything about.
>
> (Beccy)

Identifying abuse as a failure to heal not only positions victims as potential abusers but can also be used by victims to construct their abusers as victims. This feature of the literature was drawn on by a number of women to explain the behaviour of those who had abused them, and those they held partly responsible:

> What leads people to sexually abuse children – I think mostly because they've been abused themselves... I think its true. If its my father, I don't know if he's been sexually abused but he's certainly been emotionally abused and neglected so that would definitely explain. My mother was quite emotionally abusive and she was, she failed to protect me and she was emotionally and sexually abused.
>
> (Beccy)

Beccy not only identified her parents as responsible for failing to break their own cycles of abuse, but used this in support of her own biography. All the women read the recovery literature but this was not their only source of information as they were also informed through a variety of other sources, including some of the many biographies and autobiographies currently in circulation. Survivor auto/biographies were an important source of information particularly in relation to healing and moving forward. I am not suggesting women simply borrowed the plots and storylines they found in the pages of survivor biographies but they did provide women with a way to make sense of their own lives and an interpretive framework for understanding the lives of others who populated their accounts. The cycle of abuse that features in the accounts of Tracey and Beccy for example resonates with the storyline contained in Sylvia Fraser's popular biography *My Father's House* (1987). Here Fraser, although appearing to accuse her parents, does at the same time avoid blaming them by positioning them as lacking the resources necessary to forgive and heal. As Fraser suggested:

> I was the first generation of my family to receive the education and the social resources and the personal support to fight back... mine is a middle-class story with built in loopholes and rescue stations and options and time locks and safeguards.
>
> (Fraser 1987:253)

Tracey and Beccy did not simply appropriate Fraser's storyline, but were able to draw on her 'middle class story', to write their own biographies. Whilst Tracey and Beccy held their parents responsible for a failure to heal, in believing this 'middle-class story' was not available to their parents, they could also use a lack of resources to mitigate the level of blame attributed to them. This was a mitigating factor unavailable to Tracey and Beccy who, like Fraser, had the education, social resources and personal support to construct a 'middle class story'. With the growth in therapeutic / self-help culture healing resources are becoming more widely available, not only to those whose stories feature in this book, and therefore a failure to heal is increasingly used to blame victims for a catalogue of ills, including responsibility for abuse committed by others. Angela was sexually abused by her brother, but also used the cycle of abuse to identify evidence of sexual abuse in her mother's childhood and construct her mother as a victim:

> I think there is a cycle but I don't think the cycle necessarily goes along those lines... Well in my family erm, it was my brother that abused me. Now I'm certain in my mind that my mum was abused... Sexually abused when she was little. She's never told me and I wouldn't talk about it to my dad or anybody else – but the patterns I see and the connections I've made, I can see in the way my mum has behaved with me.
>
> (Angela)

Angela appeared to identify with her mother but went on to distance herself as she blamed her mother and believed she should have protected her:

> In my mind I was quite certain that she had been abused and therefore she should have seen what was happening to me.
>
> (Angela)

Angela's account not only constructed her mother as liable but rendered the perpetrator, her brother, largely invisible. Angela focused on a lack of healing to explain, but not excuse, her mother's failure to protect her and drew on explanations she found in the literature to position her mother as the family guardian who could be seen as both cause and explanation when things went wrong (Dinsmore 1991, Parks 1990). None of these women believed they were abused by their mothers but they did hold them responsible and were determined not to repeat what they saw as a cycle of abuse. The focus on women's mothers left abusers largely absent from their biographies and this reflected the general lack of attention paid to perpetrators in much of the literature, where the emphasis is on victims breaking the cycle. Warnings of future victimisation and cycles of violence, although heeded by many, were felt most acutely by Jay whose male partner had also been sexually abused as a child. For Jay and her husband CSA, which positions the male survivor as a likely abuser of his own and others' children and the female survivor as a potential victim unable to protect those for whom she is responsible, was particularly significant and frightening. They both accepted they would have difficulties as a result of their sexual abuse, and accepted the gendered dimension to those difficulties which was, at the time they got married, the only sexual abuse story available to them. Neither had any other reason to think their children would be at risk, but it was a story that created concern and suspicion:

> So Simon was terrified that he would end up being an abuser because he was abused. There was no other reasoning, just that, which was pretty scary for us both.
>
> (Jay)

The story available to Jay and Simon in the early years of their marriage only identified male victims as potential abusers and they were therefore not concerned about the possibility of Jay abusing their children. In spite of defining Simon as a potential abuser they were able to develop a trusting relationship:

> Because we were totally open about it from the beginning. He said he was abused by his brother and he was concerned about himself because he's read these reports, so he said would I watch him. And I said well that doesn't make me feel very comfortable and he said well I don't think there's any chance of it happening but keep an eye on me.
>
> (Jay)

Although Jay had initially been concerned about her husband there was nothing in what she said to indicate her fears were substantiated. The construction of formerly abused as potential abusers created problems for Jay and Simon but it also enabled them to develop a degree of openness, albeit one in which Jay kept an eye on her husband:

> And I thought well that's a relief actually, rather than having to do it on the sly which I would have done anyway, it's been brought out into the open.
>
> (Jay)

Monitoring was a course of action Jay had already decided on but having the idea out in the open made it easier for her. However, it also helped to reinforce Jay's role as wife and mother with responsibility for the well being of her family. A different storying of sexual abuse might have negated their need to keep an eye on Simon, who might not have been defined as a potential threat. In constructing her own narrative Jay not only had to deal with the effects of her own traumatic childhood and effects of sexual abuse experienced by her partner, she also had to take on the role of 'protector of the family', which in this case was constructed as particularly vulnerable in need of additional protection. Jay and Simon were first introduced to the idea of a cycle of abuse in the early 1970s, but others did not become familiar with cycles of abuse until much later. Although some did heed the warnings contained in the literature, women dealt with this message in different ways and some found it not only offensive but potentially harmful:

> I was insulted by the idea that abusers abuse...I don't believe that's so.
>
> (Emma)

> I can't remember how she said it but it was along the lines, 'people who have been abused when they were younger are likely to become abusers when they are older' and you know that was like a slap in the face to me (Fiona).

> I think it could be damaging to be told that you could go on to be an abuser.
>
> (Emma)

Women were presented with information and advice that covered a range of issues and although, as victims, they were often constructed as weak, vulnerable, gullible and easily influenced by therapists and the writers of self-help texts, they did not necessarily believe the information or follow the advice. Whereas Jay and her partner accepted that abusers were likely to go on to abuse, at least when applied to male victims, both Emma and Fiona rejected this message. How women viewed the cycle of abuse was related to the degree to which they felt they could heal. It was easier for women to accept a cycle of abuse if they felt it did not have long-term negative consequences but was something they could break. It was therefore also easier for those who felt more positively about recovery or had invested more heavily in a therapeutic solution, as they could break the cycle through healing. What the women objected to was any suggestion that they were permanently damaged but unable to heal or undo that damage.

Improving the self

There is a contradiction in the self who inhabits much of the CSA recovery literature but it was the concept of a core self untouched by abuse that was particularly significant to women's understanding of healing. Whilst many women recognised the continuing effects of sexual abuse, and (at least at times) believed their experiences could not be left behind, many also embraced the idea of a self that could be freed and, once healed, go on to live a happy, fulfilled and successful life. This was the self who enabled women to engage with therapeutic discourses and not only (re)construct themselves as damaged but also remake themselves as all-powerful. Recognition of a true or inner self did not exclude the idea of the self as a project to be worked on, to be improved and developed. Whilst some women envisaged an end to this work others saw it as an ongoing process, in which work on the self was never finished but rather the self was something in need of constant attention.

For the majority of the women, their engagement with the recovery literature was part of a project of self-improvement and self-development, and they made little distinction between healing work and self-development. Women had different reasons for embarking on this project including a desire to lose weight, address a physical illness or condition, dissatisfaction with relationships and a general feeling that all was not well, and for some it was a project that extended to included the body. Whatever the focus, much of this work was done in conjunction with self-help literature. Women read books on diet, health and illness, tried alternative therapies including massage and aromatherapy, and became involved with various organised and less organised religions, including Christianity, Buddhism and Shamanism. Some went on courses for assertiveness and building self-esteem and confidence. They were also involved in a variety of other activities that included meditation, dance, exercise, tai chi, reflexology, hypnotism, painting, walking and writing, all of which were seen to further healing and self-improvement or self-development. Whilst some women continued with these activities beyond their healing, often simply because they enjoyed them, others stopped when they were healed and no longer needed them or felt they should not need them. For some women however, their ability or willingness to continue with such activities related to the relationship they developed with an inner child and/or what they understood to be appropriate for healthy adult women. For those who were only able to engage in these activities with the help of an inner child if, when they were healed, their inner child was no longer available to them they would have no way to continue.

Women were advised that healing could be a long process that might take years of hard work and commitment and the time they devoted to their own healing ranged from a few years to over 20. How they viewed this time spent working on themselves, and whether they saw an end to it, possibly when they were healed and could write a new chapter, also varied. Some women's biographies remained focussed on sexual abuse, but others shared life stories that began with or developed around other themes. Anne's narrative, written over many years, initially featured a difficult and traumatic childhood before moving on to include incest and, eventually featured years of sexual and ritual abuse. Beccy's biography, also written over many years, illustrates ten years spent working on her self. Hers is a biography that drew on a range of self-help and self-improvement texts including those dealing with diet, sexual dysfunction, and sexual abuse but it was in the CSA recovery literature that Beccy recognised her own life and it was through her engagement with this literature that she felt she had made progress:

> It's not a question of just going to therapy forever, there's an end to it and the end is being completely healed at the end and being free. So there's a beginning, a middle and an end and there's a process to go through and that's very clear. So you feel that there's hope at the end.
>
> (Beccy)

Titles such as *Reach for the Rainbow: Advanced Healing for Survivors of Sexual Abuse* (Finney 1990) suggested that healing was an ongoing process in which victims would always have work to do. Although this was a view taken up by a number of women the majority did see an end to their healing. Beccy was clear that healing should have 'a beginning a middle and an end'. She was also clear that the work she needed to do related to having been sexually abused as a child. Beccy had yet to uncover memories of abuse but had invested heavily in the harm story and its therapeutic corollary healing discourse and believed that once healed she would no longer need to work on her self. Jay had also spent a long time in counselling and although her experiences seemed more painful and her view of life less optimistic, she shared Beccy's view that counselling should eventually come to an end. Jay had finished counselling and believed she had left a difficult phase of her life behind:

> I didn't expect it lasting so long or being as painful or causing so many problems...I'm pleased that part of my life's behind me as well.
>
> (Jay)

Not all the women had such a clear idea of an ending or break between healing and the life that would follow. Those who did believe in an end point to their recovery or healing did not necessarily believe this should signal an end to the work they did on themselves. Tracey distinguished between healing and becoming whole, where she could address experiences of abuse, and other work she might choose to do on her self:

> I think you can be healed on one, on, entirely if that was the only thing that you want to have healed but I think there is always something that we can always work on for ourselves. I think yeh, definitely

> it can come to a halt yeh, I think you can be a whole person without any blocks.
>
> (Tracey)

Even Beccy, who was clear about the end of therapy, felt she might need a 'top-up', particularly if she experienced other difficult life events:

> It could be that every now and then it comes back or something. You know if something bad happens in my life suddenly I'll have a dip. I'll immediately maybe go back for a couple of sessions. I'm not sure. But no, the idea is that at the end it's over.
>
> (Beccy)

It is hard to say how much this reflects women's view of their self as a project and how much it reflects their lack of confidence in themselves and their ability to deal with difficulties. They are also likely to have been influenced by the recovery literature itself which encourages women to identify a range of difficulties in their lives and through this to construct themselves as damaged. This was after all the route by which the majority of women identified themselves as victims of sexual abuse and in need of healing. Fiona also, at least in theory, saw an end to her recovery, a time when she had dealt with her abuse and was able to move forward:

> That's what the counselling was about, moving through all that, not ignoring it, working through it and getting past it and moving on after it.
>
> (Fiona)

Like Tracey, she did not see this as signalling an end to working on her self. However, the idea of an end to the recovery process was not shared by all the women. Angela linked recovery with finding herself:

> Well I don't think we ever do stop recovering ... I think it's something that would drive you, yeh drive me more and more and more about who I am really.
>
> (Angela)

Angela's view of recovery was linked to her belief in a makeable self but was also tied up with how she viewed her own self. She seemed unsure of herself and was constantly judging and measuring her self, possibly as a gauge of her healing and how strong she was. However, she lacked the confidence to do this in her everyday life:

> I do have a certain inclination to try and put myself into a situation that I feel will be difficult and I need to see how I'd cope with it. But rather than doing that in life I try to do that on courses.
>
> (Angela)

It may be that Angela would eventually gain the confidence to engage more fully with life, beyond the confines of her courses, but at the time of this research she was content and did not desire to leave her 'practice runs' behind.

Time out for the self

Some women wanted to turn their back on therapeutic lifestyles and some felt they should continue working on the self, but others simply wanted to look after their 'new' selves. For some this remained tied up with their recovery, seen as fragile and in need of monitoring, but for others it represented an attempt to look after themselves, and not only reflected moving forward but recognition of their own value, something many had previously found difficult. Therapeutic culture of the twenty-first century does itself encourage us to take time out to work on, look after and pamper our selves. This idea of taking time out to work on the self, whether as part of their recovery or in relation to a programme of self-improvement or self-development, featured in a number of women's accounts. The time they invested in support of their healing often continued in relation to work the women did on themselves and often took the form of reading:

> I spend at least a couple of hours on my own a week you know just to be with myself.
>
> (Tracey)

> Then I'd make notes and do the exercises.
>
> (Tracey)

Whilst some took a causal attitude others took a more rigorous approach, often dedicating fixed periods each day to this self work:

> Sometimes I listen to self-help tapes, relaxation tapes or positive thinking tapes. I have books that I dip in and out of... positive thinking books that I like, affirming type books, religious books, directional kind of books that I might spend ten minutes reading. I might chant, I might meditate, I might pray, but for half an hour in the morning I have a time to myself... most mornings and that's my habit. So that's the time when I would also look at self-help books but they're much more positive and general.
>
> (Fiona)

Even women who did not engage with the recovery or self-development literature on a regular basis continued to turn to reading at times of difficulty:

> I mean I still read self-help books. I still get them. If I'm going through a difficult time then I might go back to some of them I've got and go over stuff.
>
> (Angela)

A self in need of ongoing work was an idea shared by a number of women although not all saw it as separate from their everyday lives. For Jenny working on her self was an integral part of her daily life, or possibly her daily life was a project which involved healing and personal development in relation to both her self and her body. There was some separation between healing and the world outside but this was something Jenny was hoping to bridge:

> I will continue work with my own sexuality and releasing pain, letting go of fear in my womb area by belly dancing – creating and maintaining sexual health here.
>
> (Jenny)

> Dancing more, sharing in circles. I want to come out into the world more again and be sociable after my long retreat!
>
> (Jenny)

Ending her account with the words 'Our journey continues...' Jenny made it clear that she saw her self-work as an ongoing process, and although others also saw self-work as a long term commitment, this was not necessarily an attitude they continued to maintain, and may reflect a desire or a need to move on with their lives and leave their formerly abused selves behind. It may also have been a desire to embrace life more fully, something they now felt ready for. Sarah was in the seventh year of her ten-year cycle when she began to question the value of her heavy investment in her self-work. Sarah's decision to reject her life plan, with its carefully laid out goals and attainments, may reflect a more confident view of herself and her place in the world, a place occupied by someone who no longer needed her life meticulously mapped out. However, like many of the women, although she was leaving therapy behind, Sarah had not completely put it behind her.

> I'm going to have a break from the therapy and if I need to come back to it at a later stage I will.
>
> (Sarah)

For many their involvement with self-help and self-development was very intense. A level of intensity can be seen in Anne's account, although Anne's investment was not so much in the world of her adult self but in the therapeutic world of inner children. Like Jenny and Sarah, Anne's engagement with therapeutic discourses could also be seen as a way of life or, perhaps more accurately in Anne's case, to have taken over her life. It was a life in which her adult self was in some respects lost to her inner children. Anne worked hard on her healing but the majority of this work was not done on her adult self but on, or with, her inner children. She wrote poems, drew pictures, sent cards and brought presents and, whilst ostensibly for her inner children, these 'packages' could also be seen to function as part of a project to look after, work on, pamper and take time out for her self, albeit as a project not fully recognised or acknowledged by the adult Anne. There were occasions where Anne did work on her adult self, but even these were seen by Anne as something that would benefit, or facilitate the surfacing of, her inner children.

Whether as distinct personalities or aspects of her self, Anne's alters did provide her with an opportunity to address emotions such as anger and sadness and to express other emotions such as happiness and joy. Although it was not how she articulated the work she did with her alters or inner children, this work did enable Anne to address areas she might otherwise have found difficult. It was also through her inner children that the adult Anne was able to engage in activities that could be interpreted as indulging or pampering, but which might also be described as therapeutic. This reflected the central role Anne's inner children had come to play in her life. Anne had constructed a life story in which the important characters were her inner children and it was they who she devoted her time and energy to. At the same time Anne did not believe her front person, the adult Anne, had much value and therefore did not feel she deserved the kind of attention bestowed on her children. However, there were also times when she felt her inner children prevented her doing emotional work:

> I can't do that amount of disciplined work because you know, I can't do it. I need to, I mean I see why now, because of the children inside me who need to play in different ways.
>
> (Anne)

Jenny and Anne had both devoted to their lives to dealing with the consequences of sexual abuse they believed they suffered as children. Whilst Jenny had dedicated her life to healing and moving forward it could be argued that Anne had dedicated her life to her inner children. Anne's life centred on her inner children who she discovered might have inner children of their own, and through them Anne had found a way of maintaining her situation. Whilst some of Anne's work involved helping her children heal and (through them) express feelings and emotions, her principal motivation did seem to be to make contact. Anne was also concerned how others viewed her, not only in relation to her biography and her inner children, but also in relation to healing. In writing her life story Anne not only rejected childhood memories she had access to, but positioned herself as 'the most severe case in anything I read' which helped her justify, to herself as much as to others, why her healing was such a lengthy process.

Beyond healing

Not all the women devoted so much time to looking after themselves, and many wanted to leave behind their healing as it could act as a reminder of their sexual abuse, although some did make a clear distinction between healing work and other self-work. Fiona, for example, identified work she needed to do on her self, and was not only clear when this work should take place but also careful to keep it separate from other work that need to be done and even identified different times of the day when it could be done:

> I wouldn't use that time to do any work that's going to be upsetting or that's going to bring a wee bit of discord to my day. I'd rather do something that's going to bring a bit of calmness and peace to

> my day and I would do that in the morning. But they are more sort of general, positive thinking, self-help spiritual type of things that I use.
>
> (Fiona)

The women engaged with discourse around sexual abuse and recovery because they identified something wrong in their lives or themselves. They also believed the more general messages of self-help and self-development literature that we all have work to do on ourselves, and this enabled many to continue with some form of self-work after they were healed. It also enabled women to move beyond the identity of victim and reconstruct themselves as survivors, even if they still needed to work on themselves. The women did not articulate it as such but the idea of the self as a project to be worked on featured in many of their biographies. This project was informed by their experiences of abuse but they did not all see those experiences as the sole cause of any work that needed to be done:

> Everybody has got work to do their whole life. Nobody gets to 30 and thinks that's me grown up, I'm happy, sits back... Everybody's got ups and downs and things that they have to deal with, things that they have to learn, growth that they have to meet right up to the day they die and I'm no different to anybody else.
>
> (Fiona)

This enabled women to cast aside their identity as victim, at least of CSA, but it reinforced the belief that they should look inwards for the cause of and solution to their difficulties, an idea they had already accepted when they identified symptoms of sexual abuse in their adult lives. Through writing their life stories the majority of women had attempted to develop a character who could move beyond the identity of victim, but many found it harder to develop a character who would not need to engage with therapeutic discourses to deal with the 'ups and downs' of everyday life.

The measure against which success is judged in self-help and self-improvement literature, including that aimed at adult victims of childhood sexual abuse, is the degree to which fear and despair give way to hope and inner confidence (Kitzinger 1993) and this is also the blueprint for the survivor accounts identified by Davis (2005). However, these are written within a context in which we are led to believe that we should be happy and successful and encouraged to believe that if we are not it is because of some traumatic experience that we may or may not remember. The literature appears to be empowering but this is achieved by encouraging the reader to identify problems and find fault with things they were previously satisfied with. It is very often these, previously unacknowledged, problems that readers are empowered to address. This was an idea picked up by Jay. Jay recognised we all experienced good and bad times, and feeling happy all the time was neither possible nor even desirable. Jay rejected the underlying message that we should be able to avoid these bad times and identify any failure to do so as evidence of abuse, or at least a lack of healing. She also rejected the suggestion that we should always make connections between present unhappiness and past, childhood traumas and believed much of the advice offered was dangerous. Rather than empowering and positive, Jay believed it could have a negative effect on the reader as it directed them to focus on the negative aspects of themselves, and could encourage readers to cure themselves of problems that did not exist or could not be changed. It was a lesson learnt through her own experiences:

> All they [self-help books] do reinforce to me is what's negative ... And send you searching for things that aren't there ... And at the end of the day you're creating illusions to try and kid yourself that it's working.
>
> (Jay)

Offering some advice of her own Jay suggested:

> Don't try and fix what isn't broken.
>
> (Jay)

Reading and seeing a therapist provided important sources of information and support but women also gained this from self-help and support groups, and survivor organised conferences and newsletters in addition to activities and groups that could be accessed by those who did not identify themselves as victims of abuse. Whilst support groups offer advice and support there is also a danger:

> Too many women in them, longing for community and conversation, come to incorporate the language of victimhood and survival into the sole organizing narrative of their identity. It becomes their

> major story, a story whose moral rarely goes further than 'Join a group (or write a book) and talk about the problem'.
>
> (Tavris 1992:329)

Although harsh, this assessment of self-help groups reflected a concern felt by some of the women who participated in this research. Fiona, for example, recognised the dangers of support groups which provided community but a community which kept its members confined to their sexual abuse narratives rather than somewhere where they could learn to write new narratives or at least new chapters:

> It was a self-help group that was just supporting you where you were. It wasn't a group to do anything therapeutic or to move on and people had been going to it for years and years and years and were still going to it.
>
> (Fiona)

Fiona did identify periods when healing might require more time and distinguished between her real life, and the one she occasionally dipped into in order to work on areas that were difficult or would benefit from further work but was clear that life beyond therapy was her real one:

> My idea is that you go to a group for a while but then you get back to your real life but that group's not your real life, it's a therapeutic place to be and you wouldn't want to keep going to it for years and years. You go to it for a while, when you're grown or when you no longer need it then you would leave and get back to normal life.
>
> (Fiona)

The world of support groups was not somewhere Fiona wanted to stay, nor did she believe others should, but recognised that it may prove difficult for some to leave. Support groups might be healthy places to go if they facilitated growth and development but, as Fiona recognised, they could be very unhealthy places when they did not. In addition to healing Fiona shared with a number of others a recognition that there might be times when she might feel a need to return to counselling or to working on her self, both her adult and her child self, in response to some difficulty. However, she also introduced the idea of a self as an ongoing project to be worked on and improved, and it was not always clear if this work was a result of her, as yet unremembered, abuse or part of a general project:

> I know there are things that are just not quite right and I would like to get them quite right. But that involves a wee bit of effort, a wee bit of work but it's hard work so quite often I avoid doing it because I don't enjoy it but it needs doing.
>
> (Fiona)

As a subscriber to *Cisters'* newsletter, Fiona also welcomed the occasional timely reminder that the arrival of the newsletter gave her of the need to pay attention to her self:

> It's a good reminder that there's things to deal with because in my daily life it's quite easy to get complacent and a wee bit lazy, not wanting to be working on it and just wanting things to be... just wanting to toddle along in your life everything ok and so you don't tackle issues and sometimes issues need tackling. So a wee reminder like *Cisters* coming in every now and again gives you a little jolt like yeh, I'll have to do some work on this cos this is still here I still want to deal with it.
>
> (Fiona)

Although Fiona had no memories of having been sexually abused, she had invested a lot of effort in her healing and recovery, experienced by her as difficult and at times upsetting. She was critical of those who turned therapy into a way of life but not if their therapeutic endeavour was directed to work on the self. There were clearly times in Fiona's life when she was not upset or dealing with the effects of abuse but rather than seeing this as an end to her healing and the opportunity to leave her abuse behind, Fiona used it as another reminder that she still needed to work on her self:

> I hadn't been getting as upset recently so maybe I've not been doing that much work so I'll maybe go and feel I'm getting a bit out of touch with my wee self.
>
> (Fiona)

Fiona appeared unable to move beyond healing and like those she criticised, had allowed healing to become a way of life. This may have reflected Fiona's lack of memories and a concern with when she would be healed. Fiona had no memories of her abuse or her abuser and this made it difficult for her know she had dealt with it and was healed. Fiona's healing was founded on buried memories of abuse and therefore, even if she felt healed, she could not be sure she had uncovered memories of all the abuse from which she needed to heal. This lack of certainty may help to maintain a therapeutic link but without a clear end to her search for knowledge it is a link that Fiona may never be able to break.

Limitations of healing

When they engaged with the self-help / self-development and the sexual abuse recovery literature women were furnished with advice on how to heal and therefore live happier more successful lives. At the same time as they were confronted with warnings telling what might happen if they failed to heal. Women heeded much of the advice but they did not simply follow a set of instructions in order to achieve a predetermined end result. Rather, they played an active role in writing their own life stories, or guides to living, which they understood as better, more uplifting and more hopeful, than the stories they were living in before. However, many were motivated by a fear of what would happen to them and some by a fear of what might happen to others, if they failed to heal. Whilst not many believed they would be responsible for the abuse of others, this was largely because, they believed, they had healed. The majority of the women felt they had benefited from their engagement with therapeutic discourses, but many also identified dangers or limitations to healing and recovery. This literature could encourage women to identify problems where none existed and hold themselves responsible for these newly perceived difficulties. It might also encourage them to view unhappiness or feeling bad as something to get rid off, and failure to do so as evidence of, possibly hidden, trauma and a failure to heal. There was also the problem, identified by a number of women, that a therapeutic lifestyle might be difficult to leave behind, particularly problematic within the context of needing to remove all unhappiness or dissatisfaction.

As part of healing women were encouraged to work on their selves and their lifestyles, and for many this was often hard work. Sometimes they did this work in response to perceived threats or warnings and sometimes in the hope of creating a better, happier life for themselves. Whilst they invested considerable time and energy in this self-work, it was not always all work and no play. As Rae said of her reflexology sessions:

> It's my treat to myself once a month.
>
> (Rae)

10
Compulsory Sexuality?

I just had a problem with sex and I didn't know where it came from
(Beccy)

Introduction

Whether it is through the childhood sexual abuse recovery literature, therapeutic and psychological literature, the popular imagination, or any of a wide variety of other cultural texts, we are led to believe that sexual abuse in childhood is likely to have a negative impact on adult sexuality. In the context of adult sexuality, there are some who argue that not all those who were sexually abused as children will be traumatised by it (McMillen et al 1995, Rind and Tromovitch 1997), but the dominant view is one of sexual dysfunction, albeit defined in different ways. Adult victims of childhood sexual abuse are said to frequently report sexual unhappiness (Bartoi and Kinder 1998, Jackson et al 1990), to feel shame or guilt about how they respond sexually and have difficulty trusting sexual partners, and in the case of women to often engage in sexually risky behaviours through which they might be exposed to sexually transmitted infections and sexual assaults. Much of this discussion is conducted within a discourse of sexual rights and sexual entitlement within which abuse victims are encouraged to claim their rights to sexual pleasure and satisfaction.

This message is mirrored in the recovery literature where readers are told that sexual abuse damages women's relationship with sex but through healing they can reclaim their right to a healthy, happy and fulfilling sex life. There is no option to choose a life without sex, except by continuing with a life story in which the writer constructs herself as damaged and in need of continued or further healing. Although even here women are reminded that they cannot say 'No' forever (Bass and Davis 1988, 2002). On reading the recovery literature women are confronted with the twin ideas of the child as sexually innocent and devoid of any sexual desire and the healthy adult woman as sexually knowledgeable, active and desirous. Childhood sexual abuse is believed, in both therapeutic and self-help literature and the popular imagination, to disrupt both of these states and therefore sexual feelings, activity or knowledge in childhood and/or their lack in adulthood can be used as evidence of sexual abuse. This not only allows for the identification of symptoms in the lives of adult women but also introduces the possibility of identifying symptoms or evidence in the lives of children. Armed with this knowledge, women can revisit the time of their childhoods and identify, or reinterpret, symptoms in the lives of their child selves. In addition, by suggesting a traumatic experience is the likely cause of any lack of desire or sexual difficultly, this literature reinforces the popular belief that all women should be sexually desirous – unless they have been victims of some experience from which they need to be healed. From here it is only a short step to arguing that women need to be healed from their lack of desire, an argument that can be found implicitly in much of the recovery literature and other self-help literature. At the same time the idea of the (non abused) child as lacking sexual knowledge and desire is also reinforced, as knowledge and desire are in themselves seen as evidence of sexual abuse which can only be introduced to the child through sexual abuse. The idea that inappropriate thoughts and knowledge must come from without is not limited to children but, like sexual knowledge in children, disturbing sexual imagery or unwholesome thoughts (such as rape fantasies) are defined as problematic and said to have an external origin and as such can be seen as evidence of abuse (Haaken 1998b, 1999, Showalter 1997). Constructing thoughts and images as problematic further reinforces women's 'need' to look for explanations if or when they have such thoughts (Haaken 1999). Although not a central feature in their accounts, the idea that inappropriate sexual activity, in childhood and adulthood, indicated a history of sexual abuse was one the majority of participants touched on. A number of women also identified sexual difficulties in their lives but again their engagement with the recovery literature was not straightforward or uncritical.

Sex in the childhood sexual abuse recovery literature

Childhood sexual abuse is often portrayed as a 'profoundly deforming experience' (Contratto and Gutfreund 1996) and its victims as 'not well adapted to adult life' (Herman 1992:110). There is an expectation that victims of sexual abuse will develop symptoms and their suffering will be long and severe (Lamb 1999) and this enables perceived effects of childhood sexual abuse to be identified in the lives of adult victims. Much of the childhood sexual abuse recovery literature encourages the reader to connect the past with the present, and view the present through the lens of the past (Gavey 2003). When the past is sexually abusive it is seen as central in the development of adult sexual 'problems' (Hacking 1995, Kitzinger 1993, O'Dell 2003, Reavey 2003). The CSA recovery literature also has a tendency to locate both childhood sexual abuse and female sexuality within a liberal discourse of 'choices' (Kitzinger 1993, Reavey 2003) thereby making it easier to identify (sexual) difficulties experienced by survivors as individual (internal) problems, and to render invisible or irrelevant the wider power dynamics and imbalances that inform these 'choices' (Gavey 1993, Haaken 1998b, 1999, O'Dell 1997, Reavey and Warner 2001, Woodiwiss 2005).

Whatever aspect of our lives we attempt to chronicle we cannot escape the influence of currently circulating cultural texts. For the majority of us these texts include magazines, books and literature, film and television, and radio but even those of us do not read self-help literature, whether or not it is aimed at adult victim of sexual abuse, are to some extent informed by the underlying messages that this pervasive literature promotes. When women do read this literature they are therefore likely to have already been introduced to many of these messages. For some women, it was reading aspects of general self-help and self-development literature that led them to believe they were victims of sexual abuse and engage with the CSA recovery literature. Most of this literature includes sections on sex and relationships, and like other sections of the literature, readers were encouraged to identify (sexual) problems in their adult lives. They were shown, through examples, checklists and vignettes a variety of sexual and relationship problems from which they might suffer, from having too much or not enough sex through to problems with intimacy or failure to reach orgasm. One of the most popular self-help texts, *The Courage to Heal* (Bass and Davis 1988, 2002), in addition to a variety of checklists aimed at different aspects of readers lives, included checklists of symptoms relating to sex and perceived sexual difficulties. Not only do the writers of this manual encourage readers to identify these symptoms in their own lives but, as they were identified in the text as evidence of CSA, readers are also encouraged to interpret these symptoms as evidence of their own childhood sexual abuse. As with other checklists employed throughout

The Courage to Heal, the checklist aimed at identifying sexual difficulties involved a series of questions, thereby giving the reader an active role in identifying her own evidence:

- Are you able to stay present when making love?
- Do you go through sex numb or in a state of panic?
- Do you try to use sex to meet needs that aren't sexual?
- Do you find yourself avoiding sex or going after sex you really don't want?
- Can you say no?
- Do you feel your worth is primarily sexual?
- Are you sexual with partners who respect you?
- Have you ever had partners who sexually abused you?
- Do you experience sexual pleasure? Sexual desire?
- Do you think pleasure is bad?
- Are you turned on by violent, sadistic or incestuous fantasies?
- Do you have sex because you want to, or because your partner wants it?
- Have you been a prostitute?
- Or used your sexuality in a way that had elements of exploitation?

(Bass and Davis 1988:37–38)

A similar range of symptoms can be found in other texts aimed at adult victims of CSA. Some of the sexual abuse recovery literature does acknowledge that in contemporary western societies women are bombarded with cultural messages which mean that sex can be problematic and complex for women (Bass and Davis 1988) and that many of the 'symptoms' identified in the recovery literature are associated with women generally (Haaken 1998b, 1999, 2003, Reavey 2003, Showalter 1997, Tavris 1992). However, this is then dismissed as any difficulty is said to be compounded for victims of sexual abuse and it is their reaction to having been abused that is constructed as problematic. Parks (1990), for example, identifies a number of 'problematic sexual experiences' that can be found among formerly abused women:

> Women who cannot be penetrated, women who cannot have an orgasm, women who are not interested in sex at all and women who are not interested in men at all. On the other hand, there are also women who have a great deal of sex without physical satisfaction, women who have orgasms but cannot form a loving relationship,

and women who think they must have sex with every person they go out with in an effort to feel loved and important.

(Parks 1990:143)

Readers are told there are wrong, and by implication right, ways to relate sexually (Haaken 1999, Kitzinger 1993, Woodiwiss 2007b). These messages come at a time when the margins for women between being too sexual and not sexual enough have narrowed to produce 'an even more slippery tight rope for women to walk' (Jackson and Scott 2004:248). The literature promises women a route to a happy and successful sex-life but does so by shifting attention from the cultural messages women are bombarded with to the psychology of the survivor, whilst drawing on those messages to suggest what is appropriate, and what is problematic.

There is a compulsory element implicit in the message of sexual abuse recovery. As Kitzinger (1993) points out, although many sexual abuse recovery texts have a section on sex, they do not have a section on how to maintain celibacy in our sex-obsessed culture. This literature gives a clear message to its readers as to what they should and should not want, in which the reader is encouraged to equate healing and recovery with a healthy sexuality and to see this state as a goal to aim for. It is a goal the reader would already have achieved if only she had not been sexually abused in childhood and as such is seen as a natural state that we should all aspire to. At the same time, like other elements of healing and recovery, the achievement of this healthy and active sexuality, may need hard work and commitment. However, although the reader is told she does not need to do anything she does not want to, she is also told she cannot necessarily wait until she is feeling sexually desirous and is given advice as to how she might arouse her sexual feelings.

There is no place in this literature to acknowledge that our contemporary understanding of healthy sexuality is anything other than natural. There is also no place to recognise that it might not be what all women, sexually abused or not, might want. Readers are told that 'Sexual healing is a beautiful gift a survivor can give herself' (Maltz and Holman 1986:138) and that 'there must be an active attempt to accept sexuality as a good and natural thing – which it is!' (Parks 1990:148). Those who were not sexually active were told they did not need to fully develop their sexuality immediately and should 'allow yourself the freedom to do only what feels good' (Bass and Davis 1988:243). However, they were also advised that at some point they would be ready and warned that they 'can't simply say no every time' (Bass and Davis 1988:250). In what is claimed to be a liberating approach which helps to make sex more accessible, Bass and Davis encourage their readers to begin sexual activity 'even if you're not feeling physical longing, emotional excitement or desire of any kind' (Bass and Davis 1988:254). To help them get started women are encouraged to use a vibrator, especially if they have not used one before and (somewhat alarmingly!) to 'try a little teenage sex' (Bass and Davis 1988:250). No longer told they 'owe it to their man' women are now told they 'owe it to themselves'. Women are also encouraged to write to their 'inner child' telling them 'what the correct attitude is and how to adopt it' including such advice as 'sex is good. It really is' (Parks 1990:144–145). Not only are the readers of this literature encouraged to engage in sexual practices they might not want or enjoy but, as Kitzinger (1993) observed, we can also see similarities between the messages found in this literature and the grooming practices undertaken by some paedophiles. There is also no place in the literature to acknowledge either why some women might not want to be sexual, or why they might not want to be sexual with men. As such it also fails to recognise the implicit message/s it promotes – that women can only be 'real women' if they are sexually active, itself a dangerously short step to measuring women on their (visible) sexuality.

The majority of the CSA recovery literature is not specifically heterosexual, but claims instead to be gender neutral, and operates on the understanding that gender is irrelevant to women's (and men's) sexuality, sexual desire and sexual activity. Many advice manuals do not mention the gender of a woman's partner and some do include a section on lesbian sex. Instead, as Kitzinger argues (1993), they present a gender-neutral analysis of sexual violence which fails to acknowledge different socio-political and personal meanings between lesbian sex and sex with men and assume there is nothing about childhood sexual abuse that might have implications for women's relationships with men. This literature fails to recognise some of the lessons (female) child victims might have learnt about sex and sex with men, and therefore why they might choose a life without sex. Instead such a life is, within the context of sexual abuse recovery, constructed as unhealthy, barren and unnatural – a symptom of childhood sexual abuse and a sign of their need to heal. The recovery literature does recognise women's vulnerabilities but within a context that promotes the idea of liberation, choice and women's agency (Kitzinger 1993, Reavey 2003, Woodiwiss 2008). Reinforcing rather than challenging cultural pressures on women to behave as sexual beings, much of the literature holds up the achievement of an intimate sexuality as a measure of women's recovery from childhood sexual abuse and therefore as a goal to be achieved or aimed at. There is, as Bass and Davis cajole, 'no finish, no goal except intimacy, honesty and pleasure' (Bass and Davis 1988:248). Within the context of healing and recovery the survivor is not only expected eventually to embark on a happy and fulfilling sexual relationship but she is also held responsible if a sexual relationship does not measure up. Failure is seen as evidence of ongoing damage and her failure to heal. The message of compulsory sexuality, within which they should be sexual active and desirous as well as responsible for any failings, is one that female readers of this literature take on board.

Cultural understandings about women and sex, and the effects of childhood sexual abuse on women's 'healthy sexuality' are not simply reflected in women's sexual abuse narratives. Rather, women draw on these understandings and the narrative frameworks of the harm story and the healing discourse in order to identify themselves as victims and construct their own narratives, which not only make sense of their lives but also offer them guides to living, which may or may not include a sexual element. A sexual abuse storyline might provide some women with an explanation of, and therefore way to address sexual difficulties they experience. However, it can also encourage women to reinterpret their lives and identify sexual difficulties that they were previously unaware of, or that they had not previously interpreted as difficulties or as problematic, and as a result of a perceived failure to heal, to see themselves as the cause of any such difficulties. Although often used to identify problems that need to be addressed it is worth noting that women can also use such a story line to avoid or excuse a sexual relationship that they do not want. However, they must still construct themselves as damaged in some way and maintain this identity for the time they wish to avoid a sexual relationship. The sexual abuse story may provide an escape from sexuality for some women but it does so at some cost to their sense of self and their position as healthy adult women.

Some of those who tell stories of CSA draw on those readily circulating storylines which encompass ideas and cultural understandings not only about childhood sexual abuse and its consequences but also contemporary constructions of what it means to be a healthy adult. However, it is also possible to base a childhood sexual abuse narrative solely on a belief in the idea of childhood sexual innocence and / or a link between childhood sexual abuse and problems with sex in adulthood. In other words some women's stories of having been sexually abused as children are based entirely on what is seen as healthy and appropriate sexual activity in adults and a lack of sexuality in children, and how they fit within this understanding. This was the basis for the stories told by a number of women whose accounts are featured in this book such as Beccy:

> I just had a problem with sex and I didn't know where it came from.
> (Beccy)

Whilst I am not suggesting that they were not sexually abused as children I am pointing out that without such understandings they would not have been able to identify themselves as victims of childhood sexual abuse or tell of having been sexually abused in childhood. As Beccy reflects on reading Blume's *Secret Survivors* (1990):

> When I read it I still didn't have any memories then but I went yes, I mean if that's what happened that would explain it so much.
> (Beccy)

This proved to be an adequate explanation for Beccy and fitted with what she identified as problematic in her life and offered a way to overcome these difficulties, but we should remember that it is not the only explanation for how she feels about sex and her own sexual narrative. It is perhaps simply the one that is most readily available and culturally acceptable.

Childhood and sexual innocence

In contemporary western societies childhood is often constructed as a time of sexual innocence with children seen as asexual beings (Green 2001, Jackson 1982, 1996a) who need to be shielded from sexual knowledge (Evans 1994), and sexual abuse of children is often viewed as a violation, not just of an individual, but of (a) childhood (Kitzinger 1997). Both childhood (Jackson 1996b) and child sexual abuse (Burman 1995, Jackson 1996b) are also gendered and therefore, not only is sexual abuse in childhood experienced differently by girls and boys but how we respond to children and to sexual abuse is to some extent mediated by the gender of (and what we think that says about) the child or victim. As we saw in the previous chapter the consequences of sexual abuse is in important respects seen to be very different for girls and boys.

The idea that children are or should be innocent and that childhood is a time of innocence, particularly sexual innocence, is a central theme underpinning much of the CSA recovery literature (Kitzinger 1997). This also represented a significant story line for a number of the women in this study, as they were able to return to their childhoods and identify or reinterpret 'symptoms' as evidence of CSA in their own childhoods. The majority of women whose stories are featured here had no memories of sexual abuse and therefore an abusive childhood was reconstructed through the identification of symptoms in their adult lives. However, a number of women were also able to revisit their childhoods, and in doing so were able to identify or explain sexual or other behaviours which they believed to be wrong, inappropriate or in some other way problematic. For some this represented a significant piece of information without which their sexual abuse stories would not have carried the same weight.

Rae remembered a particular act that she had engaged in as a child. She recounted a single incident from her childhood in which, whilst having a bath, she had 'removed faeces' from herself and placed it under the bath. This was an act that she had come to see as problematic and, with no satisfactory explanation, she looked to the recovery literature which enabled her to make a connection between this behaviour and the sexual abuse she believed she experienced as a child. On revisiting her childhood this was an act which Rae thought both strange and problematic and for which, as a child, she had had no explanation. In adulthood, and with the help of a sexual abuse narrative, Rae had been able to explain this problematic childhood behaviour and in doing so, she added support to a sexual abuse narrative that was based entirely on a correlation of perceived symptoms with abuse. It was her familiarity with contemporary understandings of sexual abuse and its consequences, both in children and adults, that had enabled Rae to link a childhood act with sexual abuse and thereby explain why she behaved as she did:

> I do wonder why I did that ... so that was another thing that added to me thinking that I had been abused.
>
> (Rae)

This knowledge enabled to Rae to construct herself as a victim of childhood sexual abuse and although she did ultimately reject that part of her sexual abuse story that named her father as the abuser, her knowledge of sexual abuse enabled her to remain open to the possibility that she had been sexually abused by someone other than her father. This in turn enabled her to maintain the identity of victim and left intact her explanation for problematic childhood behaviour.

An understanding of the child as sexually innocent together with a view of what was appropriate and inappropriate for children also informed Fiona's life story. Like Rae, Fiona also revisited her childhood and identified behaviour that she engaged with as a child that she felt was problematic and shameful. Armed with a contemporary understanding of CSA and childhood innocence, Fiona not only found evidence that she had been sexually abused as a child and which explained why she felt different, but she used the messages found in the recovery literature to feel better about her child self:

> It made sense of why I felt the way I felt... I kept things hidden and I was ashamed of things like I used to masturbate a lot when I was very very young and when I was at primary school.
>
> (Fiona)

This literature proved invaluable to Fiona who used it to reinterpret what she perceived to be problematic childhood behaviour. Fiona's new story enabled her to overcome the shame she felt for her child self. However, it was the definition of childhood as a time of sexual innocence, and the 'normal' child as one lacking any form of sexual knowledge or feelings promoted in this literature, that helped to construct the behaviour of Fiona, together with other children who may in some way be sexually active or knowledgeable, as both problematic and shameful. Much of this literature, supported by contemporary understandings of children, childhood innocence and sexual abuse, fails to acknowledge that 'normal' (non-abused) children are or can be sexual and might engage in sexual activities, such as masturbation and touching themselves in a sexual way and eliciting sexual feelings or sexual pleasure. Therefore when such behaviour is identified it can often only be recognised as originating from an external source, and therefore seen as evidence of sexual abuse (Kitzinger 1997, Woodiwiss 2007b). It was such an understanding that Fiona, and to a lesser extent Rae, drew on to construct their own stories of childhood sexual abuse. An alternative construction of childhood, which accommodates children's sexuality and allows for the possibility of sexual activity, at least when viewed from an adult perspective (Gagnon and Simon 1974, Jackson 1982, 1996a), would not define this behaviour as problematic and in need of explanation, would not need us to look for an external source for the emergence of sexual feelings in children, and sexual activity in children would not inevitably be seen as evidence of sexual abuse (Jackson 1996b, Kitzinger 1997).

Whilst it is clear that the idea of the normal, healthy child as sexually innocent can be used to support a sexual abuse narrative, reinterpret childhood sexual behaviour as evidence of sexual abuse, and overcome feelings that might otherwise be experienced as shameful, there were those who found it both unhelpful and potentially dangerous. Not all those who engaged with contemporary discourses around childhood sexual abuse or read the recovery literature accepted or found the (western) construction of childhood as a state of innocence to be realistic or helpful. For some such a construction of childhood was deeply problematic, particularly during a childhood that was experienced as sexually abusive, and may even have contributed to their ongoing sexual abuse. It may in retrospect have enabled some women to overcome feelings of guilt and shame for sexual feelings experienced or acted upon in childhood but for others, particularly at the time of their abuse, it may have contributed to their feelings of guilt and shame. This in turn may have contributed to their abuse as it lead them to believe that there were no longer children and therefore anything sexual that was done to them was no longer abuse. Sexual abuse is often said to rob children of their childhood or their innocence but the very idea of childhood innocence may rob some children of their ability to see themselves as wronged and potentially defend themselves against further abuse. Jay was a victim of years of abuse throughout her childhood, much of it sexual, perpetrated by a number of men:

> I was a woman in my granda's bed from three years old and I got swapped for being my stepfathers' mistress and my stepbrother's mistress and then the other rapes and abuse went on around it.
>
> (Jay)

Jay was acutely aware of the problems inherent in constructing the 'normal' child as sexually innocent both for the abused child at the time of the abuse, and later for the adult dealing with the aftermath of abuse. The message Jay received from the recovery literature suggested to her that as a child she was or should have been (sexually) innocent. However, when Jay revisited the period of her abuse she did not believe she was returning to a time of innocence or even to a time of childhood:

> I didn't feel I was a child and I think that's part of why I couldn't accept it as abuse.
>
> (Jay)

Jay had not felt like a child when she was abused and found the idea of childhood innocence unhelpful as it was this idea that helped to distance her from (innocent) childhood and therefore also distance her sexual experiences from (child) sexual abuse. However, the idea of childhood innocence did form the background against which she interpreted her childhood experiences, both at the time and later in adulthood. It was her understanding of childhood sexual innocence that prevented her identifying herself as a child, and therefore seeing her experiences as sexual abuse.

The sexual abuse recovery literature writes of childhood as if it were a natural category and, although there is 'no benchmark of undisputed truth' to tell us the difference between the child and the adult (Stainton Rogers 2001), much of this literature is written as if there were. As sexuality is central in maintaining the boundary between childhood and adulthood (Burman 1995), it takes on added significance within the context of sexual abuse. Sexual abuse more than other forms of child abuse is said to disrupt the child's natural development to adulthood but it can also obscure the transition (Woodiwiss 2007b). As Jay's account shows, at the same time as abuse is defined as sexual it can mark the transition to adult status and therefore not only can it be defined by some (both abusers and victims) as not abusive, but the abused child can then be constructed as no longer innocent and deserving of protection (both in the mind of the abuser and in the mind of the abused), and is therefore vulnerable to further abuse (Davies 1995, Green 2001, Kitzinger 1997, Sgroi 1982, Summit and Kryso 1978). Not only is the dominant western construction of childhood as a time of sexual innocence problematic for the child who is sexually abused (and no longer innocent) but maintaining this idea of sexual innocence through secrecy and withholding of sexual knowledge and education may itself leave children vulnerable to sexual abuse (Callery 1998, Green 2001, Jackson 1996b, Kitzinger 1997). Abusers can use secrecy and children's lack of sexual knowledge to manipulate, abuse, and silence children (Green 2001). In addition, as innocence has become sexualised (Jackson 1996b), children's sexual innocence and purity can itself be seen as sexually attractive or fetishized (Green 2001, Kitzinger 1997). Although it does not feature in the sexual abuse recovery literature read by those who participated in this study there is some movement towards recognising that some sexual activities engaged in by children, such as masturbation and sexual play, are not only harmless but possibly also 'natural', even if they are discouraged (Stainton Rogers and Stainton Rogers 1999).

The adult woman: Identifying problems and learning to be sexual

Whereas sexual knowledge and desire is used to identify the sexually abused child, it is a lack of sexual knowledge and desire that is used to identify the formerly abused woman. In both professional and popular discourses, talk about sexually abused women is often based on an assumption that those who have not been sexually abused have been allowed to progress along a 'normal' developmental path to a healthy sexuality, whilst those who were sexually abused are believed to have had this developmental path blocked. Past abuse can therefore be used to explain a failure to adhere to a normative sexuality (Reavey 2003) and failure to adhere to a normative sexuality seen as evidence of past sexual abuse. This is an understanding that enables women who have no memories of childhood sexual abuse but who have, or come to redefine themselves as having, a problematic relationship with sex, or who do not conform to a particular version of healthy sexuality, to construct a sexual abused narrative. Such a relationship with sex can also be used to support or reinforce a sexual abuse narrative, and might be particularly useful to those whose story is based on a correlation of symptoms rather than concrete memories. It can of course also be used by those who have a problematic relationship with sex or who identify sexual difficulties in their lives to alleviate pressure on them to have sex or as a way to address any sexual difficulties they have identified. However they came to the sexual abuse recovery literature women were presented with a clear message regarding sex and the sexual abuse victim:

> They said in the book that you know, sex is not an enjoyable experience for someone who has been abused in that way at an early age.
>
> (Tracey)

Women in contemporary society are constantly bombarded with messages around sex and sexuality, and the dominant understandings of what it means to be a normal, healthy, and therefore sexually active and desirous, woman. Therefore, the majority of women, when they engaged with the CSA recovery literature were to some extent aware of the pressures on them to conform to a particular ideal. This literature provided them with some alternatives should they choose to follow a different path and not to conform to this sexual ideal. Sexual difficulties, including a lack of interest in sex, was a theme which permeated many of the accounts featured in this book, although for most of the women it was not identified as a major issue and came to the surface only occasionally. Where women did engage with discourses around sex and sexuality this was complex and reflected not only their need to make sense of their lives up to and including the present but also their need or wish to negotiate a future which they may or may not wish to include sexual relationships.

For some, although they did not dwell on their lack of interest in sex, it was this which contributed to their coming to 'know' they had been sexually abused:

> Because I had no interest in sex and that to me was the reason why I was not interested in sex.
>
> (Hazel)

> I thought well maybe that's what it is, I've been raped at some stage and just blocked it out or you know something has happened. Because I was very, I wouldn't let anybody really touch me at all.
>
> (Pat)

Pat and Hazel were among those who had believed themselves to be victims of sexual abuse but had since identified themselves as victims of false memory syndrome. Whilst they rejected the idea that they were abused by their fathers, the idea that they had been sexually abused as children did continue to make sense to them and so, whilst claiming the identity of a FMS victim, they also maintained their identities as victims of childhood sexual abuse. The basis of the beliefs on which their sexual abuse stories were founded came from a correlation of symptoms of which a lack of interest in sex, although less prominent, was hugely significant. Without this particular 'symptom' the stories told by Hazel and Pat would have carried less weight and one might argue they may have come to reject them sooner or ultimately more completely than they had done. Pat also recognised that she imposed contemporary attitudes about sex and sexual abuse onto her past without which her lack of interest or engagement in sexual activities might not be considered evidence of abuse:

> Even when I had boyfriends I wouldn't go near them or...have a sexual relationship with anybody...that was quite normal.
>
> (Pat)

Pat used a contemporary view of sex to interpret a past lack of interest in sex and an unwillingness to have a sexual relationship as evidence of a problem but, as she did later acknowledge, at the time she was a young woman this would not have been seen as problematic or indicative of sexual abuse.

Some women used perceived sexual problems to identify and or support a history of childhood sexual abuse, but for others the literature helped them to construct a story that would not only help to explain sexual difficulties experienced in adulthood but more importantly would, they hoped, help them overcome those difficulties. As such these stories were as much guides to living, as they were accounts of a life. Tracey had identified sex and relationships as a problematic area of her life and one that she wanted to address. Whilst she had tried to deal with these issues before, she had not been successful. It was when she engaged with the recovery literature and saw therapist who specialised in adult victims of CSA, that Tracey heard an explanation that not only made sense to her but which she believed would help her overcome her difficulties. Tracey believed her new therapist when he told her:

> You've got a reason anyway why you're blocked, maybe if you weren't blocked you wouldn't be a virgin you would be enjoying a sex life.
>
> (Tracey)

This advice can be reassuring as it provided women with a reason for sexual difficulties they might experience. Although it helped to construct them as the problem, by identifying a 'block' or area to be worked on, it also offered women the possibility of a happy and fulfilling sex life.

The women whose stories feature in this book all drew to varying degrees on discourses, found in a range of popular, cultural texts, which promoted the idea that the healthy, adult woman should adhere to a particular construction of female sexuality. When they engaged with discourses around child sexual abuse they were therefore often tapping into ideas already familiar to them. Some used the literature to explain or excuse a lack of interest in sex whilst for others the problem in need of explanation was the amount of sexual activity they engaged in or their reasons for doing so. As the healthy adult woman is expected to desire the right amount of sex and for the right reasons, readers of the CSA recovery literature were given the message that those who engage in too much sexual activity are unhealthy, or psychologically damaged, and said to confuse sex and love. Among those who were sexually abused as children there may be:

> Women who are not interested in sex at all...women who have a great deal of sex without physical satisfaction, women who have orgasms but cannot form a loving relationship, and women who think they must have sex with every person they go out with in an effort to feel loved and important.
>
> (Parks 1990:143)

The idea that victims of childhood sexual abuse engage in excessive sexual activity was a message taken up by Jenny and Sarah. Not only did they identify the amount of sexual activity as problematic and evidence of sexual abuse, but they also, in keeping with much of the advice found in self-help and CSA recovery literature, both focussed on identifying aspects of themselves as problematic rather than identifying problems with their sexual partners or those with whom they had an intimate relationship:

> I hadn't had a boyfriend for a year and fell obsessively in love over and over again, a kind of love and sex addiction with no real intimacy.
>
> (Jenny)

> Then I was having a rough time in a relationship and the only way I could relate to anything at the time was on a sexual basis.
>
> (Sarah)

The circumstances and life choices that Jenny and Sarah sought to address were very different from those who identified a lack of sex or sexual difficulties as the problem. Both women were involved in relationships, or types of relationships, they were unhappy with:

> At the same time a longing for love and attention got mixed up with sex and led me into repetitive short-term affairs that never developed into the relationship I craved.
>
> (Jenny)

The literature offered an explanation for such unsatisfactory relationships, together with the possibility of finding or building the kind of relationships readers wanted. However, the focus is on the largely female readers who were held responsible, not their partners who were rendered invisible. Failure to recognise external factors not only puts women under additional pressure to engage in sexual relationships but also puts them under pressure to make sure those relationships are healthy and fulfilling.

Jay also learnt from the literature that her use of sex as a tool to help her negotiate other aspects of her life was wrong. However, unlike Jenny and Sarah, Jay did eventually reject this message:

> I'd have sex just to placate him... I just found I was having sex for all the wrong reasons... I realise I use sex as a tool erm, it's just very rarely I'll have sex because I feel affectionate and loving and just want to make love. It made me really concerned about it for a while and now I've decided that basically if that's how I am, that's how I am and I just live with it rather than worrying about it... and creating more problems.
>
> (Jay)

Jay acknowledged that her attitude to sex could be considered problematic but she also recognised that identifying it as such could create additional problems and she was ultimately able to reject the construction of herself as the problem. Others were unable to reject such a negative construction and believed the source of any sexual difficulties lay with themselves, albeit as a result of sexual abuse in childhood. As one woman observed:

> It made me more precocious, more insular, promiscuous, frigid... unloving and unloved.
>
> (Frances)

For some women, it was the identification of sexual difficulties that first led them to engage with self-help literature and therapy. Tracey's first experience of therapy was related to what she identified as a sexual problem.

> The first therapy I went to was a couple of years ago before I met Mike and erm that was talking to someone about sexuality because I wasn't comfortable with that as well, sex and it just wasn't... you know if I wanted to lose my virginity I didn't feel comfortable because I had been tampered with.
>
> (Tracey)

Tracey had continuous memories of sexual abuse and identified a clear link between her sexual difficulties and the abuse she remembered from her childhood. For others, it was through identifying sexual problems that they came to believe they had been sexually abused in childhood and it was these difficulties that represented their most convincing, and for some only, 'evidence' for that abuse. However, this was not an easy or straightforward conclusion to draw. It could take some time and was reached because it represented an explanation for adult difficulties. It also offered some women a way to address those difficulties:

> I didn't know the source of the problem then I just had a problem with sex and I didn't know where it came from, I didn't have a clue.
>
> (Beccy)

Beccy did eventually attribute her sexual problems to sexual abuse, but they were also the only evidence she had of having been sexually abused. Beccy had identified difficulties for herself, but for some women the idea that they were sexually damaged was an idea introduced to them by others. In Fiona's case it was her boyfriend:

> He feels as if it's a barrier and as if it's like a thing that's broken and it's unfortunate that that thing doesn't work properly. That our sexual intimacy, my sexuality is kind of damaged. It's not whole it's been damaged by what happened.
>
> (Fiona)

Whatever sexual difficulties Fiona and her boyfriend were having, it is clear that he identified Fiona, and not himself, as the cause of those difficulties and this was an understanding she found reinforced in the literature. It was also an understanding available to her partner and which he could not only use to interpret any sexual difficulties they were having as Fiona's fault, but one that he could draw on to support any previously held views that she was at fault for any difficulties they might have experienced in their relationship, including any occasional lack of interest, and thereby hold her responsible for maintaining a healthy and active sexual relationship.

Having alerted the reader to possible difficulties, the literature does offer them a way to become fully functioning sexual beings. Whilst this did encourage some to look for examples of sexual problems in their own lives, or redefine as problematic, experiences or practices they were previously happy or content with, it also helped others to explain and tackle symptoms they had already identified as problematic or wanted to address:

> They said in the book that you know, sex is not an enjoyable experience for someone who has been abused in that way at an early age and they don't have, orgasmic, you get an orgasm from yourself but you don't get it so much from someone else. And I had that you know.
>
> (Tracey)

In a culture that defines healthy womanhood in terms of sexuality and measures women according to their relationship with their sexuality, such explanations for why they don't measure up are invaluable to many of those who are made to feel inadequate, unwomanly or in some other way a failure. The healthy woman as sexual being is a message women receive from the CSA recovery literature but it is also a message they are bombarded with in their everyday lives. Sexual abuse may be more about power and control than it is about sex, but the consequences are often measured in terms of women's sexuality. It is therefore easy to construct a sexual abuse narrative based purely on how one measures up on a scale of sexual activity, pleasure and desire.

Identifying problems and failures was not the only purpose or function of the literature which included suggestions for how women might overcome these problems. It was as a way to access solutions to sexual problems, sometimes ones they had already identified, that women might engage with this literature:

> There was a book on sexual, sexual genitals and how to relax them and how to feel safe with them. I used them you know, relaxing the abdominal muscles and diaphragm and just doing breathing exercises and just you know, walking naked in the flat and just feeling comfortable. Looking at yourself in the mirror and going, you're beautiful and just looking at yourself.
>
> (Tracey)

Tracey may have been encouraged to see herself as damaged but at the same time she followed advice that helped her to feel more comfortable in and happy with her own body. As guides to living women's sexual abuse stories were as important to the area of sexuality as they were to other aspects of their lives. Whilst some women used the literature to help them develop a fuller, more active sexuality, for others it offered the possibility to negotiate something very different. Hazel initially believed her memories of sexual abuse, uncovered during hypnotherapy, because they made sense to her, but over time she learnt that a biography of sexual abuse also offered her a way to avoid the pressures to conform to contemporary construction of the modern healthy woman. Hazel first went to hypnotherapy because she was having difficulty losing weight but she was also disinterested or disliked sex. A history of sexual abuse offered Hazel a plausible explanation for both of these problems but she did not simply accept the explanations and solutions put forward in the CSA recovery literature. She was aware of the cultural pressures on women to conform to a particular stereotype of healthy womanhood, whether or not it was framed within a rights discourse, but she was also aware of some competing discourses available to her if she wanted to resist conforming to this stereotype. She was therefore able to recognise different reasons for why she, and therefore also others, might choose to identify themselves as victims of sexual abuse. Of these competing discourses one, which identified hormones as a possible cause, offered Hazel a physical explanation and solution whilst another, which identified sexual abuse in childhood as a possible cause, offered her an emotional explanation and solution. Whatever the cause of her difficulties (if indeed she had any beyond the pressure to conform), Hazel recognised that her narrative, which also served as a guide to living, did not necessarily reflect childhood experiences':

> It could be my hormones; it could be anything couldn't it?
>
> (Hazel)

> I really do not know... Whether it's an excuse to... because my sexual life is horrendous and whether that's, I don't know. I don't know whether that's sort of an excuse if you like.
>
> (Hazel)

A third, much harder (feminist) discourse for Hazel to follow, suggested that she should be able to choose whether or not to engage in a sexual relationship.

> It's everybody to their own, there's too much pressure on us. Far too much pressure on us, you should do it when you feel like it not because you have to do it and that's how it should be.
>
> (Hazel)

The discourses available to women who, like Hazel, wished to negotiate a life without sex, are not without problems. They, like Hazel, must negotiate their own path and whilst we could argue that a sexual abuse narrative is not ideal, it does represent for many women the best available option in a culture where they do not feel able to assert their wishes. Hazel believed women should only engage in sexual activities if and when they wanted to, but she found this contradicted by the norm of the healthy adult woman as sexually active. A hormonal/medical discourse and a sexual abuse discourse both offered Hazel a way to negotiate a life which avoided sexual activity, but maintained a loving relationship with her husband. It would seem that for Hazel a sexual abuse narrative offered the best way for her to be able to maintain an asexual relationship with her husband but it did involve constructing herself as a victim of sexual abuse and accepting the possibility that she had been abused by her father. At the time of this research she had not fully rejected either, but believed she might have been abused by someone other than her father. To do so Hazel had rejected her earlier narrative and rewritten her life story within an alternative narrative framework of FMS. This new story enabled her to maintain a positive image of her father whilst also claiming the 'benefits' of a sexual abuse life story, including a way to avoid sex. However this was a narrative she was not entirely happy with.

In contrast, both Tracey and Beccy wanted to develop or improve a sexual aspect of their relationships and were happy or willing to accept that a history of childhood sexual abuse was the cause of their present difficulties. It was important for them to be able to identify a cause, as this would in turn enable them to find a solution. Neither saw the literature as simply providing an explanation but importantly both also saw it as offering a way forward:

> So the self-help books really helped with that because they show you what, people who have been sexually abused, these could be the symptoms and what you could do.
>
> (Tracey)

Although they accepted the construction of themselves as psychologically damaged they were engaged with an aspect of the literature they believed would help them improve certain aspects of their lives. Both women had read widely in the area of self-help and self-improvement and previously been involved in therapy specifically to address sexual problems. It may be that, out of the currently available options, the childhood sexual abuse recovery literature also offered them the best way to achieve their goals.

Alternative readings

Many of the women whose accounts are featured in this book drew on the CSA recovery literature to explain, excuse, or negotiate their own sexuality, but some of their accounts also included experiences which could be read differently. It is interesting that these women chose the particular interpretations that they did. Alternative possibilities were particularly noticeable in the accounts of those who had continuous memories of abusive childhoods. Tracey, for example, connected her sexual difficulties with having been sexually abused in childhood but her account included references to her mother which provide the foundations for a different explanation for any sexual difficulties she might experience in adulthood:

> I wasn't educated properly in these things I wasn't at all. And no one ever talked about it in the household and my mum just put me right off at the beginning, she put me off when I was about 18 when I first approached her and asked if she could talk to me about sex and stuff. She went oh no sex is horrible; it's like a knife going through inside you... Afterwards those words followed and followed until I was 21.
>
> (Tracey)

Tracey presented a dramatic image of her 'sexual education' but for others their lessons were more by way of example. Emma also accepted the link made in the CSA recovery literature between adult difficulties and childhood sexual abuse when she identified herself as:

> Emotionally retarded when it comes to relationships with the opposite sex.
>
> (Emma)

However her account also introduced an alternative explanation:

> I am single and have been for a long time and I can't imagine that I'll ever be happily married. I think that's because my parents' marriage was a sham.
>
> (Emma)

Jay also had unbroken memories of a childhood and adolescence in which she was sexually abused. Perhaps more significantly she also remembered how she negotiated the power imbalance of those abusive relationships and the lessons she learnt and brought with her to adulthood:

> Saying 'No' didn't work, but if I co-operated...So if I don't fight I don't get hurt. If I feel pressurised sexually and I feel it is a real threat then it's like a different side of me comes out. Then it's a bit like well, what's the best way to manage it, what's the best way to try and keep myself safe and that's, as I say I suppose 'No' never worked.
>
> (Jay)

An important lesson learnt by Jay was that resistance to sexual assault could be dangerous and submission, at times, the safest option. Jay recognised the knowledge she gained during childhood had at times helped to keep her safe, but she did see another side to that experience. Whilst she drew on this knowledge both she and her partner also identified a problem she sometimes has with men and with sex, which they both linked to her childhood experiences:

> I don't have a lot of confidence and that can come out in different ways. I'll chatter or I can be flirtations and various bits and pieces but Simon says I can give very mixed signals but I think that people should still check. And he doesn't feel that I'm particularly safe on my own either. Because he says men will interpret them the way they want and most men won't care and he feels I have an inability to say no if I'm in a pressured situation.
>
> (Jay)

Although Jay engaged critically with the literature, here she accepted her problem with men was largely of her own making and in doing so she rendered these men and their actions irrelevant. She may have redirected some attention onto them when she suggested they 'should still check' but ultimately dismissed their attitudes and behaviour and held herself to blame.

A sexuality of one's own

In a (Western) world increasingly informed by therapeutic discourses, childhood is constructed as a time of sexual innocence, at the same time as we are led to believe that we can and should (and have the right to) live better, brighter, happier, more fulfilling, satisfying and successful (sexual) lives. This has enabled a lack of childhood sexual innocence or a lack of sexual knowledge and desire in adulthood to be identified as evidence of childhood sexual abuse but, as I have shown, there are a number of problems with using sexual activity in this way. It denies children's sexuality and constructs children who do not conform to childhood sexual innocence (whether they are victims of sexual abuse or children beginning to explore their own sexuality) as problematic. It also constructs as problematic, women who 'deviate' from what (drawing on Rich 1980) I have called 'compulsory sexuality', and thereby puts pressure on all women to adhere to the norm of a healthy, and therefore sexually active womanhood, a message they are continually bombarded with throughout their everyday lives.

Whatever messages they took from the child sexual abuse recovery literature, women did not engage with it uncritically. Women used this literature to achieve an active and fulfilling sex life, either with a partner or by themselves, to explain 'excessive' sexual activity or a lack of interest, or to excuse them from sexual relationships. It was also used by some to maintain a positive self-image, within which problematic or difficult sexual thoughts and/or behaviours (both in childhood and adulthood) were explained with reference to childhood experiences for which they were not to blame. However, using sex as a measure of well-being, and deviation as evidence of childhood sexual abuse, also encourages those with no memories to identify themselves as victims, when other stories might better explain, and potentially improve, their situation. The stories told by the women who participated in this study did not simply reflect the cultural understanding of what childhood sexual abuse does to healthy sexuality. Rather, they drew on this understanding to construct their own narratives, at time when deviation from a sexual norm, dissatisfaction and lack of interest are themselves seen as both problematic and in need of explanation.

In a society where sex carries such weight it is possible to construct a sexual abuse narrative following the identification of 'sexual problems', even where such problems do not feature strongly in ones life. Sex did not feature strongly in most women's accounts and the majority did not talk about sex in much depth, but for some, identifying 'sexual problems' even though they did not feature greatly in their lives, was the only evidence, or alternative memory, they had for believing they were victims of sexual abuse in childhood. Even for others it was often seen as an important clue. In the short term the CSA recovery literature may represent the best available framework within which women can negotiate their own sexuality – whether or not they were sexually abused as children. However, we should not force women into 'compulsory sexuality', either as a measure of well-being and conformity to the norms of womanhood, or as an indication of their healing and recovery. Instead we should be looking to create a space and a language where women are really free to make their own choices and negotiate the conditions and experiences of their own lives which might, but equally might not, include intimate relationships and/or sex – whether or not they were sexually abused as children.

11
A Role for the Storytellers

> *Narratives of the self don't simply rest within us to motivate and guide our actions, nor do they lurk behind our backs as social templates to stamp us into selves according to the leading stories of the day.*
>
> (Holstein and Gubrium 2000:3)

To say that women construct and reconstruct stories which feature childhood sexual abuse as an organising principle is not to argue that they are creating works of fiction but to indicate the degree of choice they have and are able to exercise in constructing life stories that not only make sense of their lives but might also act as guides for living. The current orthodoxy on childhood sexual abuse constructs victims as inevitably damaged and in need of healing and this has allowed women's unhappiness and dissatisfaction to be reinterpreted as evidence of abuse and 'symptoms' of abuse to be identified in the lives of adult women. It is these 'alternative memories' that form the basis of many women's sexual abuse narratives and this book has attempted to explore the active role some women play in constructing their own biographies, based on such memories, in the process of making sense of their lives. They may have been constrained by stories that can be told and the narrative frameworks available to them (Bauman 2001, Gergen 1994, Plummer 1995, 2001) but they were nonetheless actively engaged in constructing their own stories – stories which owe more to our contemporary storying of childhood sexual abuse and those narrative frameworks currently in circulation than they do to the recovery of memories.

The women whose stories feature in this book engaged with the sexual abuse recovery literature because they were unhappy with at least some aspect of their lives and were looking to fashion better ones. The literature aimed at adult victims of childhood sexual abuse offered them a way to make sense of those lives that also offered the promise of empowerment (Showalter 1997). Women were able to construct their own narratives, organised around a framework of childhood sexual abuse because, contrary to popular perceptions, recovered memories are not about concrete or recall memories of sexual abuse. The recovered memory wars may be constructed as a debate over the 'truth' or 'falsity' of previously unknown or buried memories but the recovered memories on which the majority of sexual abuse narratives are based are unlikely to be concrete or recall memories as it is in fact rare for such memories to be recovered (Bass and Davis 1988). This is illustrated by the stories shared by women in this book, only one of whom recovered recall memories. On reading the recovery literature they were presented with checklists of symptoms that could apply to most women at some time in their lives (Haaken 1999, Showalter 1997, Tavris 1992) and which suggest to them what is appropriate and what is inappropriate in terms of thoughts, feelings and behaviours, both in adulthood and in childhood. The majority of women who shared their stories, including those who later retracted as false the memories on which those stories were founded, did not remember 'memories of abuse' but rather they made sense of their lives through a correlation of these perceived symptoms with assumed past abuse. They might have been helped in this process by therapists or the sexual abuse recovery literature but the stories they told were very much theirs.

Not all were the first author of their story but they were able to construct or embellish on a sexual abuse narrative because it made sense, it helped to explain unhappiness, and it offered a solution. For most of the women, constructing their stories did not involve abandoning an old story in favour of a new one but rather a reworking of their biographies to include a sexually abusive childhood, for which they were able to identify evidence in their adult lives and in doing so maintain or establish a connection with a past childhood and a life already lived. Women who were not the first author of their story were also able to maintain a belief in this story if they could establish some continuity between their childhood and adult lives. This was easier for those who maintained a belief in at least some aspect of their sexual abuse narrative. Of the five women who rewrote their biographies drawing on a framework of FMS, three did maintain some belief that they were sexually abused as children, albeit probably not by the fathers they once thought guilty. Importantly, they were able to tell the stories they did because they each found a way to make sense of their lives and their experiences that also enabled them to maintain a positive image of an important figure in their lives. Had such a framework been unavailable to them they may not have rejected their memories. Only two women rejected completely the sexual abuse narratives they once told and for them their narratives, also based on FMS, represented a break from the past: not so much a reworking of their life history as a rewriting of it. Neither woman gave up the identity of victim, but rather swapped the nature of their victimhood, and used FMS to rewrite the recent past, but it was not a story that connected them to a past that predated their sexual abuse narratives. Unlike the sexual abuse narratives told by the majority of women, theirs was not a story with a happy ending: knowing they had not been abused had not been a positive experience.

The inner child is a central character in much of the recovered memory and childhood sexual abuse recovery literature, and it is she who is said to hold the key to both knowledge and healing, but the women who shared their stories here did not engage with this concept uncritically. For the majority of those whose narratives were based on alternative memories an inner child or damaged, and therefore child-like, inner self was central to their coming to know they were abused, but this could take the form of a damaged child-like inner self exerting an unhealthy influence on their adult lives. Although some manifestation of a child self featured in many women's stories she was for most very different from the inner children found in the pages of the literature. For some she was a damaged part of their adult selves, for others a discrete personality stuck at the time of their abuse, and in one woman's biography she was not alone but one of a group of alters or inner children. However, not all found her helpful and for some she was a dangerous and disturbing creation of 'inner child work'. Whilst the majority of women had no concrete memories of sexual abuse, they were able to tell the stories they did because these stories helped them make sense of their lives. Therefore, although on one level they relied on some form of child self, evidenced by symptoms identified in their lives, to provide knowledge of such abuse, their engagement with their own inner child was not so much related to their search for knowledge as it was to a desire to heal and reparent their child selves. Although this was an aspect of inner child work that can be seen as problematic as it can infantilise women and reconstruct them as childlike (Showalter 1997, Woodiwiss 2005) it was also an aspect of inner child work that enabled some women to explore or express feelings, behaviours and emotions that they might otherwise have found difficult. Whilst we could argue that women should not be forced to adopt the persona of a child in order to express or articulate a range of behaviours and emotions, within the constraints that the women found themselves in this was not always an option. Whilst she can be seen to infantilise women, the inner child did also enable women to engage in different aspects of their lives without threatening the image they had, or were trying to establish, of themselves as healthy, mature adult women. However, using the inner child as a vehicle to establish what was appropriate and inappropriate might have enabled the women to deviate from norms of acceptable womanhood but it did at the same time reinforce the idea that their 'childish' thoughts and actions were inappropriate. As much as the recovery literature claims to be empowering it does not empower women to challenge these stereotypes.

Not all the women developed a relationship with an inner child, and of those who did all but one developed a relationship with only one. However, their narratives, including those of women who did not develop such a relationship, illustrate some of the problems as well as some of the benefits of developing such relationships and engaging in inner child work. Hypnosis, either because it is thought useful in encouraging alter personalities to come forward (Bliss 1986, Putnam 1989) or because it is said to help in the creation of personalities (Ofshe and Watters 1995), has been seen as central in the field of multiple personalities. However, the accounts of the women in this book suggest alternative routes for the surfacing of personalities, in which the 'front person' might themselves play an active role. Some women identified inner child work as the point at which the seeds of the inner child or children were germinated, particularly where abuse was believed to have taken place over a long period of time. We can see in the stories of others that it might also be a continued search for knowledge, held by another inner child, that may lead to the creation or recognition of additional alters. This is more likely to be the case for women who have no concrete memories, have invested in a sexual abuse narrative and a therapeutic solution to their unhappiness or dissatisfaction, but who have yet to achieve the promised land of a brighter, happier future, or left healing behind. A number of women were aware of the possibility that there may be another inner child that they had yet to contact who might hold knowledge of additional or more extreme abuse that might explain their ongoing difficulties. Unlike the inner child of the sexual abuse recovery literature the inner children who feature in the world of multiple personalities are not needed to provide knowledge of abuse as their existence is seen, at least by those on the side of believers, as evidence enough. This can be seen in the story of the one woman who had made contact with many inner children. Anne's life story had developed from one which featured a difficult and traumatic childhood, to one which featured incest, before it moved on to ritual abuse during which she believed her abused child self had split many times. Anne did not feel the need to search for knowledge but was content to contact and look after her inner children to the extent that most of her life was dedicated to the children.

The inner child was not forced upon women, although some did feel pressured to make contact, and not all developed a relationship with an inner child. Those who did took a creative and pragmatic approach to the inner child, or children, with whom they came to share their lives. These children were not prescribed by the recovery literature but reflected the needs, wishes and circumstances of those women who shared their lives with them, whether they saw her as a separate part of their adult selves, or as a discrete personality. Women developed ambiguous, at times problematic relationships with an inner child and, although some found her disturbing, she did offer an outlet that was otherwise lacking within the confines of their lives. However, in the case of Anne it may be that multiplicity also offered a new way to be an unhappy person (Hacking 1995). She had rewritten her life story many times within which the latest version not only featured inner children, but some of these inner children had inner children themselves. However, it was in many ways a story of isolation in which her only companionship was her family of alters and the end of a telephone, and where she seemed a long way from writing a happy ending. Her ever-extending family provided an explanation, to both Anne and others, for why she might after over 20 years be so far from such an ending.

The watchword of self-therapy is 'recover or repeat' (Giddens 1991:79) and in the context of adult victims of childhood sexual abuse this message is often presented as both a promise and a warning. Women were presented with a relentless tide of optimism and negativity within which claims of empowerment were set against warnings of ongoing vulnerability and victimisation; women were told they not only owed it to themselves but also to others to break the cycle and heal from their abuse. To do so the recovery literature relies on a contradictory formulation of the self as both makeable and innate, both a thing and a process. Women were encouraged to make contact with their true inner self and at the same time to work on a self that was damaged and in need of healing. Far from being problematic it was through negotiating a path between the contradictory selves they found in the literature, that women were able to construct a self with whom they could live. They could find who they 'really' were, their 'true' self, and construct who they wanted to be, by working on their makeable self. As many relied on the symptoms they identified in their adult lives to know of past abuse they needed to establish and maintain a connection between a self of the past and a self of the present. In order to realise the promise of the recovery literature – empowerment and a better life – they also had to leave their damaged self behind. The different formulations of the self presented in the literature not only enabled women to find a formulation that accorded with their own understandings and needs but they could draw on different formulations as those needs changed. Although they were presented with two formulations of the self there was another self present in women's accounts. Some gave names to this third self: it was their spirit, their soul or their front person; others spoke of a true self. This was the self who navigated a path between the contradictory selves of the literature and helped them connect their adult selves to a past whilst at the same time distancing those selves from the damaging effects of that past. It was also this self who connected their core and their makeable selves. It was the occupier of this 'inner space' (Craib 1998) who established or maintained a connection between their adult selves, the subjects of their stories, and their child selves, the selves who were sexually abused. It was through this connection that women were able to maintain a continuity in their life stories; whether or not they remembered their abuse. It was this self who was able to identify or recognise elements of their core self. This third self was responsible for working on the makeable self, the one who chose who and what they wanted to be, and who and what they did not want to be, and was a constant presence in women's accounts. Deciding who and what they wanted to be, as well as who and what to discard, helped women establish and maintain a distance between their adult and child selves. It was this that enabled them to construct themselves as victims at the same time as they constructed themselves, or worked towards constructing themselves, as healed and therefore no longer damaged by their abuse; as 'strong at the broken places' (Sanford 1991). However, it is a self that, within the discursive framework of sexual abuse recovery, can only be maintained through a constant self-monitoring which might with luck keep them free from further unhappiness or dissatisfaction but which can be held responsible if that state is not reached or maintained.

The majority of women drew on the literature aimed at adult victims of childhood sexual abuse to construct a story that made sense to them, explained present difficulties, connected them to a life already lived and offered them a brighter future. This is not to argue that their stories were 'true', only that they fulfilled, or at least promised to fulfil, these criteria, but they were not the only stories that could be told. Other stories could also be told which acknowledge the conditions of women's lives and recognise the social, material, economic and political constraints which restrict their possibilities. Indeed, many of the women who did share their stories also included a range of experiences and knowledge that could have been used to construct very different narratives, within which they recognised the, albeit limited, degree of choice they had in the stories and subplots they chose. These alternatives to the stories promoted in the sexual abuse recovery literature are narratives in which women do not have to construct themselves as damaged and ultimately responsible for their own unhappiness and well-being, and do not prescribe a life of self-monitoring or define women as damaged and in need healing if or when things go wrong or as a result of the everyday ups and downs that we might all reasonably expect to experience. In order to write such stories women would have to look beyond personal healing to the outside world and not direct their gaze exclusively within. In the current climate of therapeutically influenced story telling, in which we are schooled in 'a therapeutic discourse of the emotions' (Rose 1989:257), such narrative frameworks are not widely circulating and therefore these alternative stories are difficult to tell and difficult to have heard.

This book has been about women's engagement with the contemporary sexual abuse recovery literature; the stories they have told of coming to believe they were abused, of living with that knowledge and sometimes rejecting it, and of moving forward, and the characters who populated their stories and accompanied them in the telling of their lives. I have shown that the women who tell these stories are far from being the weak vulnerable subjects constructed in the recovered memory wars, and have demonstrated the active, imaginative, pragmatic role women take in writing their own stories, constructing their own lives and creating for themselves a self, or selves, with whom they can approach the future. Whilst I would not argue that these are the only, or even the best, stories that can be told of their lives, they are the stories the women chose to construct for themselves, albeit drawing on a narrative framework that was severely limited and a model of childhood sexual abuse that was flawed. The stories they told included possibilities for other stories, with different subplots and endings, some of which the women may go on to write for themselves in the future, but I have not been able to explore these different storylines. The women who shared their stories were either still in therapy or had not long since finished, and therefore I have not explored how their different endings or new beginnings served them and what problems, if any, they encountered. Nor have I explored what might happen to those women who, based on recovery and healing, wrote a happy ending which is at some later date threatened, an occurrence which, as it could also be interpreted as further evidence of abuse, may direct some women back into 'recovery'. A significant group who do not feature at all in this book are those formerly abused women who do not see themselves as psychologically damaged and in need of healing. That their stories are missing should not be taken to indicate that they are unimportant; indeed their stories may prove to be the most important of all.

In looking at the telling of narratives of sexual abuse I have had to engage to some degree with the recovered memory wars. I have taken as my starting point women's claims to have been victims, either of sexual abuse or false memories, and have therefore avoided the questions of truth and falsity, except to acknowledge that women's claims were true to them. However, we should recognise that the stories they told were constructed from the vantage point of the present and this present itself contributed to what they understood to be true. In exploring the role played by those at the centre of these stories I hope to have moved the debate beyond the simplistic confines of a true/false dichotomy and a search for 'truth', in part by demonstrating that those stories based on 'alternative memories' are not based on verifiable 'facts' but subjective correlations. I argue instead for a space within which we can recognise women's agency in negotiating their own paths through the literature on CSA, recovered memories, multiple personalities, narratives of abuse, and the self and in doing so believe I have highlighted the limitations of currently available discourses and narrative frameworks within which women are attempting to make sense of and improve their lives. I hope this also contributes to the creation of a space within which it is easier for women to formulate different stories to those in which they are encouraged to look inward and construct themselves as damaged and in need of healing, and where they are no longer constrained by the dominant discourses of femininity and do not need recourse to an inner child. Women, whether or not they are the victims of sexual abuse, would be better served if future research were to open up the potential for them to tell different stories and construct different selves, no longer the selves whose only hope of a brighter future is to admit they were 'programmed to self destruct' (Bass and Davis 1988:179). As part of this project we need to revisit women and children's experiences of sexual abuse and challenge the prevailing orthodoxy of the harm story. In doing so we must not dismiss the wrongfulness of child sexual abuse but equally we should not equate wrongfulness with inevitable long-term psychological damage.

The tellers of contested stories of childhood sexual abuse are usually constructed as victims of either sexual abuse in childhood or malicious or misguided therapists. However, I would argue that they are victims as much if not more so of the limiting and inadequate stories currently in circulation, toing and froing between limited options (Bauman 2001) whether or not their memories (concrete or alternative) reflect sexual abuse in childhood. It is these that provide frameworks for women to make sense of and improve their lives and it is these that direct them to look inward for both cause of and solution to perceived inadequacies and difficulties. The stories women shared in this book may have helped them make sense of their lives but they are also likely to find themselves constrained by the stories they have come to tell. That they were drawn to stories of sexual abuse and recovery says more about the world in which we live and the pervasiveness of therapeutic culture, the harm story and the healing discourse than it does about either 'recovered memories' or childhood sexual abuse.

Bibliography

Adams, K (1991) *Silently seduced: When parents make their children partners – Understanding covert incest* Deerfield Beech, Fl: Health Communications Inc.

Ainscough, C and Toon, K (1993) *Breaking free: Help for survivors of child sexual abuse* London: Sheldon Press.

Ainscough, C and Toon, K (2000 2nd revised edition) *Breaking free: Help for survivors of child sexual abuse* London: Sheldon Press.

Aldridge-Morris (2000) *bfms newsletter* 11.

American Psychiatric Association (1994) *Diagnostic and statistical manual of mental disorders 4th edition (DSM-IV)* Washington: American Psychiatric Association.

Armstrong, L (1978) *Kiss daddy goodnight* New York: Hawthorn Press.

Armstrong, L (1994) *Rocking the cradle of sexual politics: What happened when women said incest* London: The Women's Press.

Armstrong, L (1996) 'In the footsteps of Doctor Freud and down the proverbial garden path'. *Feminism and Psychology* 6 (2): 298–303.

Arnold, R (1994) *My Lives* New York: Ballantine.

Atwood, M (1994) *The robber bride* London: Virago.

Baker, C D (2002) *Female survivors of sexual abuse: An integrated guide to treatment* Hove: Brunner-Routledge.

Bartoi, M G and Kinder, B N (1998) 'Effects of adult and child sexual abuse on adult sexuality'. *Journal of Sex and Marital Therapy* 24: 75–90.

Bass, E and Davis, L (1988) *The courage to heal: A guide for women survivors of child sexual abuse* London: Cedar.

Bass, E and Davis, L (2002 4th edition) *The courage to heal: A guide for women survivors of child sexual abuse* London: Vermilion.

Bauman, Z (2001) *The individualized society* Cambridge: Polity.

Bliss, E (1986) *Multiple personality, allied disorders, and hypnosis* New York: Oxford University Press.

Bloom, S (1994) 'Hearing the survivor's voice: Sundering the wall of denial'. *Journal of Psychohistory* 23: 461–477.

Blume, E (1990) *Secret survivors: Uncovering incest and its effects in women* New York: Ballantine Books.

British False Memory (August, 1999) Society *bfms newsletter* 7 (1).

Brown, L (1996) 'Politics of memory, politics of incest: Doing therapy and politics that really matter' in Contratto, S and Gutreund, M J (eds) *A feminist clinician's guide to the memory debate* London: Harrington Park Press.

Burgess, R (1982) (ed.) *Field research: A source book and field manual* London: Allen and Unwin.

Burgess, R (1984) *In the field: An introduction to field research* London: Allen and Unwin.

Burman, E (1995) 'What is it? Masculinity and femininity in cultural representations of childhood' in Wilkinson, S and Kitzinger, C (eds) *Feminism and discourse: Psychological perspectives* London: Sage.

Caine, L and Royston, R (2004) *Out of the dark* London: Corgi.

Callery, P (1998) 'Sex and children in the past and present' in Harrison T (ed.) *Children and sexuality*. London: Bailliere Tindall.
Cameron, C (2000) *Resolving childhood trauma: A long-term study of abuse survivors* London: Sage.
Chase, T (1987) *When rabbit howls* New York: Jove Books.
Contratto, S and Gutfreund, M J (1996) 'Introduction' in Contratto, S and Gutfreund, M J (eds) *A feminist clinician's guide to the memory debate* New York: Harrington Park Press.
Coons, P (1980) 'The differential diagnosis of Multiple Personality'. *Journal of Clinical Psychiatry* 42: 330–336.
Courtois, C (1992) 'The memory retrieval process in incest survivor therapy'. *Journal of Child Sexual Abuse* 1: 15–31.
Craib, I (1998) *Experiencing identity* London: Sage.
Davies, M (1995) *Childhood sexual abuse and the construction of identity: Healing Sylvia* London: Taylor and Francis.
Davis, J (2005) *Accounts of Innocence: Sexual abuse, trauma and the self* Chicago: University of Chicago Press.
de Rivera, J (1997) 'The construction of False Memory Syndrome: The experience of retractors'. *Psychological Enquiry* 8 (4): 271–292.
de Rivera, J (1998a) 'Evaluating believed-in imaginings' in de Rivera, J and Sarbin, T R (eds) *Believed-in imaginings: The narrative construction of reality* Washington DC: American Psychological Association.
de Rivera, J (1998b) 'Relinquishing believed-in imaginings: Narratives of people who have repudiated false accusations' in de Rivera, J and Sarbin, T R (eds) *Believed-in imaginings: The narrative construction of reality* Washington DC: American Psychological Association.
Dineen, T (1999) *Manufacturing victims: What the psychology industry is doing to people* London: Constable.
Dinsmore, C (1991) *From surviving to thriving: Incest, feminism and recovery* New York: State University of New York Press.
Driver, E (1989) *Child sexual abuse: Feminist perspectives* London: Macmillan Education.
Engel, B (1982) *The right to innocence: Healing the trauma of childhood sexual abuse* Los Angeles: Jeremy Tarcher.
Enns, C, McNeilly, C, Corkery, J and Gilbert, M (1995) 'The debate about delayed memories of child sexual abuse: A feminist perspective'. *The Counselling Psychologist* 23: 181–279.
Ernst, S and Goodison, L (1981) *In our own hands: A book of self-help therapy* London: The Women's Press.
Evans, D (1994) Falling angels: The material construction of children as sexual citizens. *International Journal of Children's Rights* 2: 1–33.
Evans, R M (1995) *Childhood's thief: One woman's journey of healing from sexual abuse* Bantam Dell Pub Group.
Faludi, S (1991) *Backlash: The undeclared war against women* London: Chatto and Windus.
Finkelhor, D and Associates (1986) *A sourcebook on child sexual abuse* London: Sage.
Finkelhor, D (1990) 'Early and long term effects of child sexual abuse: An update'. *Professional Psychology: Research and Practice* 21: 325–330.

Finney, L (1990) *Reach for the rainbow: Advanced healing for survivors of sexual abuse* Malibu, CA: Changes publishing.
Forward, S (1989) *Toxic parents* New York: Bantam.
Fraser, S (1987) *My father's house: A memoir of incest and of healing* London: Virago.
Fredrickson, R (1992) *Repressed memories* New York: Simon & Schuster.
Furedi, F (2004) *Therapy culture* London: Routledge.
Gagnon, J and Simon, W (1974) *Sexual conduct* London: Hutchinson.
Ganway, G (1989) 'Historical truth versus narrative truth: Clarifying the role of exogenous trauma in the aetiology of Multiple Personality Disorder and its variants'. *Dissociation* 2: 205–220.
Gavey, N (1993) 'Technologies and effects of heterosexual coercion' in Wilkinson, S and Kitzinger, C (eds) *Heterosexuality: A feminism and psychology reader* London: Sage.
Gavey, N (2003) 'Writing the effects of sexual abuse' in Reavey, P and Warner, S (eds) *New feminist stories of child sexual abuse: Sexual scripts and dangerous dialogues* London: Routledge.
Gergen, M (1994) 'The social construction of personal histories: Gendered lives in popular autobiographies' in Sarbin, T R and Kitsuse, J (eds) *Constructing the social* London: Sage.
Giddens, A (1991) *Modernity and self-identity: Self and society in the late modern age* Cambridge: Polity.
Glaser, D and Frosh, S (1993 2nd edition) *Child sexual abuse* London: Macmillan.
Green, L (2001) 'Children, sexual abuse and the child protection system' in Foley, P, Roche, J and Tucker, S (eds) *Children in society: Contemporary theory, policy and practice* Basingstoke: Palgrave Open University.
Grodin, D and Lindlof, T (1996) 'The self and mediated communication' in Grodin, D and Lindlof, T (eds) *Constructing the self in a mediated world* London: Sage.
Haaken, J (1998a) 'Women's stories of hidden selves and secret knowledge: A psychoanalytic feminist analysis' in de Rivera, J and Sarbin, T R (eds) *Believed-in imaginings* Washington DC: American Psychological Association.
Haaken, J (1998b) *Pillar of salt: Gender, memory and the perils of looking back* London: Free Association Books.
Haaken, J (1999) 'Heretical Texts: The courage to heal and the incest survivor movement' in Lamb, S (ed.) *New versions of victims: Feminists struggle with the concept* New York: New York University Press.
Haaken, J (2003) 'Traumatic revisions: Remembering abuse and the politics of forgiveness' in Reavey, P and Warner, S (eds) *New feminist stories of child sexual abuse: Sexual scripts and dangerous dialogues* London: Routledge.
Hacking, I (1991) 'The making and moulding of child abuse'. *Critical Enquiry* 17: 253–288.
Hacking, I (1995) *Rewriting the soul: Multiple Personality and the science of memory* Princeton: Princeton University Press.
Hall, L and Lloyd, S (1989) *Surviving child sexual abuse: A handbook for helping women challenge their past* London: Falmer.
Hall, S (1996) 'Who needs identity' in Hall, S and du Gay, P (eds) *Questions of cultural identity* London: Sage.
Hay, L (1984) *You can heal your life* London: Eden Grove Editions.
Herman, J (1981) *Father-daughter incest* Cambridge MA: Harvard University Press.

Herman, J L (1992) *Trauma and recovery: From domestic abuse to political terror* New York: Basis Books.
Herman, J L (2000) *Father-Daughter incest* Cambridge MA: Harvard University Press.
Hocking, S (1992) *Living with your selves: A survival manual for people with multiple personalities* Launch Press.
Hocking, P (formerly Hocking, S) (1996) *37 to One: Living as an integrated multiple* Brandon Vermont: The Safer Society Press.
Holstein, J and Gubrium, J (2000) *The self we live by: Narrative identity in a postmodern world* Oxford: Oxford University Press.
Hovdestad, W and Kristiansen, C (1996) 'Mind meets body: On the nature of recovered memories of trauma' in Contratto, S and Gutreund, M J (eds) *A feminist clinician's guide to the memory debate* London: Harrington Park Press.
Huskey, A (1990) *Stolen childhood: What you need to know about child sexual abuse* Westmont, Illinois: Intervarsity Pr.
Jackson, J L, Calhoun, K S, Amick, A E, Maddever, H M and Habif, V L (1990) 'Young adult women who report childhood intrafamilial sexual abuse: Subsequent adjustment'. *Annual Review of Sex Research* 13: 346–388.
Jackson, S (1982) *Childhood and sexuality* Oxford: Blackwell.
Jackson, S (1996a) *Childhood and sexuality revisited* Basingstoke: Palgrave Macmillan.
Jackson, S (1996b) 'Lost childhood or sexualised girlhood?' in Jackson S (ed.) *Heterosexuality in question* London: Sage.
Jackson, S (1998) 'Telling stories: Memory, narrative and experience in feminist research and theory' in Henwood, K, Griffin, C and Phoenix, A (eds) *Standpoints and differences: Essays in the practice of feminist psychology* London: Sage.
Jackson, S and Scott, S (2004) 'Sexual antinomies in late modernity'. *Sexualities* 7 (2): 241–256.
Jenks, C (1996) *Childhood* London: Routledge.
Kaminer, W (1993) 'Feminisms identity crisis'. *Atlantic Monthly* Issue 66.
Kelly, L (1988) *Surviving sexual violence* Cambridge: Polity Press.
Kelly, L (1996) 'Weasel words: Paedophiles and the cycle of abuse' in *Trouble and Strife* 33: 44–49.
Kirkwood, C (1993) *Leaving abusive partners* London: Sage.
Kitzinger, J (1993) 'Sexual violence and compulsory heterosexuality' in Wilkinson, S and Kitzinger, C (eds) *Heterosexuality: A feminism and psychology reader* London: Sage.
Kitzinger, J (1997) 'Who are you kidding? Children, power and the struggle against sexual abuse' in James, A and Prout, A (eds) *Constructing and reconstructing childhood* London: Falmer Press.
Kitzinger, C and Perkins, R (1993) *Changing our minds: Lesbian feminism and psychology* London: Only Women Press.
Lalor, K (2001) *The end of innocence: Child sexual abuse in Ireland* Cork: Oak Tree Press.
Lamb, S (1999) 'Constructing the victim: Popular images and lasting labels' in Lamb, S (ed.) *New versions of victims: Feminists struggle with the concept* New York: New York University Press.
Lasch, C (1979) *The Culture of narcissism* New York: Norton.

Lawler, S (2002) 'Narrative in social research' in May, T (ed.) *Qualitative research in action* London: Sage.
Levenkron, S (2008) *Stolen tomorrows: Understanding and treating women's childhood sexual abuse* New York: Norton.
Levett, A (2003) 'Problems of cultural imperialism in the study of child sexual abuse' in Reavey, P and Warner, S (eds) *New feminist stories of child sexual abuse: Sexual scripts and dangerous dialogues* London: Routledge.
Lew, M (1988) *Victims no longer: A guide for men recovering from sexual child abuse* London: Cedar.
Lew, M (2004 2nd edition) *Victims no longer: A guide for men recovering from sexual child abuse* New York: Harper Paperbacks.
Loftus, E and Ketcham, K (1994) *The myth of repressed memories: False memories and allegations of sexual abuse* New York: St Martin's.
Love, P (1990) *The emotional incest syndrome* New York: Bantam.
Maguire, A (1992) 'Power: Now you see it now you don't. A woman's guide to how power works' in McDowell, L and Pringle, R (eds) *Defining women: Social institutions and gender divisions* Cambridge: Polity Press.
Maguire, T (2007) *Don't tell mummy: A true story of the ultimate betrayal* South Africa: Harper Element.
Maltz, W (1987) *Incest and sexuality: A guide to understanding and healing* Lexington, MA: Lexington Books.
Maltz, W (1991) *The sexual healing journey* New York: Harper Collins.
Maltz, W and Holman, B (1986) *Incest and sexuality: A guide to understanding and healing* Lexington, MA: Lexington Books.
Maslow A H (1970) *Motivation and personality* New York: Harper and Row.
McHugh, P R (1993) 'Multiple Personality Disorder'. *Harvard Mental Health Newsletter* Autumn 1993: 4–6.
McMillen, C, Zuravin, S and Rideout, G (1995) 'Perceived benefit from child sexual abuse'. *Journal of Consulting and Clinical Psychology* 63: 1037–1043.
McNally, R (2003) *Remembering trauma* Cambridge Mass: Belknap Press Harvard University.
Miller, A (1987) *The drama of being a child* London: Virago.
Miller, A (1991) *Banished knowledge* London: Virago.
Norwood, R (1985) *Women who love too much: When you keep wishing and hoping he'll change* London: Arrow.
Norwood, R (1994) *Why me, why this, why now* London: Arrow.
O'Dell, L (1997) 'Child sexual abuse and the academic construction of Symptomatologies'. *Feminism and Psychology* 7 (3): 334–339.
O'Dell, L. and Reavey, P. (2001) 'Listening and speaking: The lost and found voices of women survivors of sexual violence'. *Psychology of Women Section Review* 3: 4–14.
O'Dell, L (2003) 'The "harm" story in childhood sexual abuse: Contested understandings, disputed knowledges' in Reavey, P and Warner, S (eds) *New feminist stories of child sexual abuse: Sexual scripts and dangerous dialogues* London: Routledge.
Ofshe, R and Watters, E (1995) *Making monsters: False memories, psychotherapy, and sexual hysteria* London: Andre Deutsch.
Olio, K (1989) 'Memory retrieval in the treatment of adult survivors of sexual abuse'. *Transactional Analysis Journal* 19: 93–100.

Parks, P (1990) *Rescuing the 'inner child': Therapy for adults sexually abused as children* London: Souvenir Press.
Park, S M (1997) 'False Memory Syndrome: A feminist philosophical approach'. *Hypatia* 12 (2): 1–50.
Pelzer, D (1995) *A child called it* Florida: Health Communications.
Pelzer, D (1997) *The lost boy* Florida: Health Communications.
Pelzer, D (1999) *A man named Dave* Florida: Health Communications.
Pelzer, D (2000) *A child called it* London: Orion.
Pelzer, D (2001) *A man named Dave* London: Orion.
Pelzer, D (2003) *The lost boy* London: Orion.
Pendergrast, M (1997) *Victims of memory: Incest accusations and shattered lives* London: Harper Collins.
Pendergrast, M (1999) 'From Mesmer to memories: A historical, scientific look at the recovered memories controversy' in Taub, S (ed.) *Recovered memories of child sexual abuse* Illinois: Charles C Thomas.
Peters, D (1986) *Betrayal of innocence: What everyone should know about child sexual abuse* Waco, Texas: W Publishing Group.
Plummer, K (1995) *Telling sexual stories* London: Routledge.
Plummer, K (2001) *Documents of life 2: An invitation to a critical humanism* London: Sage.
Prout, A and James, A (1997) 'A new paradigm for the sociology of childhood? Provenance, promise and problems' in James, A and Prout, A (eds) *Constructing and reconstructing childhood* London: Falmer Press.
Prozan, C (1993) *The technique of feminist psychoanalytic psychotherapy* Northvale NJ: Jason Aronson.
Putnam, F W (1989) *Diagnosis and treatment of Multiple Personality Disorder* New York: Guildford Press.
Reavey, P and Warner, S (2001) 'Curing women: Child sexual abuse, therapy and the construction of femininity'. *International Journal of Critical Psychology*, Special issue on Sex and Sexualities 3: 49–71.
Reavey, P (2003) 'When past meets present to produce a sexual "other": Examining professional and everyday narratives of child sexual abuse and sexuality' in Reavey, P and Warner, S (eds) *New feminist stories of child sexual abuse: Sexual scripts and dangerous dialogues* London: Routledge.
Renvoize, J (1993) *Innocence destroyed: A study of child sexual abuse* London: Routledge.
Rich, A (1980) 'Compulsory heterosexuality and lesbian existence'. *Signs* 5 (4): 631–660.
Rind, B and Tromovitch, P (1997) 'A meta-analytic review of findings from national samples on psychological correlates of child sexual abuse'. *Journal of Sex Research* 32: 219–233.
Rogers, C R (1970) *On becoming a person: A therapists view of psychotherapy* Boston: Houghton Mifflin.
Rose, N (1989 2nd edition) *Governing the soul* London: Free association books.
Ross, C (1995) *Satanic ritual abuse: Principles of treatment* Toronto: Toronto University Press.
Rush, F (1980) *The best kept secret: Sexual abuse of children* New York: McGraw-Hill.
Russell, D (1982) *Rape in Marriage* New York: Macmillan
Sanford, L (1991) *Strong at the broken places* London: Virago.

Sarbin, T R (1998) 'Believed-in imaginings: A narrative approach' in de Rivera, J and Sarbin, T R (eds) *Believed-in imaginings: The narrative construction of reality* Washington DC: American Psychological Association.

Scott, S (2001) *The politics and experience of ritual abuse: Beyond disbelief* Buckingham: Open University Press.

Sennett, R (1976) *The fall of public man* New York: Knopf.

Sennett, R (1993) *The fall of public man* (New edition) London: Faber and Faber.

Sgroi, S (ed.) (1982) *Handbook of clinical intervention in child sexual abuse* Massachusetts: Lexington Books.

Showalter, E (1997) *Hystories: Hysterical epidemics and modern culture* London: Picador.

Simonds, W (1992) *Women and self-help culture: Reading between the lines* New Brunswick NJ: Rutgers University Press.

Simonds, W (1996) 'All consuming selves: Self-help literature and women's identities' in Grodin, D and Lindlof, L (eds) *Constructing the self in a mediated world* London: Sage.

Smith, M (1993) *Ritual abuse* San Francisco: HarperSanFrancisco.

Spence, D (1998) 'The mythic properties of popular explanations' in de Rivera, J and Sarbin, T R (eds) *Believed-in Imaginings: The narrative construction of reality* Washington DC: American Psychological Association.

Spring, J (1987) *Cry hard and swim: The story of an incest survivor* London: Virago.

Stainton Rogers, W (2001) 'Constructing childhood, constructing child concern' in Foley, P, Roche, J and Tucker, S (eds) *Children in society: Contemporary theory, policy and practice* Basingstoke: Palgrave/Open University.

Stainton Rogers, W and Stainton Rogers, R (1999) 'What is good and bad sex for children?' in King, M (ed.) *Moral agendas for children's welfare* London: Routledge.

Summit, R and Kryso, J (1978) 'Sexual abuse of children: A clinical spectrum'. *American Journal of Orthopsychiatry* 48: 237–251.

Tavris, C (1992) *Mismeasure of woman: Why women are not the better sex, the inferior sex, or the opposite sex* New York: Touchstone Books.

Tietjens-Meyers, D (1997) 'The family romance: A *fin-de-Siecle* tragedy' in Nelson, H L (ed.) *Feminism and families* London: Routledge.

Walker, L (1979) 'How battering happens and how to stop it' in Moore, A (ed.) *Battered women* Beverly Hills, CA: Sage.

Walker, L (1984) *The battered woman syndrome* New York: Springer.

Ward, E (1984) *Father daughter rape* London: The Women's Press.

Warner, S (1996) 'Constructing femininity: Models of child sexual abuse and the production of "woman" ' in Burman, E, Alldred, P and Bewley, C (eds) *Challenging women: Psychology's exclusions, feminist possibilities* Buckingham: Open University Press.

Weiner, N and Robinson-Kurplus, S E (1995) *Shattered innocence: Practical guide for counselling women survivors of childhood sexual abuse* London: Taylor & Francis.

Weldon, F (1994) *Affliction* London: Harper Collins.

Whitfield, C L (1987) *Healing the child within: Discovery and recovery for adult children of dysfunctional families* Deerfield Beech, Fl: Health Communications Inc.

Whitfield, C L (1995) *Memory and abuse: Remembering and healing the effects of trauma* Deerfield Beech, Fl: Health Communications Inc.

Whitman, T C and Shore, S (1994) *The multiples guide to harmonized family living: A healthy alternative (or prelude) to integration* New York: Artistic Endeavors Pub.

Whyte, W (1982) 'Interviewing in the field' in Burgess, R (ed.) *Field research: A source book and field manual* London: Allen and Unwin.

Woititz, J (1983 expanded edition) *Adult children of alcoholics* Deerfield Beach, Fl: Health Communications Inc.

Woodiwiss, J (2005) *Stories to live by, selves to live with: Constructing the self through narratives of childhood sexual abuse,* unpublished PhD thesis University of York.

Woodiwiss, J (2006) 'Alternative memories: Searching for knowledge, telling a story' in Milnes, K et al (eds) *Narrative, memory and knowledge* Huddersfield: Huddersfield University Press.

Woodiwiss, J (2007a) 'Politics, Responsibility and Childhood Sexual Abuse'. *Sociological Research Online* 12 (2) [online] Available at: http://www.socresonline.org.uk/12/2/woodiwiss.html (5 February 2009).

Woodiwiss, J (2007b) 'Narrating a sense of (sexual) well-being: Beyond the "harm story" of childhood sexual abuse' in Milnes, K et al (eds) *Narrative, memory and health* Huddersfield: Huddersfield University Press.

Woodiwiss, J (2008) ' "Compulsory sexuality": A guide to healing?' *Culture, Health & Sexuality* 10 (4): 345–359.

Woodiwiss, J (2009) 'Alternative memories of childhood sexual abuse' in Haaken, J and Reavey, P (eds) *Memory Matters: Contexts for understanding sexual abuse recollections* London: Routledge.

Worrell (2003) 'Working at being survivors: Identity, gender and participation in self-help groups' in Reavey, P and Warner, S (eds) *New feminist stories of child sexual abuse: Sexual scripts and dangerous dialogues* London: Routledge.

Yapko, M (1994a) 'Suggestibility and repressed memories of abuse: A survey of psychotherapists' beliefs'. *American Journal of Clinical Hypnosis* 36 (3): 163–171.

Yapko, M (1994b) *Suggestions of abuse: True and false memories of childhood sexual traumas* New York: Simon and Schuster.

Index